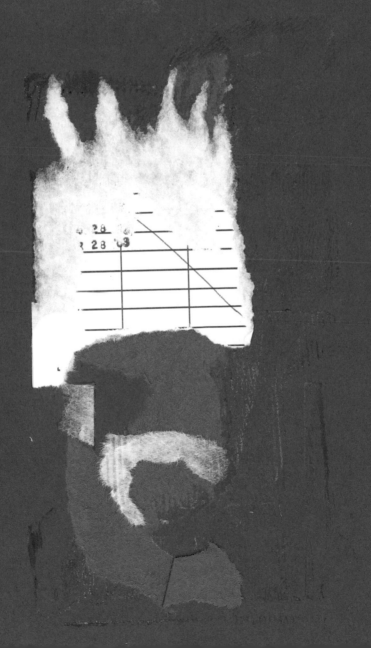

Argentina 1943-1976

Argentina
1943-1976

The National Revolution and Resistance

Donald C. Hodges

UNIVERSITY OF NEW MEXICO PRESS

Albuquerque

Library of Congress Cataloging in Publication Data

Hodges, Donald Clark, 1923–
   Argentina, 1943–1976 : the national revolution and
resistance.

   Bibliography: p.
   Includes index.
   1. Argentine Republic—Politics and government—
1943–   2. Peronism.   3. Government, Resistance to.
I. Title.
F2849.H6   982'.06   76-21544
ISBN 0-8263-0422-2
ISBN 0-8263-0423-0 pbk.

To

RAIMUNDO ONGARO

and the other heroes of the Resistance

Preface

In July 1974 three cardboard boxes of proscribed documents written by the Peronist and Guevarist left were smuggled out of Argentina on a Mexican presidential aircraft. Thanks to Dr. Leo Gabriel, the Austrian sociologist and coordinator of the Grupo Informe of Cuernavaca, these documents were later placed at my disposal. Among them were a complete set of *Militancia* and nearly complete sets of *El Descamisado* and *Nuevo Hombre*—journals banned by the Peronist government in April 1974. The Grupo Informe also had most of the back issues for the period July 1973 to July 1974 of *Estrella Roja* and *El Combatiente*, the principal publications of the outlawed People's Revolutionary Army (ERP) and its political counterpart, the Workers' Revolutionary Party (PRT). It had tapes of discussions with Roberto Santucho and Mario Firmenich, the leaders respectively of the PRT-ERP and the Montoneros, as well as scores of taped speeches and interviews with the Peronist Youth, the Peronism of the Bases, the Peronist Urban Squatters' Movement and the combative trade unions of Córdoba. These materials were crucial to my research on the Peronist resistance and the developing struggle by the Peronist left against the new wave of repression launched by the rightist camarilla which had assumed control of the Peronist movement.

Originally my plan had been to return to Buenos Aires, where I had lived from 1929 to 1941 and revisited in 1971, for the purpose of gathering documents and interviewing Peronist leaders. But with Perón's death on July 1, 1974, the prospects of a civil war between the left and right wings of the Peronist movement and of renewed intervention by the armed forces along the lines of General Augusto Pinochet's coup in Chile emerged. By September these fears had been partly confirmed by news of the vendetta between the Argentine military and the ERP. At the same time, I received the shocking news of Professor Silvio Frondizi's assassination and of the scores of other political murders by the Argentine Anti-

Communist Alliance (AAA)—the equivalent of Brazil's infamous Death Squadron.

I expressed my forebodings in a letter to Abraham Guillén, the Spanish anarcho-Marxist and Civil War veteran, who was then teaching at the University of Buenos Aires. "You can come with tranquility," he wrote on October 30, 1974. "In Spain there is a refrain which says 'fear is free and each one takes what he wants, though it is hardly convenient to take all of it.' " Guillén's letter and the news that Isabel Perón (Juan Domingo's widow) had convened a multisectoral junta on October 8 for the purpose of combating political violence in Argentina, an effort supported by most of the leftist parties, was enough to induce me to reschedule my trip for November.

Within two days, however, the Chief of the Federal Police had been assassinated by the Montoneros. The government's response was to proclaim a state of siege on November 6 with all that it entailed—immediate arrests, police and army dragnets, and the suspension of habeas corpus. Several weeks later I was to hear from Guillén, in a letter dated November 29 and addressed from Lima, Peru: "I expect that you did not make the trip to Buenos Aires because of the foul political air in that city, which effectively obliged me to leave."

Accordingly, I postponed my trip until the state of siege might be raised. But in another letter dated January 16, 1975, Guillén was not encouraging: "I doubt that the state of siege will be lifted. At least, for the moment, that is impossible. On the contrary, I fear that the repressive methods used in Brazil will be applied to Argentina: detention without knowledge of where the detained are held—dead or alive. Thus I anticipate that your trip will be again postponed, and for a considerable time." By the end of May the state of siege was still in effect. I resolved to make the trip anyway.

If I did not leave immediately for Argentina it was because I had just made my first contact with the community of Argentine exiles in Mexico City. Ex-President Héctor Cámpora had made his home there as had the deposed governor of Córdoba, Ricardo Obregón. Through Adriana Puiggrós, a former dean at the University of Buenos Aires and the daughter of Peronist militant Rodolfo Puiggrós, I was put in touch with the Argentine journalists working on Mexico's daily newspaper *El Día.* I am also indebted to her for reading the first draft of my manuscript and for her comments concerning some of its finer points.

More important for my research were the Argentine "tourists," members of the Peronist Youth (JP) and Montoneros, who were passing through Mexico as self-styled "visitors" or "commercial travelers." They were more difficult to interview, but were also better informed about the current state of the resistance movement in which they were actively engaged. For reasons of security they used fictitious names; they were continually on the move or in the course of changing residence; they could not be reached by telephone.

They had good reason to take precautions. On June 18 they had collected sixty million dollars in ransom for the brothers Jorge and Juan Born. (That was a world record, the previous high having been the fourteen million dollars paid by Esso to Argentina's People's Revolutionary Army for the release of its executive, Victor Samuelsson.) The Born brothers, co-directors of Bunge and Born, Argentina's largest multinational corporation, had been kidnapped on September 19, 1974, shortly after the Montoneros had returned underground in opposition to the government of Isabel Perón. Agents and collaborators of the Argentine police were presumably combing Mexico City and the exile community for traces of the missing money.

Through the official Peronist exiles the "tourists" learned of my work, expressed an interest in it, read the first draft and made many useful notations on the margins. They contacted me; I had no way of contacting them. We would arrange to meet outside a bookshop or restaurant in downtown Mexico. I learned from experience that they would just as likely not show up. Occasionally, they would travel over the mountains to Cuernavaca to help in the editing of Leo Gabriel's film on Argentina, put together from the film archives of both the Montoneros and the People's Revolutionary Army. Their plan was to help edit the film, to show it abroad, and eventually to use it for clandestine showings in Argentina. Much of my information concerning the armed operations and internal structure of the Montoneros-JP came from interviews with militants of the organization in Mexico City and Cuernavaca.

Toward the end of the summer I was obliged to return to the States to a teaching position at Florida State University. However, I arranged for a leave during the Winter Quarter and again made plans to travel to Argentina. I had reason to be apprehensive about the trip. I had edited a book on the *Philosophy of the Urban Guerrilla* (1973) and authored another on *The Latin American*

Revolution (1974), both testifying to my connections with revolutionary groups operating in Argentina. I also had a police record in neighboring Uruguay, where I had been detained and questioned by military intelligence in June 1971 on charges of aiding and abetting the Tupamaros.

I made the trip between two military coups, arriving in Buenos Aires on January 12, 1976, exactly three weeks after the abortive coup of December 18–22, and leaving at the end of February, approximately three weeks prior to the successful coup of March 23. Prudence dictated that I research the ultraright and right wings of the Peronist movement and keep shy of the contacts I had made in 1971. Accordingly, I concentrated on the politics and strategy, first, of the ultraverticalists in the president's so-called "entourage" and, second, of the principal labor bureaucrats in the Confederation of Labor (CGT) and the "62 Organizations." The Montoneros-JP, I discovered, had not fully appreciated the scope of the divergence between the Peronist labor bureaucracy and the "entourage," nor the importance of labor's participation and the extent of labor's stake in the Peronist government. The outright sabotage of government measures by employers' associations and the menacing role of the armed forces, likewise committed to halting the "advance of organized labor," indicated that the Peronist government was basically left of center and still predominantly populist in character.

Before returning to the States I stopped over in Lima at the invitation of Abraham Guillén, who had become an "international bureaucrat" and the top foreign expert on social property and workers' self-management to be employed by the Peruvian government. Guillén had himself fought as a militant during the resistance. Actually, he had thrown the first stone.

At the request of John William Cooke, later to become Perón's personal representative and chief of tactical operations from 1956 through 1959, Guillén had drawn up the first plan for massive Peronist resistance based on guerrilla warfare. Well-versed in military and guerrilla strategy because of his experience during the Spanish Civil War, he was also active in organizing the first Peronist rural guerrillas. As the military assessor of the so-called *Uturuncos* ("tiger men" in Quechua), operating along the borders of Santiago del Estero and Tucumán in December 1959, he planned the first successful assault on police headquarters in the provincial town of Frías where the guerrillas seized arms and munitions. Imprisoned during the first three months of 1961 on suspicion of having been involved in this action, he shortly afterwards left for Cuba where from April through December he instructed Peronist militants in urban guerrilla strategy and tactics. Guillén had warned me against being too accepting of the Montoneros-JP. But I needed to know his specific criticisms of their politics and strategy, and I visited him in Lima for that purpose.

On my arrival Guillén took me to see Raimundo Ongaro, once secretary-general of the outlawed Graphic Workers Union and former head of the combative "CGT of the Argentines." Ongaro's apartment had become a Mecca for labor militants from Argentina, who had traveled to Peru to consult with him on labor matters. A charismatic figure, a kind of Che Guevara of organized labor, Ongaro was as much sought after for his keen political intelligence as for the lasting friendship and loyalty he instilled in his followers. No longer able to exercise his rhetorical gifts directly on the rank and file, he practiced on his visitors.

He was then up to his neck in correspondence with leaders of the resistance, including army commanders intent on a Peruvian-style, or populist, military coup. Ongaro had established links with the Movement of the Armed Forces (MFA), a nationalist lodge of young army officers supported by their peers in the air force and navy. The MFA was committed to a program of nationalizing the economic infrastructure and establishing a state monopoly over foreign commerce. It was openly anti-imperialist. While critical of the labor bureaucrats in control of the CGT and "62 Organizations," it was sympathetic to labor leaders democratically elected and responsive to the rank and file. Ongaro was such a leader, and he filled a lacuna in my research. Even more than the Peronist armed formations, he argued, the combative trade unions had played the decisive role in pressuring the military to abdicate. I was also surprised to learn that the 1969 "Cordobazo" (a mass uprising in the industrial city of Córdoba) had not been spontaneous, as was generally believed, but the result of careful planning months in advance of the historical occasion that made it possible.

Through Ongaro I made contact with other Argentine exiles. If Mexico City had become the foreign headquarters for militants of the Montoneros and Peronist Youth, Lima had come to harbor militants of the Peronist Armed Forces (FAP) and Peronism of the Bases (PB). A large two-story house had been rented in a Lima suburb where a dozen or so cadres were temporarily cooling their heels.

Beginning roughly in October 1974, the FAP changed its mode of operations to semilegal actions directly linked to the workers' struggles inside the factories. Consequently, the FAP cadres in Lima had little to fear from international agents on the scent of new bank "expropriations." The FAP's old leadership, decimated by repression and torn by internal splits, had given way to a new one under the Villaflor brothers. One was in charge of armed operations; a second with the political direction of the movement; a third, with labor matters. I interviewed the last. To him I owe an understanding of the linkage between the FAP and PB, and of the FAP's newly assigned importance to anonymity in the armed struggle. Yet I wondered whether the FAP's virtual disappearance from the political scene was a consequence of its new strategy of maintaining a low profile or of the combined effect of military repression and the loss of its principal cadres to the ERP and Montoneros. In any case, the FAP-PB had been superseded by the Montoneros-JP in the struggle for survival within the Peronist left. Perhaps that explained why the cadres I interviewed in Lima were so consistently pessimistic and morose.

Timetable of the Peronist Resistance, 1955–1973

Background 1943–1955

4 June 1943: Military coup led by nationalist officers of the Group of United Officers (GOU), including Juan Domingo Perón, ousts Conservative President Ramón S. Castillo.

October 1943: Perón appointed to reorganize the National Department of Labor.

November 1943: Perón appointed Secretary of Labor.

February 1944: Perón appointed Minister of War in addition to Secretary of Labor.

July 1944: Perón becomes Vice-President without relinquishing his cabinet positions.

October 1945: Perón detained and imprisoned by the military after being compelled to resign from the government.

17 October 1945: Mass demonstrations in Plaza de Mayo lead to Perón's release.

February 1946: Perón elected President, with the support of former Radical Party members and the new Labor Party.

June 1946: Radical Party members and Labor Party join to form the United Party of the National Revolution (PURN).

January 1947: PURN officially renamed the Peronist Party.

June 1952: Perón inaugurated as President for second term.

26 July 1952: Death of Evita Perón.

September 1955: Perón ousted by military coup and exiled.

Stage 1:
1955–1958

Objective: to overthrow the military regime through mass industrial unrest and armed struggle.

January 1956: Secret directive from Perón officially launches the resistance. The National Command is formed: serves as the principal coordinator and center of Peronist resistance. Members include all Peronist groups and organizations that survived the purges of 1955.

1956: Movement of National Recovery formed by Gen. Juan José Valle and other Peronist military officers who were imprisoned. Released in 1956, they launched an abortive coup on June 9. Valle and his colleagues executed by Pres. Pedro Aramburu.

August 1957: The government-intervened General Confederation of Labor (CGT) splits into the "62 Organizations" loyal to Perón and the "32" liberal trade unions opposed to Perón.

Stage 2:
1958–1962

Objective: the normalization of the CGT and the legalization of the Peronist Party, with the expectation of returning to power through an electoral victory.

1958: Perón-Frondizi Pact. Perón trades approximately 2 million of his followers' votes for the promise from presidential candidate Arturo Frondizi of legality for the Peronist Party and general amnesty for exiled or imprisoned leaders. Amnesty granted May Day 1958; CGT normalized 1961; but Peronist Party not returned to legal status until 1962.

1958: Peronist Youth (JP) formed. Purpose, to provide the bulk of cadres for armed struggle and a revolutionary tendency within the Peronist movement aimed not only at restoring Perón to power, but also at establishing a form of national socialism.

January 1959: National Command calls nationwide labor strikes. Conciliatory executive council of the "62 Organizations" dissolved and more militant leaders chosen.

December 1959: First guerrilla movement launched in Tucumán Province, with name *Uturuncos* ("tiger men" in Quechua).

Stage 3:
1962–1966

Objective: systematic creation of chaos aimed at paralyzing the country economically, and the use of armed struggle to pressure the military-backed pseudoconstitutional government into allowing Perón's return.

1959–1961: Guerrilla training camps, based on Cuban model, established.

1962: Peronist Party restored to legality. Military coup ousts Pres. Arturo Frondizi.

Late 1962: "62 Organizations" adopts revolutionary program of Huerta Grande.

1962–1963: Organization of two guerrilla groups: a rural foco under Ricardo Masetti called the People's Guerrilla Army (EGP), and the first urban foco under "Joe" Baxter, head of the Revolutionary Nationalist Movement (Tacuara).

1963: Augusto Vandor replaces Amado Olmos as the principal influence in the "62." Rejects program of Huerta Grande in favor of negotiations with newly elected Pres. Arturo Illia. Perón assumes role of moderator, from exile, between Vandor's reformist wing and John William Cooke's revolutionary tendency.

1964: "Battle Plan" for Perón's return. Country paralyzed by successive strike waves and occupations of factories.

April 1964: EGP wiped out by armed forces. Major leaders of Tacuara arrested. Baxter flees to Montevideo where he works with Tupamaros until 1966.

August 1964: Founding of Peronist Revolutionary Movement (MRP), successor to the National Command. Program formulated by Gustavo Rearte proposed to carry on the resistance under conditions of semilegality, in which the struggle would be a protracted one and the seizure of power a prelude to a continuing revolution. "From today forward we shall know how to use armed struggle as the principal means of political action."

1964: Vandor launches campaign against the MRP and the Confederation of Peronist Orthodox Associations (CAOP) led by Jorge Di Pasquale.

Stage 4:
1966–1973

Objective: the end of military dictatorship through the combined tactics of labor unrest, mass mobilizations, armed struggle, and the organization of a political front.

1965: Vandor openly proclaims his differences with Perón. José Alonso reelected secretary-general of the CGT for a second two-year term.

January 1966: MRP and CAOP form the "62 on Foot with Perón," precursor of the "CGT of the Argentines." Major leaders include Amado Olmos, Gustavo Rearte, Jorge Di Pasquale, and Armando Jaime.

February 1966: Crisis in the CGT. Alonso obliged to resign as secretary-general under pressure from Vandor. With Perón's support, Alonso becomes head of the "62 on Foot."

June 1966: Pres. Arturo Illia ousted by military coup.

1966: Armed Forces of Liberation (FAL), a non-Peronist, Guevarist group organized by dissidents of the Communist Youth to implement Che's call for a Latin American Viet Nam.

1966–1967: Split between the "62" and remnants of the "62 on Foot" widens. Vandorist "62" conciliatory with military government.

1968: Split in the CGT. CGT-A, led by Raimundo Ongaro, reaffirms program of Huerta Grande.

Mid 1968: Envar El Kadri and militants of JP revive rural armed resistance which had disappeared following the defeat of the EGP in 1964. Form Peronist Armed Forces (FAP).

June 1969: CGT-A intervened following the Cordobazo in May. Vandor assassinated by pre-Montonero commando.

October 1969: CGT-A dissolved because military repression destroyed its effectiveness.

December 1969: Gustavo Rearte organizes the Revolutionary Movement 17th of October (MR-17): designed to overcome the limitations of the MRP by developing a political vanguard rooted in the trade unions. To replace CGT-A and to mobilize masses for a popular war.

1969: Montoneros founded by Fernando Abal Medina. Named after gaucho contingents in Argentina's 1810 War of Independence. Urban guerrilla group formed in direct response to the Cordobazo. Medina succeeded in 1970 by Mario Firmenich. Influenced by both Guevarism and Camilism.

1969: Revolutionary Armed Forces (FAR) founded. First Guevarist organization on the continent to learn the lessons of Che's failure in Bolivia by adapting Guevarism to a national context. In December 1970 merged with Peronism.

1970: Montoneros kidnap and execute former Pres. Pedro Aramburu. Begin to use spectacular armed operations to raise the political consciousness of the nation.

June 1970: Pres. Juan Carlos Onganía ousted by fellow military officers. Replaced by Gen. Roberto Marcelo Levingston.

July 1970: Unity Congress of CGT elects José Rucci its new secretary-general. Workers' Revolutionary Party (PRT), affiliated to the Trotskyist Fourth International (Unified Secretariat), forms an armed branch called the People's Revolutionary Army (ERP).

August 1970: Alonso assassinated by Peronist commandos who later join the Montoneros.

November 1970: Coalition of proscribed political parties called "Hour of the People" formed. Includes Radical, Popular Conservative, Progressive Democratic, Socialist parties, and the Peronist movement. Purpose: to pressure the military government into abdicating and calling new elections.

March 1971: Second Cordobazo. Pres. Levingston ousted by fellow military officers. Replaced by Gen. Alejandro Lanusse.

1971: Pres. Lanusse announces the "Great National Accord" and pressures Perón to renounce the revolutionary tendency in return for an easing of the repression of the Peronist Party. Perón refuses and instead chooses leftist Héctor Cámpora to represent him in Argentina. Political parties legalized in July.

1972: Perón forms the Civic Front of National Liberation (FRECILINA), renamed the Justicialist Front of Liberation (FREJULI) in December, an electoral coalition of 25 organizations led by Peronist Party.

August 22, 1972: The Trelew massacre of sixteen political prisoners belonging to the ERP, FAR, and Montoneros occurs.

March 1973: National elections in which the FREJULI receives approximately 50% of the vote. Hector Cámpora elected president.

May 1973: ERP-22 formally breaks with the PRT-ERP over the issue of Cámpora's candidacy, which the 22 August faction supported.

June 1973: The PRT-ERP breaks with the Trotskyist Fourth International and rejects the "Trotskyist" label.

July 1973: Resignation of Pres. Cámpora under pressure from Peronist right wing. Replaced by provisional Pres. Raúl Lastiri.

September 1973: Perón elected President for the third time. Rucci assassinated. Launching of campaign of "ideological purification" against Marxist infiltrators in the movement.

October 1973: Organizational merger of the FAR and the Montoneros, called the Act of Unification. Name Montoneros retained. Intended as contribution to the reorganization, institutionalization, and unification of the Peronist Youth movement.

1973: FAR-Montoneros organize subsidiary groups: Peronist University Youth (JUP); Union of Secondary Students (UES); Agrupación Evita; Peronist Working Youth (JTP); and Movement of Peronist Urban Squatters (MVP). Had support of older Peronists who were in the Association of Authentic Peronism (APA). All geared to cooperating with the new Peronist government.

Interim—1973

Peronist movement split into two sectors: "movementist" and "classist."

Movementist sector: composed of FAR-Montoneros and the Peronist Youth. Felt that the resistance had come to an end, and made a major policy shift aimed at working within the legal and political mainstream of the Peronist movement. Armed struggle was used to defend the government, and was subordinated to the political effort to implement the Peronist program of national liberation.

Classist sector: composed of the FAP and Peronist Bases, the latter being the successor to the "62 on Foot" and the CGT-A. Made common cause with non-Peronist guerrilla organizations since they believed that the resistance should continue until the establishment of a "Socialist Fatherland." Declared independence from the official Peronist movement, and planned to confront Peronist political and trade union bureaucracies, the reactionary armed forces, and the multinational corporations.

Contents

Argentina 1943-1976

The National Revolution and Resistance

Introduction

If Argentine politics are crucial to the future of Latin America it is because the Peronist resistance against military dictatorship has become a model for the popular resistance movements in neighboring Chile, Bolivia, and Uruguay, with the prospect of also becoming the model for the Brazilian resistance. Following the military coup against General Juan Domingo Perón in September 1955, the majoritarian Peronist Party was banned. It took eighteen years of combined legal and armed struggle against the pseudoconstitutional governments of Presidents Arturo Frondizi and Arturo Illia, and against a new series of military regimes beginning in 1966, for the Peronist Party to be restored to full legality. The resistance was ultimately successful in pressuring the military to abdicate and to call new elections in March 1973, the first free elections held in more than two decades.

In Argentina in 1955 the military intervened in the political process as an interim measure aimed at displacing a populist and majoritarian political party. The military ruled directly from 1955 to 1958, and then indirectly from 1958 to 1966. Beginning in 1966 the armed forces initiated a new phase of military rule designed not as an interim measure, but to perpetuate the military bureaucracy in power. The congress was shut down and all political parties were banned, since they were supposedly unfit to rule. Between 1966 and 1973 there occurred in Argentina, although on a lesser scale, the same kind of repressive decrees, systematic violation of civil rights, police and military torture, and massive attacks on the trade unions that also characterized the Brazilian dictatorship beginning in 1968, and the Bolivian, Uruguayan, and Chilean dictatorships during the 1970s.

There were, of course, differences between the authoritarian military regime imposed in Argentina in 1966 and the military coups that followed among its neighbors. The Brazilian coup-within-a-coup of December 1968 was a response to the emergence

1

of a broad front against the government, a coalition of virtually all the old political parties, followed by the largest oubreak of urban guerrilla warfare on the continent. The Bolivian coup of August 1971 and the Chilean coup of September 1973 were directed at the threat represented by the Communist, Socialist, and other leftist parties which actively shared in the government. In Bolivia there was the first soviet-type Popular Assembly in the Americas; in Chile, Salvador Allende's government of Popular Unity. The Uruguayan coup of June 1973 was aimed at curbing a rebellious congress that was resisting military pressures and efforts to launch a full-scale internal war against subversion. Congress and the Communist-dominated National Confederation of Workers (CNT) were dissolved in June, followed by political parties of the left in December.

The extent of repression seems to have varied with the cause. In Chile, where the Socialist and Communist parties occupied the executive branch of government and were gaining ground in congress, the extent of political sadism exceeded even that in Brazil. The Brazilian military was reported as having gone to the length of crucifying some of its political prisoners, which created problems with the Church besides causing an international scandal in 1969–70. Yet a Brazilian army officer attached to his embassy in Santiago remarked to a Bolivian exile then working for the United Nations: "At least we were surgeons; these people are butchers!" After Chile and Brazil, Uruguay has established a record in military-police tortures. Although the left was closer to taking over in Bolivia than in Uruguay, special features of the Bolivian situation account for its seeming exception to the rule that repression varies directly with the menace of a socialist revolution. In Bolivia the dictatorship counted on the active collaboration in the government of the country's two principal political parties, the Revolutionary Nationalist Movement (MNR) and the pro-fascist Bolivian Socialist Falange (FSB). In Argentina, where the Peronist movement was itself anti-Communist, the extent of repression was even less. Although the torture of political prisoners first became prominent under General Juan Carlos Onganía (1966–70), it never reached the Uruguayan degree of cruelty and barbarism or the Bolivian scope of the repression. There were enough similarities between these new military regimes, however, to warrant the same type of resistance. Hence the relevance of the Peronist model.

In each of those countries the armed forces had originally justified their intervention as an interim measure aimed at crushing the political left, revising the electoral laws, and calling new elections. That they later decided to rule on their own for an indefinite period indicates their defiance of the traditional parties of the right and, more important, their independence of the landed and business oligarchies supporting these parties. Beginning in Argentina in 1966 a new political order emerged that soon spread to neighboring countries. The economic order was left unchanged, but the levers of power were no longer manipulated by propertied interests. Henceforth there was a division of privileges between the military and the owners of property: the former enjoyed a monopoly of power; the latter continued as the principal economic beneficiaries of the system. In this scheme an absolute majority of the population, consisting of wage earners, peasants and small farmers, independent artisans and shopkeepers, petty bureaucrats, and sectors of the political and labor bureaucracies, was to be denied both property and power. Hence the popular basis of a resistance patterned on the Peronist model.

Because the example of the Argentine resistance contributed to shaping the Chilean Popular Resistance Movement (MRP) and the Bolivian Alliance of the National Left (ALIN), the backbone of the resistance in both countries, the Argentine model acquired during the 1970s an international significance. Although critical of the model of an insurrectionary catalyst disseminated by Che Guevara and Régis Debray during the 1960s, the Peronist resistance was actually continuous and consistent with Fidel Castro's strategy of the "people in arms" which helped the July 26 Movement to victory in the armed resistance to Fulgencio Batista. As in Cuba under Batista's dictatorship, the fundamental problem in Argentina between 1966 and 1973 was not how to make a socialist revolution but how to unmake an oppressive regime.

The Peronist resistance harbors negative as well as positive lessons for the Latin American left. Although successful in toppling a repressive regime, it failed to crush the military as a reactionary social force in Argentina. Since the military was never thoroughly purged of its anti-Peronist elements, its backbone remained intact and actually, if not formally, independent of the Peronist Party in control of the government. The military survived the resistance and remained the principal pressure group on the various Peronist governments that succeeded one another during 1973–76. In effect, the Argentine resistance achieved only a partial and limited triumph, having removed the visible part of the cancer but not its roots.

From its inception the resistance had an absentee leader, which contributed to an early rupture within the Peronist ranks. In exile, whether in Paraguay, Panama, Venezuela, the Dominican Republic, or Franco's Spain, Perón was never in a position to lead directly the struggle for his return. The shaping of revolutionary Peronism, whose historical origins date back to Evita Perón, his first wife, was less his work than that of John William Cooke and other Peronist militants. It was they who had to organize the resistance and combat the pseudoconstitutional governments intermittently permitted by the armed forces.

During the resistance the tactics of the reformist or conciliatory wing of the movement came to be known as "Peronism without Perón," a seemingly straightforward description of a political group whose putative leader was in exile. However, the Peronist left applied this phrase disparagingly to those who had betrayed Perón, to those who rejected his confrontationist tactics applied by the movement's left wing. After his return the same reformist political and trade union bureaucracy adopted a different tactic, that of isolating Perón from the Peronist masses followed by the purging of the movement's left wing—a tactic referred to by the Peronist left as "Perón without Peronism." Evidently, the reformist wing, even with Perón's newly found support, did not have an exclusive claim to being Peronist.

Following the military coup led by General Onganía in June 1966, Perón publicly supported the movement's left wing, the Peronist Youth (JP) and its special armed formations, the Peronist Armed Forces (FAP) and Montoneros. Then, after his return from exile in June 1973, he called for legalizing the struggle for national and social liberation. When the FAP and the Guevarist-oriented People's Revolutionary Army (ERP) continued their armed actions against the multinational corporations, he initiated a new series of repressive laws that ultimately resulted in a rift in the movement. The first rupture was formalized by the FAP and the Peronism of the Bases (PB) in February 1974, when they qualified their allegiance to Perón; the second, by the Montoneros in September 1974, when they denounced the government of Isabel Perón, Juan

Domingo's widow, as "illegitimate" and called for a resumption of the resistance.

The Peronist movement has survived several crises, but the most damaging was the formal split in the movement beginning in 1974. The special armed formations and their mass fronts, which had pressured the military to abdicate, found themselves persecuted by the very movement they helped restore to power. The Chilean, Bolivian, and Uruguayan leftists are in a position to learn from such mistakes by not permitting their own resistance movements to evolve in a rightward direction. The lessons of the Argentine resistance include the politics and strategy not only of overcoming military dictatorship, but also of preventing a restoration of the status quo ante.

Since the military coup which overthrew the government of Isabel Perón in March 1976, the Peronist model of resistance has again become broadly applicable to Argentina. Only this time the Peronist armed formations have learned the lessons of the first resistance by calling for an independent front of national and social liberation under the political, as well as military, hegemony of the left. A basic lesson of the experience in power from 1973 to 1976 was the need for the left to democratize the Peronist movement, to reconstruct it on the basis of a left-of-center coalition free of control by the labor bureaucracy and the party's ultraright wing.

Following Perón's death on July 1, 1974, the government of Isabel Perón stepped up the repression against so-called "Marxist infiltrators" within the movement. Within the government the "hard-liners," in favor of repression, were led by the Minister of Social Welfare José López Rega. They succeeded in imposing their will against the "soft-liners," led by the Minister of Economics José Ber Gelbard. This victory encouraged an escalation of police and paramilitary terrorism against the left, culminating in Gelbard's resignation in October and the imposition of a state of siege in November. At the same time these developments deepened the already existent fissure in the movement, and undermined all hope of future reconciliation. With Perón's death the movement's left and right wings could no longer be held together, while the populist coalition that he had cemented between organized labor and the national bourgeoisie began to dissolve. In effect, Peronism was to become polarized into a right and left wing: a self-dominated "official" version ostensibly aimed at repeating in

Argentina the reconciliation of political opposites institutionalized
with success by the Mexican Revolution; and a self-denominated
"authentic" version endeavoring to adapt Marxism and Leninism
to specifically Argentine conditions and the outlook of Peronist
workers in particular.

This is a study, then, of Argentine politics since World War II
and their relevance to the future of Latin America. More precisely,
this is a study of Argentine Peronism, with emphasis on the
Peronist resistance, its lessons and international significance. The
focus is on the most important periods in recent Argentine history:
the national revolution under Perón (1943–55); the resistance
movement to military dictatorship and intervention (1956–73); and
the crisis of Peronism following victory, the sharpening of tensions
within the movement, and the revival of the resistance (1974–76).

Three fundamental theses are explored. First, a bureaucratic
political revolution occurred in Argentina between 1943 and 1955,
tantamount to the transference of political, if not economic, power
from the landed and business oligarchies to a bureaucratic class
within which the representatives of organized labor played a
conspicuous role, and as a result of which labor benefited both
economically and politically. Second, among the principal armed
formations of the resistance between 1956 and 1973, the Montoneros and the ex-Guevarist Revolutionary Armed Forces (FAR)
were the most successful in integrating a revolutionary vanguard
with the politics of a mass movement, in part overcoming the
dilemma of "arms without people" and the "people without arms."
Third, the model of resistance developed mainly by the FAR and
Montoneros has become a major rival to Guevarist-type movements
in Brazil, Bolivia, Uruguay, and Chile, and in several instances has
displaced them, precisely because it offers the most viable strategy
for popular-based revolutionary struggles during the 1970s.

1

The Argentine National Revolution

Fundamental to an understanding of contemporary Argentine politics is the self-styled national revolution of June 4, 1943, the military coup that, in an effort to maintain Argentine neutrality during World War II, overthrew Conservative President Ramón S. Castillo. Because of the pronounced Axis sympathies of the new military regime, its indefinite prolongation of the state of siege decreed in 1941, its dissolution of congress, and its legal ban on all political parties, it evoked extensive civilian opposition. The deposed Conservative Party joined the majoritarian Radical Party and the Socialist and Communist parties to denounce the "totalitarian" blight which had descended upon the country. In January 1944, the government finally broke off diplomatic relations with Germany and Japan. Nonetheless, Argentina was the only nation in the Western Hemisphere that did not declare war against the Axis powers until the outcome of World War II was already decided, and then only to avoid becoming isolated and the subject of recriminations by the United States.

The colonels, or "young Turks," who masterminded the coup not only launched an internal war against Marxist subversion, but also put an end to the political hegemony of the export-oriented landowning class and commercial bourgeoisie, which had dominated Argentine politics for almost a century. The hegemony of the oligarchy had been shaken from 1916 to 1930 when there was a brief interlude of rule by the Radical Party—a broad coalition including the new industrial bourgeoisie and a petty bourgeois popular base. However, the overthrow of Radical President Hipólito Yrigoyen on September 6, 1930, in a military coup led by General José Uriburu, initiated the so-called "infamous decade" during which the political power of the oligarchy was again firmly secured.

The military coup of September 6 had two wings or factions: a nationalist wing led by General Uriburu, and a liberal wing led by General Agustín P. Justo. Uriburu sought to replace the old bourgeois political regime with a corporate state modeled on that of Italian fascism, whereas the moderate or liberal faction of the army opted for a restoration of the old order of government through fraudulent elections that would guarantee the continued rule of the oligarchy. The liberal faction won, and in 1932 the military dictatorship permitted new elections from which General Justo emerged the victor. During the "infamous decade" the landed oligarchy in control of the government signed the Roca-Runciman Treaty with England, guaranteeing the British market for its agricultural exports and the Argentine market for British manufactures. This pact contributed to stifling the incipient national bourgeoisie and to obstructing the development of the new industrial sector.

Unlike Uriburu's military coup, the one which deposed President Castillo in 1943 was directed at a Conservative rather than a Radical government. It was the work of a secret nationalist military lodge, the Group of United Officers (GOU), whose "Group Work of Unification" was dominated by young colonels under the leadership of Juan Domingo Perón. Some of them, like Perón himself, had participated in leading roles in Uriburu's own coup. In 1943, however, they were not restrained by a liberal faction of the army intent on calling new elections and restoring the oligarchy to political power.

Strongly influenced by Italian fascism and profoundly nationalist in orientation, the GOU was committed to the development of an Argentine native industry as the necessary basis of a strong professional army, and to a program of social reforms as a condition of national unification. The young colonels who proclaimed the army to be the savior of the nation were intent on ruling directly, on the premise that whatever benefited the armed forces would also benefit the country. Accordingly, the military coup transferred

political power from the old landowning and commercial bourgeoisie to a new bureaucracy headed by the military. The new
military bureaucracy was not composed of agents of another class
but was accountable mainly to itself. Although it depended for
the industrialization of the country upon the nascent national
bourgeoisie, the military excluded this class from political power.
The industrial bourgeoisie received a boost from the new military
government, but at the price of continued political dependence.

Although the coup was planned and initiated by the GOU, the
latter chose to remain a secret organization and to dominate the
new government from behind the scenes. Actually, the coup was
headed by General Arturo Rawson, who was not a member of the
lodge. Proclaimed president on June 4, 1943, he was compelled to
resign three days later when his minister of war, General Pedro P.
Ramírez, was chosen by the GOU to succeed him. He in turn was
replaced as president on February 25, 1944, by his minister of war,
General Edelmiro J. Farrell. Farrell promptly appointed Perón the
new minister of war.

Throughout these changes at the helm, Perón concentrated
increasing powers in his own hands. In October 1943 he had
himself appointed to reorganize the National Department of
Labor; in November he acquired ministerial rank in the new
government as secretary of labor and security—a post he retained
after his appointment as minister of war. In July 1944 he also
occupied the vice-presidency, but his power resided in the military
lodge he headed and in the unique coalition he had created
between young nationalist military officers and the new labor
leaders unaffiliated to the traditional parties and ideologies of the
working class. The foundations of Peronism as a social and political
movement were laid with the cementing of this alliance in
February 1944, a union supported and represented by Perón in his
two key roles as minister of war and secretary of labor.

This alliance was made possible by two quite different sets of
circumstances. First, the snowballing of labor grievances, which
the trade unions had endeavored to satisfy without success during
the 1930s, encouraged a revival of labor militancy in the 1940s
calling for drastic reforms by the government. This was a period
characterized by rapid industrialization and capital accumulation
combined with massive unemployment because of the depression
and the internal migrations from the rural areas to the principal

industrial centers. Nonetheless, in the absence of state intervention, there was no redistribution of income. Second, a new generation originating within the majoritarian Radical Civic Union (UCR) had been disseminating a popular brand of Argentine nationalism which exerted a strong influence upon Perón and Peronist doctrine.

According to the standard academic interpretations of Peronist support from organized labor, that support derived mainly from a politically naïve stratum of industrial workers consisting primarily of rural immigrants to the new industrial centers of Córdoba, Rosario and the capital city of Buenos Aires. This new working class was upwardly mobile, unable to identify with the long traditions of struggle of a disciplined and independent working class, untouched by Marxist and socialist ideas and, correspondingly, an easy prey of nationalist demagogy and massive manipulation by organized political elites. Although the main opposition to Peronism within organized labor came from the stratum of skilled and highly skilled workers of predominantly European extraction, recent studies show that the principal support for Peronism did not come from the new working class of unskilled and semiskilled workers from the interior. On the contrary, the principal support for Peronism also derived from the highly politicized sectors of the old working class.

In *Studies on the Origins of Peronism,* Miguel Murmis and Juan Carlos Portantiero further show that the internal division within the Argentine working class is less significant in accounting for Peronist support than the unity of organized labor both old and new. While the newer industrial unions had been directly encouraged by Perón in his capacity as secretary of labor, the older unions were also turning to him to redress the grievances accumulated over the so-called "infamous decade." The 1930s had been a period not only of military intervention, rigged elections, economic depression, Conservative Party rule, and the economic hegemony of the landowning oligarchy, but also of strong government repression. Argentine labor desperately needed the state to intervene in the economy, but on its side instead of the employers'. Perón and his group of young nationalist officers responded to this call in an effort to cull labor's support for their own project of breaking the political stranglehold of the oligarchy and building a strong economy independent of foreign influence.

Fundamental to Perón's approach to labor was not so much the influence of European fascism as of the uniquely Argentine nationalism popularized by the Radical Orientation Forces of the Argentine Youth (FORJA). Founded by Arturo Jauretche and other Radical Party youth leaders on June 29, 1935, the FORJA initiated an anti-imperialist campaign against British interests in Argentina and against their principal allies among the native landowning and meat-exporting oligarchy. In view of the rivalries and developing hostilities between the demoliberal plutocracies and the Axis powers, it called for Argentine neutrality during World War II, a war it continued to oppose as an interimperialist one even after the German armies launched their invasion of the Soviet Union. Since, for an Argentine nationalist, Great Britain was the number one enemy because of its heavy investments in Argentina and virtual domination of the Argentine economy, the FORJA resisted the efforts by the U.S. State Department to induce Argentina to enter the war on the side of the allies. On this score the FORJA had the support of the new generation of military officers who were later to throw their weight behind Perón.

The nationalism of the FORJA was predicated on a new so-called "revisionist" interpretation of Argentine history, according to which the liberal, Europeanizing, and "civilizing" influence of the port city of Buenos Aires was conceived as a major obstacle to Argentina's economic, political, and cultural independence from Europe. This was substantially the work of Raúl Scalabrini Ortiz, whose analysis of the historic role of British imperial policy in the River Plate was basic to the FORJA's strategy. The FORJA also owed an intellectual debt to Manuel Ugarte. Expelled from the Socialist Party toward the commencement of World War I for his nationalist orientation, Ugarte favored the political unification of Latin America as the only effective defense against Anglo-Saxon imperialism. It is noteworthy that Jauretche, Scalabrini Ortiz, and Ugarte were all subsequently to serve under Perón during his first administration.

The FORJA labored diligently for a decade to disseminate through pamphlets, public speeches, and conferences its new nationalist perspective. Whatever the sources of Perón's own platform of political sovereignty, economic independence, and social justice, they were anticipated by the FORJA, which as early as 1936 had summarized its proposals for national reconstruction under the three basic themes of "popular sovereignty, economic emancipation, and social justice." Through an act of independence in 1939 the FORJA dissociated itself from the Radical Party and essentially became a process in search of a politician. When the FORJA was dissolved in December 1945, it was on the ground that Perón had become a more faithful expression of its principles than had the old Radical Party.

Although this new nationalist current lacked the theoretical depth of a Marxist-based conceptual analysis of Argentine historical and social reality, the Marxist left represented by the Socialist and Communist parties subscribed to a predominantly liberal and European-oriented interpretation of Argentina's recent past. Their respective strategies for the working class blatantly subordinated national interests either to the defense of West European social democracy or to Soviet foreign policy. Unlike the Communists, who softened their criticism of Yankee imperialism during the War, the FORJA was consistently anti-imperialist. Thus it was mainly the antinationalist role of the former leaders of Argentine labor that provided the occasion for a new crop to emerge with the support of nationalist elements within the armed forces.

The enigma of the first phase of the Argentine revolution, from June 4, 1943, to the self-dissolution of the military regime and Perón's oath of office as the newly elected president on June 4, 1946, hinged on whether there had been a revolution, as Perón claimed, or simply a continuation of the "infamous decade"—a mere change of command by which the military continued to represent the interests of the oligarchy. The established parties of the left accepted the second interpretation, which prompted them to join with the Radical and Conservative parties in the so-called Democratic Union to oppose Perón in the elections of February 1946. The Democratic Union was supported by the U.S. State Department, which in February published its notorious *Blue Book* denouncing the extent of Nazi influence in Argentina. Perón responded with the *White and Blue Book*, the colors of the Argentine flag, decrying U.S. intervention in his country's internal affairs. The issue of the election, he proclaimed to the nation, boiled down to a choice between the author of the *Blue Book*, former U.S. Ambassador Spruille Braden, and Perón. On this anti-imperialist platform, Perón won the election in the fairest and most honest contest ever held in Argentina, leading with roughly 1.5 million votes against the 1.2 million received by the opposition.

How did Perón accomplish this tour de force in defiance of all the established political parties? The answer lies in his use of the newly created secretaryship of labor and security to acquire mass support for the nationalist program launched by the military on June 4, 1943. In a speech on August 10, 1944, Perón affirmed the continuity between the redistributive and pro-union policies of his secretaryship of labor and the military coup of the year before: "The Revolution of 4 June has had two fundamental postulates which I traced with my own hand at 10 o'clock on the night of June 3rd: . . . *national unity* and . . . *social justice.* . . . This unity is to be understood, in the first place, in terms of social unity and trade union unity, which are the real foundations of the unity of the masses."

Perón succeeded in forging a political alliance with the bulk of organized labor—the old craft unions as well as the new industrial unions—through a combination of strategies that transformed the secretaryship of labor from a mere arbiter in labor-management disputes and passive intermediary between labor and government into the active champion of labor's interests on a national scale. There is little doubt that Perón stole the thunder of the traditional left and isolated it politically. After all, he had done more for organized labor during his two brief years as secretary of labor, from November 1943 to the mass mobilizations in his support in October 1945, than had the Socialist and syndicalist-oriented trade unions during the entire "infamous decade." Specifically, Perón was able to win the support of organized labor through two basic policies set in motion by the military government at his instigation. First, he developed a system of redistribution in favor of the working class, whose share of the national income during his first administration reached a record-breaking fifty percent; second, he strengthened and unified organized labor through the mass unionization of unorganized workers, the intervention of the Socialist and Communist dominated unions, the creation in certain instances of parallel unions, and the hierarchical restructuring of old unions under the authority of the secretaryship of labor.

Perón's redistribution policy was implemented through a series of legal decrees and regulations that he dictated from roughly the end of 1943 to the beginning of 1946. These included the decree concerning pensions, the establishment of labor courts, the Statute of the Peon, the regulations covering the apprenticeship of minors, the regulations governing domestic service, the regulations concerning intangible wages, the decree concerning paid vacations and a separate New Year's bonus, the regulations against arbitrary job dismissal, the statutes on tenure in selected occupations, the decree freezing rents, and the sanctions against persons or corporations obstructing the work of the secretaryship of labor.

The secretaryship of labor also initiated important changes in the field of organized labor. New unions, such as Light and Energy, the Sugar Workers of Tucumán, and the Wine Workers of Mendoza were created, as were parallel unions in textiles, woodwork, construction, and metallurgy. The intervention of the railroad unions took place. And nationalist tendencies within the tramworkers, dockworkers, and commercial employees unions were encouraged. Perón also sought to woo and co-opt labor leaders from the traditional political parties, including labor lawyers and other experts in labor matters. Among these were the ex-socialist Ángel Borlenghi, head of the commercial employees union, and Juan Atilio Bramuglia, former legal counsel for the socialist unions. At the same time, Perón encouraged the emergence of new leadership for organized labor independent of the old political parties. These new men of labor organized the first British-type labor party in Argentina in October 1945 and chose Perón as their presidential candidate in the elections scheduled for February 1946.

Perón's political ascendancy was originally made possible by the fascist-influenced, right wing nationalist officers in the GOU. It was they who had imposed upon the nation in December 1943 compulsory religious education in the schools. Perón adopted some of their principles, such as a belief in the tutelary role of the army as custodian of the supreme values of the nation embodied in Hispanic cultural tradition. He took over some of their ideas; however, he distrusted most of their men.

They did not share his conviction that a strong state must rest upon a popular basis. Many of the nationalist officers who originally followed him drew back from his efforts to link the army with the masses. Backed by liberal elements in the military, they pressured President Edelmiro Farrell on October 9, 1945, into demanding Perón's resignation as secretary of labor, minister of war, and vice-president of the nation, and into convoking elections for 1946. Perón was detained and then imprisoned by the military, but mass rallies called by Eva Duarte in Plaza de Mayo on October 17 brought about his release. From that moment he began to rely mainly upon organized labor in his struggle to return to power. Unquestionably, the betrayal by nationalist military officers accounted for his loss of confidence in them, and for their replacement in positions of influence by representatives of organized labor after he became president in June 1946.

In organizing his first electoral coalition, Perón also relied heavily upon disaffected groups and leaders within the old Radical Civic Union (UCR), the Radical Party of Hipólito Yrigoyen which still exhibited traces of its populist origins. From the UCR-Renovating Junta he chose Hortensio Quijano to be his running mate. Thus Perón became the presidential candidate of a dissident Radical organization as well as of the newly founded and electorally decisive Labor Party. On Perón's orders these two organizations officially merged in June 1946 to constitute the Unified Party of the National Revolution (PURN). The merger was resisted by the leaders of the Labor Party, who hoped to maintain their independence of the government. A rump Labor Party survived the merger, but was legally banned in 1948. And by then the PURN had come to acquire the authoritarian, hierarchical, and bureaucratic structure of the present Peronist Party, including the name which was officially adopted in January 1947.

With Perón's assumption of the presidency a new phase in the development of the revolution began. It was characterized by the most extensive political reforms and economic and social legislation Argentina had ever seen. During his first term of office, from June 4, 1946, to June 4, 1952, Perón's revolution reached its apex: the military bureaucracy, fortified by its alliance with the new labor bureaucracy, consolidated its power over the state. This was achieved at the political expense of the landowning oligarchy and the commercial bourgeoisie whose economic—as well as political—power was being eroded by government policies aimed at industrializing the country, developing the internal market, and encouraging the national bourgeoisie. Although the national revolution also contributed to the rise of organized labor, the principal political beneficiary of the revolution was the bureaucratic class as represented by its military and trade union sectors, including a budding political bureaucracy within the newly created Peronist Party.

The legislative reforms initiated during this period were designed to implement the Peronist program of political sovereignty, economic independence, and social justice. A series of basic political reforms was launched which fortified and extended the control of the bureaucracy over the nation's affairs. Simultaneously, economic and social legislation was passed which strengthened the state and the bureaucracy with regard to the traditional social classes. An ambitious program of economic reforms contributed to enlarging the public sector to the detriment of the native capitalist and imperialist sectors. At the same time, new social legislation helped to improve the conditions of the working class and to eliminate the grounds for social discontent. In effect, the Peronist pursuit of political sovereignty helped to break the political back of the export-oriented landowning and commercial interests tied to British imperialism. Its objective of economic independence contributed to boosting the economic interests of the national bourgeoisie through government subsidies to native industries. And its project of social justice led to a further redistribution of income in favor of the working class and to an increased participation of that class in political power.

Among the basic political reforms of Perón's first administration was a change in Argentina's foreign policy and the establishment in June 1946 of diplomatic relations with the Soviet Union. In the domestic field, legislation was passed in September 1947—on the initiative of Eva Duarte Perón—which gave women the vote. This action led to the foundation in July 1949 of the feminine branch of the Peronist Party with Eva Perón as president. This new branch of the party was designed to mobilize the support of Argentine women for Perón and was to constitute the third pillar of the new order, on a par with the men's branch of the party and the Peronist-dominated General Confederation of Labor (CGT). With approximately 2.5 million women voting in the presidential elections of November 1951, six women senators and twenty-four congresswomen were voted into office on the Peronist ticket—a performance unmatched during Perón's second administration.

On March 11, 1949, a new constitution based on major changes in the old one was promulgated. These included the incorporation of an historic charter on the "Rights of the Worker." The president was given the right to succeed himself in office without the lapse of an intervening term. These changes, along with the forced merger of the Labor Party and the UCR-Renovating Junta, contributed to the consolidation of the Peronist movement and to Perón's landslide vote (almost double that of his opponents) in November 1951.

Earlier in 1948 the government had begun to intervene in the field of mass communications and by 1950 had developed an extensive chain of government-owned and operated newspapers and broadcasting networks. In January 1951 the oligarchy's principal opposition newspaper *La Prensa* was closed by the government, and then expropriated by a congressional act in April. Many such changes, including the dismissal of the Supreme Court justices in April 1947, following a Senate-initiated investigation of their role in obstructing the work of the secretaryship of labor, were designed to crush political opposition to the new regime. However, when one considers that the opposition was organized mainly by the old Radical and Conservative parties, it is evident that the semitotalitarian character of Perón's reforms had a revolutionary content. By strengthening the political power of the bureaucracy, he helped to consolidate the national revolution, while preventing a revival of the counterrevolutionary oligarchy and liberal bourgeoisie.

The economic reforms of Perón's first administration included the nationalization of key sectors of the economy, the creation of new industries, the restrictions on the repatriation of profits by foreign companies, the control of credit through the Central Bank, the liquidation of the foreign debt and corresponding dependence on Great Britain and the United States, the inauguration of Argentina's first five-year plan in January 1947, and the channeling of the economic surplus from agriculture into industry through government-imposed price controls and a state monopoly over the purchase of agricultural goods.

The historic "Act of Economic Independence," presented by Perón to the nation on July 9, 1947, was a major turning point. The British-owned railroads and port facilities and the U.S.-owned electric companies were nationalized. In January 1947 German investments had been confiscated on the pretext that they constituted enemy property. As a result of these expropriations and the regulation of the repatriation of profits, the general level of foreign investments dropped off markedly. Ironically, the United States became the principal foreign investor in Argentina not because of the influx of U.S. capital but by default because of the government's policy of nationalizing foreign enterprises, the bulk of which were

British-owned. This policy contributed not only to eliminating foreign control over the economic infrastructure, but also to reducing the financial services paid to foreign companies. All bank deposits and the foreign exchange market came under government jurisdiction, which gave the Central Bank a monopoly over the country's financial resources.

Among the new industries created were the merchant marine and air transport industries, which made Argentina almost self-sufficient in those areas. Priority was given to the development of the state-owned petroleum company YPF—"You Poor Fool!"— whose initials had long been a butt of ridicule for foreigners. The financing of new industries and the promotion of old ones was channeled through one of the principal economic agencies created by the regime, the Argentine Institute for the Promotion of Trade (IAPI), which funded the industrialization program of the first five-year plan. Through its monopoly over the export of cereals, which reached a high of more than ninety percent in 1949, the IAPI bought grains at low prices on the domestic market and sold them at high prices on the world market. It was then able to funnel the monetary surplus into industry.

The principal agencies of social reform during Perón's first term of office were the secretaryship of labor and security and Evita Perón's Foundation of Social Aid, both working in close cooperation with the labor bureaucracy of the CGT. Once installed in the presidency, Perón turned his attention increasingly to political and economic matters, leaving to Evita the principal initiative for social reforms. The secretaryship of labor came increasingly under her influence, as did the bureaucracy of the CGT which she packed with her friends and supporters. Not only were women's rights one of her favorite causes, but also the welfare of the dispossessed—the so-called *descamisados* or "shirtless ones." Evita became the propelling force behind the secretaryship of labor, and the principal figure in charge of the nation's welfare program.

The Foundation of Social Aid, established in June 1947, was far from being a charity in the traditional sense. Although it began with a capital of 10,000 pesos originally donated by Eva Perón with the help of voluntary contributions from private individuals and organizations, it quickly acquired a public character. Besides occasional subsidies by the government, it benefited from the transfer during one year of twenty percent of the revenues of the

National Lottery. It was also exempted, beginning in July 1949, from all taxes. At its August 1950 congress, the CGT voted to contribute to the Foundation an annual deduction of two days' wages from each of its several million members, amounting to roughly six million pesos annually. The Foundation also served a political purpose. In response to the military veto of Evita's candidacy as vice-president in August 1951, followed by the unsuccessful coup of General Luciano Benjamín Menéndez in September, the Foundation ordered the purchase of weapons and munitions for the purpose of organizing popular militias in defense of the government and the CGT.

In contrast to the charities dispensed by the fashionable and aristocratic Beneficent Society, the Foundation initiated a comprehensive building program that included the construction of apartment complexes for workers, orphanages, homes for the aged, houses for transients, medical clinics, and schools. Of the 4,000 schools constructed between June 1943 and December 1950, for example, one fourth were erected by the Foundation. The Foundation distributed food and clothes to the needy and in 1951 opened a chain of twenty-four dispensaries in Buenos Aires, where articles of necessity might be bought at reduced prices. It also organized sports events for children, provided free playthings, and distributed refreshments worth millions during the traditional Christmas holidays. These and the many other services provided by the Foundation helped to foster Evita's popularity and to perpetuate her memory among the masses. As Perón noted in the "Twenty Truths of Justicialism" presented to the nation in his Plaza de Mayo address of October 17, 1950: "The two arms of Peronism are social justice and social aid. With them we give to the people an *abrazo* [embrace] of justice and of love."

The policy of giving priority to the interests of organized labor was another prominent feature of Perón's first administration. In 1948 real wages were almost forty percent higher than in 1943. The government raised fringe benefits, which amounted to another forty-percent increase. It increased the number of paid legal holidays, provided accident and health insurance for most workers, and initiated a new social security program. In 1943 only half a million workers had been eligible for social security; in 1946 the number had risen to more than one and a half million; and by 1952 it included as many as five million workers. The organization of unorganized workers received a tremendous boost. There were some 200,000 organized workers in 1943; there were approximately 500,000 when Perón became president in 1946; and there were roughly three million by the end of his first term of office. The social composition of organized labor had also changed. At the beginning of 1946 it had consisted of the aristocracy of labor, mainly skilled workers, European immigrants, and their immediate descendants. By the end of 1951 it consisted mainly of unskilled workers from the interior who had migrated to the big cities, the untutored and so-called *cabecitas negras,* for whom Peronism represented the only philosophy of labor they had ever known.

Under Perón, for the first time in Argentine history workers occupied important government positions. Beginning in 1945, Juan A. Bramuglia, a former lawyer for the socialist railroad union, was appointed federal intervenor in the key province of Buenos Aires. During Perón's first government workers were also appointed to important cabinet positions, an index of labor's newly acquired political power. Bramuglia became minister of foreign affairs. Ángel Borlenghi, the head of the union of commercial employees, became minister of the interior. Ramón Cereijo became minister of finance. And José María Freire, a leader of the glassworkers union, served for a brief period as secretary of labor.

The president's own wife had been a labor organizer. Eva Duarte had taken a leading role in organizing the national union of radio employees and the mass demonstrations in Plaza de Mayo on October 17, 1945. Once Perón became president, Evita moved her office to the secretaryship of labor where she assumed de facto control over all government agencies concerned with labor matters, taking charge of all collective bargaining agreements, contracts, pensions, and disputes involving organized labor. Through her control of the secretariat of labor and her encouragement of labor leaders and individual workers to come to her directly with their problems, she built up a personal following in the labor movement that soon rivaled that of the president. She actively intervened in union elections and sought to pack the leadership of the CGT with those loyal to her. Because of a falling out with Evita, Aurelio Hernández, who had been selected by Perón in 1947 to replace the former Labor Party chief Luis Gay as secretary-general of the CGT, was replaced in 1948 by José Espejo. The new secretary-general, the head of the grocers union, had also served as janitor of the apartment building where Evita and Juan Domingo once occupied adjacent suites.

So important was Evita's role as intermediary between the government and organized labor that after her death Perón took over personally the secretaryship of labor and the direction of the Evita Perón Foundation. As Evita explained the relationship of Perón and herself to the people in *The Reason of My Life,* when he became president she took his place in directly defending the interests of the workers. There could be no conflict of interest between labor and the government because "to divorce himself from the people, the head of the government would have to begin by divorcing his own wife."

Perón's second administration inaugurated on June 4, 1952, was followed shortly by Evita's death on July 26. Since nobody was capable of filling her shoes, the nation's system of social welfare failed to move forward without her. Evita's death boded a decline in the fortunes of organized labor. Under Perón's renewed direction, the secretaryship of labor failed to initiate any major social legislation. New leaders for the CGT were appointed in October including a new secretary-general, Eduardo Vuletich, but they did little to distinguish themselves. By 1952 the Peronist Party had developed a top-heavy bureaucracy dedicated to maintaining the new status quo. Once firmly entrenched in power, the political and trade union bureaucracies had no intention of rocking the boat through a showdown with the landed oligarchy and the commercial bourgeoisie, but sought instead to establish a modus vivendi with them.

With Evita's death, the national revolution came to a screeching halt not only in matters of social justice, but also in the economic and political fields. Industrial growth suffered a relapse beginning in 1951–52. Economically, the nation could no longer count on boosting its foreign trade in the wake of the worldwide beef and grain shortages following World War II. Droughts throughout the country led to a fall in grain production which, combined with the deterioration of the terms of trade, adversely affected Argentine exports. As a result, the trade surpluses that had provided the financial basis for Argentina's industrialization during Perón's first administration were gradually eroded.

Faced with a shortage of capital, congress approved a law in August 1953 favoring the investment of foreign capital in industry and mining on terms beneficial to U.S. companies. The same month Perón began negotiations with U.S. oil interests for the purpose of developing Argentina's petroleum resources. In April 1955, a contract was signed by the government with the Argentine branch of Standard Oil of California. It was opposed by the militant sector of the Peronist movement led by John William Cooke. When the financial surpluses that had accrued to the IAPI during the late 1940s were displaced by deficits because of the fall in world market prices for cereal exports, the government began to issue new money. The immediate result was widespread inflation, the erosion of real wages, and the redistribution of income at the expense of the workers. When mounting labor discontent issued in demands for higher wages, the Peronist bureaucracy responded with an exhortation to the workers to produce more and to consume less. The result was a loss of confidence in both the party and the government.

Faced with a deteriorating economic situation, the government had only one recourse: to carry the revolution forward. To go forward, however, Perón would have had to rely on the masses, not on the entrenched members of the political and trade union bureaucracies. By 1952 the Peronist bureaucracy had become a closed corporation, hierarchically organized with all initiatives coming from above. In fact, nothing was done to overcome the crisis. In the search for new sources of capital, the government could have appropriated the entire parasitic rent from the owner-ship of land, thus putting an end to the cattle-raising and grain-producing oligarchy. The meat-packing industry and foreign monopolies might have been nationalized, thereby contributing additional revenues. Although the IAPI had a virtual monopoly over grain exports, it failed to gain control of wool exports nor did it ever acquire control over the import sector. The sugar-refining industries could have been nationalized, but were not. Although it had granted diplomatic recognition to the Soviet Union, the government did not establish trade relations with the Soviet bloc. Furthermore, it neglected to develop heavy industry. Far more drastic measures were needed, especially in the areas of agrarian reform and government control of foreign commerce, than the Peronist bureaucracy and Perón himself were ever willing to take.

Perón's second administration lost the political support first of the national bourgeoisie, then of the church, and finally of the military. The failure of the IAPI to provide sufficient funds to assure continued industrial expansion encouraged the national bourgeoisie to look to the United States for new sources of capital and technology. Since the U.S. had emerged from World War II as one of the largest exporters of grains and meat products, it chose to ally itself with Argentina's new industrial bourgeoisie rather than, as Great Britain had done, with the old landowning and commercial oligarchies. The national bourgeoisie had discovered a new ally in U.S. imperialism, whose runaway factories were on the lookout for cheap sources of labor and raw materials for local production and export. Thus, when a law was passed in 1953 permitting only limited private investments in the key automobile, petrochemical, and electrical appliance industries, the national bourgeoisie became dissatisfied with the government, broke off relations with the Peronist movement, and allied itself increasingly with foreign interests.

Perón's difficulties with the church began in 1954 and were brought to a head in December by a congressional act which, for the first time in Argentina, made divorce legal. Added to this insult to the ecclesiastical hierarchy, congress approved another act in May 1955 removing religious instruction from the schools. The church replied by inciting mass demonstrations against the government, to which Perón responded by expelling two Argentine prelates from the country. On June 16 Perón was excommunicated by the Vatican; the same day the navy launched an abortive coup. The confrontation was further escalated when the Peronist masses responded to the aerial bombardment of the Plaza de Mayo by burning and desecrating churches in the nation's capital. Although Perón retreated before the opposition, the die had been cast. Thus one of the explanations of his fall from power was his violation of religious tradition, which continued to be sacred among the army, and among nationalist military officers in particular.

Perón was overthrown by a coalition of nationalist and liberal armed forces factions in a military coup reminiscent of the one that overthrew the Radical President Hipólito Yrigoyen in 1930. Both coups were directed against a majoritarian populist party in power. Each began under nationalist auspices to be followed shortly by the ascendancy of the army's liberal wing and the calling of new, if narrowly restricted or fraudulent, elections. The self-styled "Liberator Revolution" of September 16, 1955, which dissolved congress and sent Perón into exile, was originally led by the nationalist General Eduardo Lonardi. As provisional president, Lonardi adopted an economic program that was not basically different from Perón's, appointed a new pro-Peronist minister of labor, sought an accommodation with the CGT, and attempted to woo the moderate elements within the Peronist movement. Since his policy of "neither victors nor vanquished" was regarded by the army's liberal faction as too lenient, Lonardi was in turn over-thrown by a coup led by General Pedro Aramburu on November 13, 1955.

The CGT called a general strike to protest the new government's labor policy. Aramburu then organized the most repressive cam-paign in the nation's history designed to stamp out, organization-ally and politically, all traces of Peronist influence as well as resistance to the "liberal" dictatorship. The CGT was intervened by the government on November 15 and its leaders were arrested. By September 1957 it had formally dissolved into 62 Peronist unions and 32 independent ones. It was not restored to legality until the early 1960s. Aramburu decreed the Peronist Constitution of 1949 to be null and void, thus returning the country to the old political system and the liberal constitution of 1853. Elections were eventually called for February 1958. However, the Peronist Party had been proscribed, while a decree dated March 6, 1956, prohibited anyone from holding elective office who had held any position in the Peronist Party since June 1946.

Perón's fall is to be attributed to the disintegration of the populist alliance between organized labor and the military. Yet the military was not alone in its disaffection with Perón's second administration. Perón's new economic policy, which obliged him to curtail the social and economic gains won during his first administration, also contributed to alienating the workers. Following the presidential elections of November 1951, Perón sought to establish stricter measures of control over the inflationary spiral. In December he helped to establish the General Confederation of Economics (CGE) to represent the new manufacturing industrialists, and asked them to cooperate with the CGT in stabilizing wages and prices—mea-sures precursory to those of the Social Pact of June 1973. In effect, the anti-inflation campaign by the government put an end to any new wage demands by the trade union bureaucracy. This campaign reached a climax in March 1955, when the CGT and the CGE jointly sponsored a National Congress of Productivity and Social Welfare with emphasis on labor-management cooperation in the so-called national interest.

Since Perón had effectively abandoned the workers in order to neutralize the growing political opposition of the bourgeoisie, compounded by increasing restlessness and dissatisfaction within the armed forces, the workers were hardly in a mood to lay down their lives in defense of the regime. Under pressure from the opposition and fearful of a repetition of the military coup of June 16, 1955, Perón asked the leading Peronist militants in the government and the trade unions to resign—the Minister of the Interior Ángel Borlenghi and the CGT's Secretary-General Eduardo Vuletich—and permitted the military to seize the CGT's arsenal of 5,000 rifles and revolvers. These setbacks to labor's influence and power were crowned on July 15 when Perón addressed the nation in a speech announcing the end of the revolution. All revolutions, he noted, have a beginning and an end: "The Peronist Revolution has ended; now begins a new constitutional stage without revolution. . . . I have ceased to be the leader of the National Revolution in order to become President of all the Argentines."

A month later, however, as the rumblings within the labor movement mounted, he reversed himself by announcing the end of the political truce. In mid-August the CGT, in a campaign aimed at reidentifying Perón with the lost Evita, launched a series of inflammatory editorials attacking all opposition to the government. On August 31 Perón addressed a crowd assembled in Plaza de Mayo in a renewed challenge to his enemies, following which the new secretary-general of the CGT, Hugo Di Pietro, offered to place the voluntary reserves of the workers at the disposition of the army—an offer the military rejected because it foreshadowed the emergence of a workers' militia. Perón's final desperate efforts to reestablish his popularity with the workers came too late, and in September they did not respond to Di Pietro's call to fight for Perón. Furthermore, Perón never gave the order to fight until he was safely out of the country. In any case, he had collaborated with the army in depriving them of weapons.

The difference between Perón's relations with organized labor and the military at the beginning and at the end of the Perón era (1943–55) is neatly summarized in Samuel Baily's *Labor, National-*

ism, and Politics in Argentina. During the crisis of October 1945, workers united to defend Perón and the national revolution, even though Perón had given no order to fight and they had no arms. At the same time, the military was divided over the question of support for Perón and unable to win civilian backing. Together these factors contributed to the victory of the workers on October 17. In September 1955, however, the military was united in opposition to Perón and had civilian support. This time the workers were divided, even though the majority of them identified with Peronism. Since Perón had given no order to fight and they were unarmed, these circumstances favored the victory of the military on September 16.

Although Perón had long sought a solution to Argentina's predicament of economic dependency, his account of the underlying causes of his fall in September 1955 showed virtually no understanding of the changed character of that dependency. In Perón's principal work on the antecedents and significance of the so-called Liberator Revolution, *Force is the Right of Beasts,* the coup was interpreted as a showdown between two classes: the productive class of manual, technical, and intellectual workers who allegedly consumed only what they produced; and the parasitic class consisting of the oligarchy, the clergy, and the professional politicians who lived off the surplus created by the productive class. Perón's intellectual apparatus was hardly capable of appreciating the subtle transformations undergone by the Argentine national bourgeoisie during his second administration, a national bourgeoisie figuring as "productive workers" in this obsolete schematism dating from the French Revolution of 1789 and the political philosophy of Saint-Simon. Thus the coup was explained in such loose and subjective terms as the "reaction" of the parasitic class and the "treason" by sectors of the armed forces "at the service of the bastard ambitions of obscure men, generally ignorant and unqualified," who had become mercenaries in the service of a corrupting capitalism and had sold their honor from a sordid desire for money. In effect, Perón explained his fall as the product of a simple conspiracy initiated by the oligarchy with the backing of the clergy and the minority political parties, a coup allegedly "directed, financed, and controlled by domestic and foreign capital."

Missing from this account was an explanation of why the various coups against the Peronist government in September 1951, February 1952, and June 1955 failed, whereas that in September 1955 succeeded. In *The Fall of Perón from June to September 1955,* Julio Godio argues that the conditions for the success of the September 1955 coup included, on the one hand, the breakup of Perón's populist and majoritarian front and, on the other hand, the formation of a new political bloc capable of providing popular support for the conspiracy. What Perón had failed to realize was that by 1953 the national bourgeoisie had already ceased to benefit from his program of stimulating the internal market through labor reforms and higher wages for Argentine workers. Once the post–World War II and Korean War booms had run their course, the economy settled down into a condition of relative stagnation. In consequence, the former positive-sum game advantageous to both labor and capital deteriorated into a zero-sum game, in which for every winner there had to be a loser. Under those changed conditions there were only two remedies available to Argentina's growing and aspiring national bourgeoisie. First, a renewed impetus toward economic growth within the structure of Argentina's dependent-capitalist system required a new influx of capital goods and new sources of financing in the imperialist metropolises. Second, a policy of encouragement to foreign investments depended upon a cutback in the gains of organized labor. Since neither of these courses was acceptable to Perón, to the CGT, or to the Justicialist movement, the national bourgeoisie shifted within a few years from a posture of active support to one of outright hostility to the anti-imperialist and prolabor policies of the Peronist government.

The national bourgeoisie was not the only class to enter into a new political bloc with the oligarchy, the foreign bourgeoisie, and disaffected elements within the military. During his second administration Perón made the mistake of stepping up repression against the vanguard of the liberal opposition, against university students and the petty bourgeoisie, instead of against the main enemy consisting of the landed oligarchy and the big capitalists. Since the opposition Radical Civic Union was the principal spokesman for these groups, it too joined the anti-Peronist crusade pressing for Perón's resignation. The UCR's support of a military coup made the difference between the abortive coup of June 1955 and the successful attempt in September. It effectively neutralized the professional wing of the military, while raising the hopes of the anti-Peronist or *golpista* sectors.

In this situation, Perón's only hope of saving his administration was to strengthen his last remaining base of popular support—the trade unions. His widely proclaimed "State of the Workers" depended upon workers' militias to defend it. Instead, Perón turned to the army, while seeking a negotiated settlement with the military and civilian opposition to his government. Fearful of the intensified campaign being waged against him and the Peronist movement, he sought to join rather than to confront his enemies. In the effort to serve as "President of all the Argentines," he even resigned his post as head of the Peronist Party. His so-called "pacification policy" between June and August 1955 effectively made him turn his back on organized labor. Thus when the final blow came in September, even his staunchest followers hesitated to defend the national revolution.

But was the self-styled national revolution really a revolution? If not, then the Conservative and Radical parties had strong reasons for supporting it. Despite the legal ban on their activities, their fundamental interests and those of the nationalist government should have coincided. In time they would have sought a modus vivendi with the new regime. But this never happened. If the so-called revolution was in fact one, then the minoritarian Socialist and Communist parties had little cause to resist it. In any case, one would have anticipated their eventual accommodation to Peronism. This never occurred.

The question of whether Argentina did or did not experience a national revolution under Perón's leadership is still hotly debated. For the most part, the controversy hinges on how the term "revolution" is used. In the Marxist tradition, the only kind of revolution that is usually worthy of the name is a social revolution, tantamount to the transfer of economic power from one social class to another, the transformation of property relations, or the foundation of a new economic order. In this sense there was no national revolution between 1943 and 1955. Within the non-Marxist tradition, the term is most often used for a violent and abrupt change in political or economic institutions independently of the question of its class significance. Since the transfer of political power from one class to another does not always occur either violently or abruptly, it falls short of being revolutionary even though it constitutes a

major structural change. Furthermore, this usage fails to discrimi-
nate between revolutions and counterrevolutions. At least the
traditional Marxist use of the term errs by way of overprecision
rather than looseness.

Actually, the customary Marxist usage is not the only one
consistent with a Marxist conceptual framework. Just as a social
revolution consists of the transfer of economic power, so a political
revolution may be interpreted as the transfer of political power to a
new class. The significance of this distinction is that social
revolutions, at least in the twentieth century, tend to be prepared
in advance through the seizure of political power by a given class,
which then uses it as leverage to acquire the lion's share of the
economic surplus. This is not to say that every political revolution
is followed by a corresponding social revolution, but only that the
former is usually a necessary condition of the latter. The Argentine
national revolution did not issue in a corresponding social revolution, which in no way gainsays its character as a bureaucratic
political revolution that effectively eliminated, between 1943 and
1955, bourgeois control of the state apparatus.

The answer to this question also hinges on how the term
"bureaucracy" is used. If the bureaucracy is conceived not as a
class rooted in the economic structure of society but as a stratum
linked to the legal superstructure, then it is a mere agent of a class.
Exceptional conditions may arise when it is able to exert its
independence, but only when a dominant class is being successfully
challenged by a new aspiring one. Even with this qualification the
Marxist stereotype of the bureaucracy as a mere stratum is
inadmissible: first, political administrators also perform economic
functions; second, the managers of industrial, commercial, and
financial enterprises also perform legal and administrative tasks
corresponding to those of political bureaucrats; third, they, too, are
momentarily capable of asserting their independence of Marx's
principal classes; and fourth, they share in common the ownership
of a separate factor of production alternatively identified with
"expertise" or "organizational know-how." Marx's model of social
classes needs to be updated to include the political and military
bureaucracies. Since they fail to qualify either as exploited laborers
or as owners of capital, while nonetheless appropriating a share of
the economic surplus, they cannot be reduced to the status of either
proletarians or bourgeois. Ergo, they constitute a separate class.

In this perspective the Argentine national revolution was not an isolated phenomenon nor is it the only example of its kind. In fact, the revolution of June 4, 1943, was followed in Bolivia by a similar revolution on December 20, 1943. It began with a military coup led by Major Gualberto Villarroel, the head of "Patriotic Cause" (RADEPA), a secret military lodge of young nationalist officers. Like Perón, Villarroel was devoted to the modernization of the army, which made him question the monopoly of power by a traditionalist landed oligarchy. The RADEPA's program of political sovereignty, economic independence, and social justice was designed to overcome Bolivia's semicolonial status and dependency. Unlike the later revolution of 1952–64, which destroyed the landed oligarchy economically as well as politically, the revolution launched by Major Villarroel was a strictly political one. It mainly benefited a bureaucratic class led by military officers intent on ruling independently of the traditional class structure. Again, as in Argentina, the revolution ended on a sour note. On July 21, 1946, Villarroel was overthrown by a counterrevolutionary coup of "liberal" generals who not only restored the political rule of the oligarchy, but also allowed him to be unceremoniously hung from a lamppost in the public square opposite the presidential palace.

A more recent example of the Argentine model of bureaucratic political revolution is afforded by the Peruvian national revolution of October 3, 1968, led by another group of "young Turks" or so-called "Nasserist colonels"—named after the leader of the Egyptian national revolution of 1954. Actually, the terms "Nasserism" and "Peronism" are interchangeable when applied to the younger generation of left-wing officers in Latin America. Like the Peronist revolution of 1943–55, the Peruvian national revolution led to the transfer of political power from the landed oligarchy and commercial bourgeoisie to a military bureaucracy ruling in its own interests. Major political, economic, and social reforms were introduced beginning in 1968, including an agrarian reform and a new system of industrial communities based on profit sharing and labor participation in management, but without a corresponding social revolution. Like the Argentine military under Perón, the Peruvian military launched an ambitious program of nationalization of foreign enterprises designed to strengthen the public sector and to overcome the country's dependence on the multinational corporations and the world market. Although its original social basis was the peasantry rather than the industrial proletariat, it later acquired labor backing by creating the government-controlled National System of Support for Social Mobilization (SINAMOS). Argentine influence was also evident in the new regime's commitment to a "Third Position," first formulated by Perón in the 1940s, which aligned Peru with the Third World in foreign policy and, domestically, with a so-called *via media* between capitalism and socialism. In practice, this was tantamount to the coexistence of a new bureaucratic political order and a modernized capitalist sector, in which the principal political beneficiary was the army and the principal economic beneficiary was the national bourgeoisie, but in which labor too made important gains.

2

Development of the Resistance

The Peronist resistance began in response to the campaign of repression launched by the liberal wing of the armed forces, which seized power through the coup-within-a-coup of November 13, 1955. In retaliation for the general strike called by the CGT to protest the regime's labor policies, all of the trade union, professional, and cultural organizations of the Peronist movement were intervened, confiscated, or destroyed by the military, which did not hesitate to use tanks for that purpose. With most of the CGT leaders in jail and deserted by the political leadership of the movement, Perón's only recourse was to turn to new leaders and to prepare the workers for a protracted struggle against the dictatorship. This called for reorganizing the movement from the bottom up. Thus, relying mainly on intermediate cadres and on the younger generation of trade unionists to bring forth new leaders, Perón actively promoted the militant elements within the movement.

Although the resistance began without him, it was formally launched in a secret directive by Perón in January 1956. This message to the top militants in the movement was smuggled into Argentina through the Commando of Peronist Exiles in Chile. It called not only for industrial sabotage of various kinds, but also for armed struggle against the dictatorship. Rather than reorganize the movement on the basis of old slogans and strategy, it demanded a social revolution in addition to a political one. Accordingly, it rejected the reformist and gradualist tactics employed with only limited success during the decade 1946–55, and instead advocated carrying the revolution to its ultimate consequences (*Militancia,* 12 July 1973).

Perón's secret communiqué contained both general and specific guidelines on how to organize the resistance. Among its general directives was an exhortation to the Peronist rank and file to undertake actions independently of their former leaders, to recognize new leaders by their deeds, and to repudiate those who might have approached or established contact with representatives of the dictatorship. Specifically, the message directed the masculine and feminine branches of the party to turn the house of each member into a basic unit or cell under his or her direction for the purpose of building a new underground organization. It also contained directives to the trade union branch to replace old leaders with more militant ones, to organize strike committees, work stoppages, slowdowns and breakdowns aimed at demoralizing the regime. In these several ways the military dictatorship was conceived by Perón as a purifying agent destined to restore the movement's original revolutionary impetus.

In response to his letter, a clandestine National Command was created that brought together in a single organization and under a unified command all the underground Peronist groupings and organizations that had survived repression. In February 1956 it published its first "Manifesto," demanding the unconditional return of Perón. It called for a struggle of national liberation which was to be organized through Peronist bases or commandos in every factory and neighborhood—thus applying Perón's secret directives. Defining itself as the representative of the Peronist rank and file in opposition to the old leadership, which had effectively disappeared or betrayed the movement, the National Command became the principal coordinator and center of the Peronist resistance until roughly 1959.

The first concrete efforts at armed resistance were taken not by the National Command, however, but by General Juan José Valle and a group of Peronist officers who, having been imprisoned by the "liberal" dictatorship of General Aramburu, were released in March 1956. General Valle retired to a farm on the outskirts of the capital, where he and other officers organized the Movement of National Recovery. Initially, it included representatives of the nationalist faction within the army, who had been displaced by the "liberals" in November. But these elements withdrew as soon as it became evident that the leaders were working for Perón's return. Contacts were also made with trade union leaders such as Andrés Framini, the last secretary-general of the intervened CGT, although organized labor was never considered to be more than an auxiliary force by the military officers loyal to Perón. The Movement of National Recovery attempted to overthrow Aramburu on June 9, 1956, but the coup was aborted before it was born. This first insurrectionary attempt with a military origin ended with the assassination of soldiers and civilians loyal to Perón and with the abrupt and arbitrary execution of General Valle and a score of Peronist officers at the hands of a firing squad. Thus ended the first stage of militant opposition and armed struggle, to be followed after a temporary lull or letdown in the resistance by a second upsurge in January 1959.

The complete failure of Valle's military putsch does not seem to have discouraged Perón, who had adopted a different strategy based on mass resistance. The National Command was assigned the task of sowing new seeds of discontent in the expectation of forcing the march of events. In a letter to Cooke from Caracas dated May 8, 1957, Perón favored the use of psychological warfare. He advocated reliance on clandestine radio transmitters, infiltration, provocation, and the perpetration of social disorders to prepare a new climate of hostilities. "Now is the time to make war against the dictatorship without quarter and without rest, from within and from without," he wrote in his first defense of the tactical methods of the guerrillas and of the strategic conception of an "integral war" later adopted by the Montoneros. "Peronists must be persuaded to combat in all parts and under all circumstances, with all means at their command, the dictatorship that is bound to fall not through a great battle as it anticipates, but through millions of small encounters which its means are insufficient to prevent and where the enemy cannot concur to defend itself. . . ." (*Militancia*, 19 July 1973). When this climate of hostilities is in full vigor, he continued, the moment will have arrived to paralyze the economy and to launch guerrilla operations in as many places as possible and where the conditions are most favorable.

Thus Perón belatedly decided to adopt Cooke's plan of resistance based on guerrilla warfare, first formulated in response to the abortive June 1955 uprising against Perón and the precursor of the September military coup. This plan, whose details were the work of Abraham Guillén, the Spanish anarcho-Marxist and Civil War veteran who worked as a journalist on Cooke's political magazine *De Frente*, relied mainly on the experiences of the Spanish resistance against General Franco. Proposed by Cooke for adoption by the Supreme Council of the Peronist Party between June and September 1955, the plan was vetoed by generals loyal to Perón on the ground that it would create a dual instead of a unified military command.

Following the temporary ebb in the resistance in the wake of General Valle's abortive putsch, a new wave occurred during the presidency of Arturo Frondizi and his Intransigent Radical Party —elected on a popular and anti-imperialist platform with the support of the Peronist movement. Prior to the elections of February 1958, Perón had entered into an agreement with Frondizi—the so-called "Perón-Frondizi Pact"—in which he traded approximately two million votes in return for a promise of legality for his movement, a general amnesty for imprisoned and exiled Peronist leaders, and a restoration of the CGT under Peronist leadership. After being inaugurated on May Day 1958, Frondizi granted a general amnesty but postponed the "normalization" of the CGT until 1961, and did not restore the Peronist Party to legality until early in 1962. Moreover, he betrayed the nationalist and anti-imperialist platform that had contributed to his election by signing contracts with eight foreign oil companies. This provoked a general wave of protest strikes, which contributed to a new upsurge in the resistance beginning in January 1959.

From Perón's standpoint the pact with Frondizi was only a temporary measure designed to strengthen the Peronist movement in preparation for a new phase of confrontation. That he continued to share Cooke's assessment of the Argentine situation and of the need to develop an insurrectionary strategy is evident from a letter to Cooke, dated September 16, 1958, from Ciudad Trujillo in the Dominican Republic: "In a private meeting the politicians are strong, but in the street power is in the hands of those who manipulate the masses, if only they know how to unite them in action. It is necessary to abandon all political action that is not directed toward agitating the masses, who constitute our strength." The priority of an insurrectionary strategy, Perón continued, is founded on the necessity of mobilizing the masses in street actions against the repressive legislation imposed by the military: "If we, bound by a strategy of small steps that are merely political, conform to the methods that favor the politicians, then we shall no longer be able to rely on the majority, but shall go on losing time and strength until we are dominated. If, on the other hand, we raise problems in the street through an agitation without precedent, choosing well the themes of that agitation, then we shall put in evidence our superiority. . . . We should not forget that this has been Peronist procedure since 1945 and that, in all circumstances, it has yielded excellent results" (*Militancia,* 11 October 1973).

At the same time, the Perón-Frondizi Pact was being given a different interpretation by the revived trade union bureaucracy in the "62 Organizations" loyal to Perón. In August 1957 the still intervened CGT had split into two principal blocs: the "62" Peronist controlled unions and the "32" liberal trade unions led by socialists, radicals, and "independents." For the Peronist trade unions the pact was mainly a device to recover control of the CGT, to restore the Peronist Party, and to run their own candidates for public office. Since this legally oriented branch of the movement was insisting on its independence from the National Command or clandestine branch, Perón was obliged to establish a Supreme Council with authority over both—in the interest of unified direction for the resistance. As head of the National Command and chief of operations, Cooke was selected by Perón to be one of the delegates of the Supreme Council and as a counterweight to the reformist line of the "62 Organizations."

Revolutionary Peronism had been initiated and nurtured by the National Command under conditions in which the legal possibilities of the movement for bargaining and maneuver were either narrowly restricted or nonexistent. Beginning with the Perón-Frondizi Pact, agreed upon through the intermediary of Cooke, the prospect of major concessions through negotiation contributed to a resurgence of the Peronist political and trade union bureaucracies. Although the favorable consequences of the pact included the release of trade union leaders, the sanction of a law of professional associations permitting the reorganization of each union under a national leadership, and an increase in wages of sixty percent, these were offset by the growth of a conciliatory wing in the movement which began to challenge the clandestine leadership of the National Command.

The emerging conflict between the Peronist National Command and the "62 Organizations" was first publicized in January 1959, on the heels of the general strike supporting the workers' occupation of the nationalized meat-packing plant "Lisandro de la Torre." The National Command issued a declaration which publicly censured the vacillating role of the trade union bureaucracy. This declaration, dated January 30, 1959, characterized the strike as the most formidable demonstration in Argentine history of the repudiation of an unpopular government by the masses, and at the same time criticized the trade union bureaucracy for not having prepared the workers for such a confrontation (*Militancia,* 19 July 1973).

It was no ordinary strike. In response to President Frondizi's decision to denationalize the plant because of pressure on the government from the International Monetary Fund, the workers occupied it on January 15 as a sign of protest. Other work stoppages spontaneously followed along with the shutdown of small businesses in the suburbs of Mataderos, Villa Lugano, Villa Luro, and Liniers. On January 17, the police of Buenos Aires showed up in force outside the plant, supported by army cavalry and four Sherman tanks. After a violent struggle lasting several hours the workers defenses were overcome. They then took to the streets and began erecting barricades throughout the zone. For five consecutive days, from January 17 to January 21, the Peronist masses were able to hold an enormous sector of Buenos Aires. The violence and brutality of the police provoked a general wave of indignation throughout the country. The leadership of the "62 Organizations" responded by calling a general strike for January 18–19. Fearful of being replaced by militant cadres who were actively directing the struggle, the leadership, after this first timid response, changed the forty-eight-hour strike into one of indefinite duration.

The government's response to this direct challenge to its authority was to declare a state of siege and to put into execution the "Plan Conintes" (*CONmoción INTerno del EStado*), first applied in the industrial cities of Berisso, La Plata, and Ensenada which were declared military zones. The most important trade unions were intervened, hundreds of strikers were arrested, and more than half of the nine thousand workers at "Lisandro de la Torre" were fired. The coordinating board of the "62" had resisted the many efforts by the National Command to prepare for such an historic conjuncture, preferring to negotiate with the government rather than to collaborate with the Peronist underground, which for three years had been waging a campaign of subversion with Perón's support. Now, instead of mobilizing the workers in the streets and preparing to continue the struggle in clandestinity, the coordinating board let them remain quietly at home waiting for a solution from above. As a result of government intervention and military repression, the strike was left without a national leadership almost from the beginning. The Strike Committee ceased to exist, although the strike continued spontaneously and without organization from January 18 to January 21. Finally, the workers became demoralized, and the imprisoned leaders began calling them back to work to save their own hides—first one union, then another, but again without any plan or coordination.

The upshot of the *Porteñazo* (a mass insurrection in the port city of Buenos Aires) was a shot in the arm for the National Command. The coordinating board of the "62," which had become a symbol of compromise and capitulation, was dissolved. The general strike brought forth its own leaders from the rank and file and from intermediate cadres of the labor bureaucracy. These men began to push the "62" in a more militant direction and acknowledged the need for an underground apparatus, which could provide a disciplined and centralized command beyond the reach of the government. In its declaration dated January 30, the National Command called the Peronist militants to support these new leaders in their efforts to assume control of the movement.

Although the Argentine resistance emerged independently of the Cuban resistance, its left wing began to model itself as early as 1959–60 on the example of the July 26 Movement. Under the influence of Cooke, in exile in Havana, the first rural guerrilla movement was launched in December 1959 in the province of Tucumán in northwest Argentina, by a group called *Uturuncos*. Then, under Cooke's influence, guerrilla training camps with Cuban military instructors were set up for Peronist militants. Some of these camps were in Cuba, others in Argentina. Among the latter were those raided by the police in July 1961, at Coronel Pringles and Lomas de Zamora in the province of Buenos Aires.

Testifying to the influence of the Cuban resistance on the Argentine resistance were Cooke's November 1960 "Briefings on the Ideology of the Cuban Revolution." The resistance, Cooke noted, was a multiclass movement of heterogeneous and frequently opposing tendencies. It supported the interests of the national bourgeoisie by calling for the restoration of civil liberties, and it supported the interests of the workers and petty bourgeoisie with its program of national and social liberation. As in the Cuban resistance, the bourgeois, or right wing, followed a semilegal and reformist strategy based on negotiations with the dictatorship for the restoration of civil and political rights. In contrast, the left wing chose the path of armed resistance. Since the Cuban resistance had been successful owing to its choice of armed struggle, Cooke concluded that a similar strategy should be used in Argentina. Indeed, the only guarantee for Cooke that the resistance would culminate in a social revolution, over and above the restoration of bourgeois democracy, was the creation of a rebel army with popular support capable of defeating and replacing the professional army in the service of the oligarchy. On the model of Cuba, Cooke anticipated an eventual showdown between the left and right wings of the resistance. At the same time, he foresaw that the bourgeois wing of the movement would attempt to regain power through negotiations with sectors of the professional army—a strategy that could be effectively resisted only, as in Cuba, through a general strike in support of the revolutionary forces.

Early in 1962 the Peronist Party was restored to legality, which permitted it to run its own candidates in the March provincial and gubernatorial elections. Its landslide victory included the election of Andrés Framini as governor of Buenos Aires—a position second in importance only to the presidency. President Frondizi, under pressure from the military, annulled the elections, causing a third militant upsurge in the resistance. On March 29 Frondizi was removed from the presidency by a military coup. After the coup President of the Senate José Maria Guido was appointed interim president, until a new president might be inaugurated following the elections scheduled for July 1963.

In view of a renewed military decree making the Peronist Party illegal, Perón again looked for backing from other political parties. Arturo Illia, the candidate of the Popular Radical Civic Union (UCRP), a rival of Frondizi's Intransigent Radical Civic Union

(UCRI), sought Peronist support by promising to remove the ban. Unconvinced by Illia's blandishments, Perón supported the National and Popular Front (FNP) whose presidential candidate, Vicente Solano Lima, represented the Popular Conservative Party. Only after the Front was proscribed by the military did Perón order his followers to cast blank ballots. Illia won the election, but with only twenty-five percent of the vote. In effect, he was not the choice of the people since the Peronist Party had been proscribed. At least Frondizi had been elected with massive Peronist support.

Although the resistance failed to make headway politically, the revolutionary tendency nurtured by the National Command became increasingly influential in trade union circles. A new program adopted by the CGT in Huerta Grande, Córdoba, at a national conference in 1962 presided over by Amado Olmos, showed this clearly. Olmos, a close friend of Cooke and secretary-general of the Sanitary Workers Union, had become one of the most influential leaders of the "62 Organizations" on the heels of the 1959 general strike. Under his leadership the conference formally agreed to accept the following ten-point program: the nationalization of the banks and the establishment of a single centralized banking system; the imposition of state controls over foreign commerce; the nationalization of the key sectors of the economy, notably iron and steel, electricity, petroleum, and the meat-packing industry; the prohibition of all direct or indirect exports of capital; the cancellation of all financial agreements signed behind the backs of the people by the government; the prohibition of all imports in competition with Argentine industry; *the expropriation without compensation of the landed oligarchy; the imposition of workers' control over production;* the termination of commercial secrets and the rigorous taxing of business associations; and the planning of production in the interests of the Argentine nation through the fixing of priorities and outputs. Although taken separately most of these objectives had at best a reformist content, in conjunction they constituted a direct challenge to the ruling classes. Furthermore, the italicized items had an unconcealed and unquestionably revolutionary thrust.

The influence of Cooke and the experience of the Cuban Revolution on the younger generation of Peronist militants was also evident in the organization of a second rural foco under Ricardo Masetti and in the parallel organization of the first urban guerrilla group led by the notorious "Joe" Baxter—both in response to the military coup of March 1962. Masetti's foco was planned, financed and armed with the collaboration of his fellow Argentine, Che Guevara. After crossing the Bolivian frontier into northwestern Argentina in September 1963, it issued a communiqué calling on Peronist militants to join the People's Guerrilla Army (EGP). Actually, the EGP had a Guevarist rather than a Peronist orientation and was an antecedent of the current People's Revolutionary Army (ERP). Although during the months that followed it successfully recruited some Peronist cadres from the industrial cities of Buenos Aires and Córdoba, after long and arduous military preparations it was surprised and overcome by border patrols in the province of Salta in April 1964.

In contrast, Baxter's organization registered some important victories. The Revolutionary Nationalist Movement (Tacuara), reorganized by Baxter in 1963 under new Peronist leadership, had been founded in 1958 by Alberto Ezcurra Uriburu, a lineal descendent of General José Uriburu. (The latter was instrumental in the September 6, 1930, coup.) It also counted among its leaders the three Guevaras—all first cousins of Che Guevara. Originally Catholic, nationalist, and antisemitic, it was the youth counterpart of the authoritarian nationalists within the military—represented by the GOU under Perón and by the adherents of General Lonardi in the coup of September 16, 1955. It was opposed to materialism in philosophy, to liberal democracy in politics, and to capitalism as an economic system. In opposition to this bourgeois political syndrome it favored its own Christian version of national socialism, and was strongly influenced by the Spanish Falange and by the writings of José Antonio Primo de Rivera. Unlike the GOU, the Tacuara was an openly fascist organization. Nonetheless, under the combined influence of the Cuban and Algerian revolutions and of the revolutionary politics of Che Guevara and Frantz Fanon, it too developed a revolutionary tendency.

Benefiting from his association with Abraham Guillén, Baxter was the first to apply Guillén's urban-guerrilla strategy in an armed attack on the Polyclinic Bank of Buenos Aires in August 1963, which resulted in the taking of twelve million Argentine pesos. In a public declaration by the MNR (Tacuara) on May Day 1964, Baxter explained the motives of this operation. First, violence was the only means by which the oligarchy could maintain its privileges and break the will of a people used to participating in the political process. Second, the Peronist masses had no access to political power through legal channels because of the proscription of the movement by the armed forces. And third, General Perón had directly called upon the people to defend their rights through armed resistance (*Militancia,* 19 June 1973). One should remember that, although Illia had been elected president on July 7, he did not assume office until October 12, 1963. Thus Baxter's operation took place under the military-appointed President José María Guido, after the results of the comparatively free March elections had been annulled by a Radical president.

The MNR (Tacuara) claimed to be one of the few Peronist organizations to obey with strict discipline the instruction of the movement's leader: "Against brute force the only effective response is force intelligently managed." Thus Baxter announced that the national command of the Tacuara had in extraordinary session resolved upon the following: to mobilize all its cadres for the purpose of armed struggle in conformity with the directives of the general staff of the people's army commanded by General Perón; and to implement through armed struggle and mass mobilizations the program of Huerta Grande, since forgotten by the lame and bungling leadership of the "62 Organizations." Although the Tacuara was effectively destroyed in Buenos Aires as the result of the arrest in April 1964 of its leading militants, Baxter successfully shifted its operations to neighboring Montevideo where he provided military instruction to the Tupamaros and participated jointly in further bank "expropriations." Only much later, when a Uruguayan police investigation of an assault on December 22, 1966, led to the discovery of the Peronist cadres who had participated with the Tupamaros, was the Tacuara formally compelled to disband.

The organization of rural and urban focos in 1963 represented a tremendous step forward for the partisans of revolutionary Peronism. However, this advance was offset by a major defeat within the "62 Organizations," which in 1963 saw the displacement of Olmos' influence on the trade union bureaucracy by that of Augusto Vandor. As head of the powerful Metallurgical Workers Union (UOM) and of the "62 Organizations"—a position he held until 1969—Vandor effectively sidetracked the revolutionary program adopted at Huerta Grande in favor of negotiations with the newly elected government of Arturo Illia. Thus, parallel with the escalation of armed resistance against the pseudoconstitutional governments of Presidents Guido and Illia was a revival on an extended scale of a conciliatory faction within the Peronist movement, which resolved to pursue an independent policy should Perón continue to favor an insurrectionary strategy.

The increasing differences between the revolutionary line and the politics of negotiation favored by the legal and trade union branch of the movement prompted Cooke to postulate the coexistence of two rival and fundamentally opposed forms of Peronism. In a statement from Havana dated October 12, 1962, he contrasted the revolutionary strategy of the Peronist masses with the reformist politics of intermediate cadres whose claws had been manicured by an Occidental Christianity. These vestiges of the old Peronist political and trade union bureaucracies, along with the new figures just as reactionary, Cooke wrote, believed that the contradictions within the movement were being resolved in their favor. But those who constitute the vanguard during a period of negotiations, he noted, become the rearguard when the people are in open struggle. "Even admitting that their tactics of conciliation might have achieved something positive, it would be only for a short time and of only limited significance: the struggle cannot be resolved short of the defeat of one of the contending parties, and neither the oligarchy has a margin for bargaining nor can the people be bought off with charity" (*Militancia*, 2 August 1973).

As the differences within the movement threatened to explode, Perón was increasingly obliged to perform a moderating role in his capacity as supreme conductor. Accordingly, he began to favor a gradual accumulation of forces, a strategy combining legal and illegal forms of resistance that did not apparently favor either one. In a letter to Perón dated October 18, 1962, Cooke admitted to having differences with Perón over this new strategy. While acknowledging the difficult circumstances in which Perón was obliged to lead the movement, Cooke found fault with his reliance on Christian and Occidental slogans, his concessions to the reformist and legal wing of the movement, his second thoughts concerning an insurrectionary strategy, and his preference now for a reformist strategy, now for an insurrectionary one, "depending on the circumstances" (Ibid.). If the clandestine apparatus is dismantled during an electoral struggle and an insurrectionary strategy is postponed until a more opportune moment, Cooke argued, one will have to start from scratch when that moment arrives. Such a strategy for all occasions is a pendular one impelled by circumstances, a strategy of rebound incapable of independently shaping events. Moreover, negotiation is likely to take the pressure off the oligarchy, to give it a breathing spell instead of increasing its difficulties. Granted the usefulness of fomenting divisions within the ruling class and within the armed forces and of neutralizing sectors of the clergy and the industrial bourgeoisie, Cooke concluded that none of these efforts can do more than prepare the conditions for a showdown. Hence their value is strictly secondary and auxiliary to the only strategy for victory—an insurrectionary one.

Cooke's differences with Perón spelled the end of the honeymoon between the supreme conductor and the revolutionary currents in the movement. Henceforth, Perón would assume a moderating role not merely from pressures within the movement, but also because revolutionary Peronism had acquired a Guevarist complexion at odds with the populist philosophy of Justicialism. Initially, Perón had sought to use Guevara and Guevarist tendencies to strengthen the Peronist resistance, but important sectors of the latter had ended by becoming "Cubanized." The People's Guerrilla Army was only one such instance of an armed force recruited from the Peronist rank and file, but under a leadership that was Guevarist rather than Peronist.

Perón could hardly have been unaware of this development and of its potential threat to his leadership of the resistance. Within a decade the convergence of revolutionary Peronism on Guevarism was to escape his control entirely. Meanwhile, pressure was put on him to make Havana rather than Madrid his place of exile. At a plenary meeting of the CGT in January 1965, Olmos and Cooke moved the acceptance of a letter to Perón to this effect. Although the letter was not rejected, neither was it approved. This led Olmos to conclude his participation in the plenary with the remark: "Perón's residence in Spain is the tomb of the National Revolution. . . ." (*Militancia*, 7 February 1974).

Designed originally to direct the resistance under conditions of clandestinity, Cooke's National Command began to outlive its function when President Frondizi granted semilegal status to the "62 Organizations." A new organization of the resistance was evidently needed, including a new program. As the principal successor to the National Command, the Peronist Revolutionary Movement (MRP) was organized in 1964 for the specific purpose of carrying on the resistance under conditions of semilegality in which the struggle would be a protracted one and the seizure of power a prelude to a continuing revolution—an evident reference to the Cuban example. However, Cooke, the principal theoretician of revolutionary Peronism, was not destined to lead it. His own group, the Peronist Revolutionary Action (ARP), was much smaller and had comparatively little influence.

The program of the MRP, formulated by Gustavo Rearte and adopted on August 5, 1964, rejected the "false option" of 1958—the option of either forfeiting one's vote or supporting a non-Peronist candidate—which had been imposed on the movement by efforts to reach a negotiated settlement. As for those who had tried to transform the Peronist movement into just another political party, the program demanded their expulsion. In view of conflicting "Battle Plans" for the return of Perón, which the merchants of Peronism hoped to secure through negotiations rather than mass mobilizations, the program favored revolutionary struggle in all its forms. Hence its insistence on reviving the tradition of the gaucho *Montoneros* during the War of Independence and of responding blow by blow to the violence of the repression: "From today forward we shall know how to use armed struggle as the principal means of political action. . . .To that end the people must oppose to the regime's army of occupation their own armed forces and labor militias" (*Confluencia*, May 1974). Going beyond the program of Huerta Grande, the MRP called for the "total elimination of the parasitic social classes which serve the interests of international finance capital: not only the old oligarchy tied to British imperialism, but also the new sectors of the bourgeoisie which serve as an instrument of penetration by Yankee imperialism." Furthermore, the struggle for national liberation was to be organically linked with an armed struggle for social liberation against domestic exploiters, tantamount to the replacement of capitalism by a new socialist order.

By 1964 the rivalry between the left and right wings of the Peronist movement was approaching the critical point. Although set aside by the national leadership of the CGT, the program of Huerta Grande became a rallying cry for the bulk of the rank and file. With the help of cadres in the labor bureaucracy, it was translated into a "Battle Plan" designed to step up labor militancy. In 1964 three million workers were involved in strikes and take-overs of 11,000 factories and workshops. These actions also had the political objective of paving the way for Perón's return in December. The wave of strikes was finally backed by the CGT leadership. However, it supported the "Battle Plan" not in an effort to secure Perón's return, but rather to discredit him. It refused to believe that he would sacrifice a comfortable life in Spain in order to risk imprisonment by returning to Argentina. Thus by calling Perón's bluff, the trade union bureaucracy hoped to undermine his credibility and to assume formal as well as de facto control over the Peronist movement.

This maneuver of the CGT ultimately failed in its objective. On December 2, 1964, large numbers of Peronists began converging on the Ezeiza International Airport of Buenos Aires in order to greet their returning leader. At the request of the Argentine military, however, his plane was intercepted and boarded in Rio de Janeiro. Hours later the air force announced that it would be shot down should it proceed in its flight over Argentine territory. Although Perón was compelled to return to Madrid, the Argentine masses understood and accepted his predicament. Thus began a new letdown in the resistance, which was to last until June 1966 when yet another coup returned the country to direct military rule.

The rebellion against Perón led by the Vandorist faction within the CGT was designed to secure exclusive control of the movement in Argentina. Basic to its strategy was the revival of the Peronist Party under the control of the "62 Organizations" and the liquidation of Perón's chief basis of support in revolutionary Peronism. Although committed to business unionism, the Vandorists also sought to impose their political interests on the state. Moreover, they were not averse to collaborating with big capital, with the native monopolies and the U.S. multinational corporations through the intermediary of the AFL-CIO. Already in the July 1963 elections, representatives of the Vandorist tendency had refused to follow Perón's directive to cast blank ballots, choosing instead to nominate their own candidates under another name—a tactic repeated in the 1965 congressional elections. In 1963 they obtained enough votes to elect two governors, to gain control of five provincial legislatures, and to win sixteen seats in the lower house of congress.

Concurrently, the Vandorist bureaucracy stepped up its efforts to isolate Perón from the militant sectors of the movement. It mounted a campaign of vilification against the newly organized MRP and against the Confederation of Peronist Orthodox Associations (CAOP), which had likewise incurred the wrath of the "62." Unlike Cooke, the new generation of revolutionary leaders, represented by Rearte of the MRP and by Jorge Di Pasquale of the CAOP, had risen directly from labor's ranks. Elected secretary-general of the Federation of Soap and Perfume Workers in 1956–57 when he was barely twenty-five, Rearte collaborated in the reorganization of the Peronist labor movement through the "62 Organizations" in 1957 and in the creation of the Peronist Youth in 1958, serving as a member of its executive board in 1959. Di Pasquale, elected secretary-general of the Association of Pharmaceutical Workers in 1958 when he, too, was in his twenties, served as press secretary of the "62 Organizations" from 1960 to 1962, as secretary of the Coordinating Supervisory Council of Peronism in 1962, and as a personal delegate of General Perón to the socialist countries in 1963. This new generation of trade union leaders appealed directly to the rank and file over the heads of the official leadership, thus constituting a challenge from within the "62 Organizations" that was potentially more dangerous than the threat from without.

The campaign against the MRP was followed by the crystallization of the rebellion against Perón at the Avellaneda Congress of the CGT in 1965. There Vandor publicly proclaimed his differences with the leader: "One must take a stand against Perón in order to save him"—presumably from the Peronist left. The response of the left to this blatant neo-Peronism of the trade union hierarchy was to organize in January 1966 the "62 on Foot with Perón"—the immediate precursor of the "CGT of the Argentines" created in 1968. Among the organizers of the "62 on Foot" were Amado Olmos, Rearte, Di Pasquale, and Armando Jaime, the last a member of the executive committee of the MRP, a founder of the Peronist Youth, and a former member of Cooke's National Command. Vandor's response was to expel the eighteen unions supporting the "62 on Foot" from the "62 Organizations."

At the same time a split developed in the leadership of the CGT between Vandor and José Alonso, the head of the Garment Workers Union. In 1963 Alonso had succeeded Andrés Framini as secretary-general of the CGT; then, at Perón's instigation, he had been re-elected for a second two-year term in 1965. However, in February 1966 Vandor pushed through a resolution demanding Alonso's resignation, after which he was replaced by one of Vandor's own men, Francisco Prado of the Light and Power Workers Union. Supported by Perón, Alonso then assumed the leadership of the "62 on Foot." Once again the flow of the revolutionary tide, which had reached its crest in December 1964, was followed by an ebb reaching its low point in mid–1966. By then the "62 on Foot" had virtually expired. When a new allegedly "nationalist" coup led by General Juan Carlos Onganía overthrew the pseudoconstitutional government of President Illia in June, it was supported by the Vandorist-controlled CGT which sought an immediate agreement with the military.

The fourth upsurge of the resistance that followed, lasting from the overthrow of President Illia on June 28, 1966, to May 25, 1973, when the military abdicated and President-elect Cámpora was inaugurated, sustained a higher level of militancy for a longer period of time than any of the preceding flows of the revolutionary tide. While the trade union hierarchy welcomed the dictatorship's proscription of all political parties and endeavored to fill the resulting vacuum with the "62 Organizations," a revived Peronist left wing unreservedly opposed both the new regime and the capitulationist tactics of the trade union bureaucracy. In a "Briefing to the Peronist Bases," Cooke exploded the illusion of a new unity between the armed forces and the people, arguing that the military government was a mixture of the worst features of both "systems": the liberalism of free trade, free enterprise, and economic development, technologically updated and modernized by the two Radical governments of Frondizi and Illia; and the authoritarian "nationalism" of the armed forces, reinforced by fascist currents and a revival of the Christian theology and feudal hierarchies of the twelfth century. In view of this combination of the worst of the old and the new, there could be nothing left to negotiate except one's own confusion (*Confluencia*, May 1974).

The initial accord between the military dictatorship and the Vandorist bureaucracy was founded on an illusion. Although

nominally nationalist, the military regime was bent on denational-
izing the economy. In December 1966 the bureaucracy resisted the
growing movement for a general strike, but in January 1967 the
autoworkers struck in protest against the liberal economic policies
of the new Minister of Economics Krieger Vasena. Under his
direction the currency was devalued, wages were frozen, prices
were permitted to rise, and a boost was given to the penetration of
Argentine industry and the domestic market by U.S. corporations.
By February 1967 the CGT leadership had to bow to internal
pressures by calling a general strike. Then in October it publicly
denounced the government's economic program and its policy of
denationalization. Labor struggles persisted and hostility by rank
and file workers toward the Vandorist bureaucracy mounted until
in March 1968, at the "Amado Olmos" Congress in homage to the
deceased leader of the CGT, the top labor bureaucrats absented
themselves and were voted out of office. The Vandorist bureaucrats
then voided the elections. Since they retained control of the CGT's
apparatus by fiat, from 1968 to 1970 there were two CGT's: the
Vandorist CGT representing a minority of unions, although by far
the largest, still inclined to "participate" with the military
dictatorship; and the "CGT of the Argentines" or CGT(A) under
the leadership of Raimundo Ongaro, head of the Graphic Workers
Union. In this first formalized split in the Peronist movement, José
Alonso deserted the group loyal to Perón in favor of an alliance
with Vandor.

On May Day 1968 the CGT(A) reaffirmed the program of Huerta
Grande and organized lightning strikes throughout the country. By
September the continued upsurge in labor militancy had led to a
three-month strike by petroleum workers at the government
refinery in La Plata and to a revival of armed resistance. The
divisions in the labor movement prompted Perón to intervene
through his new representative Jorge Paladino, but his effort to
dissolve the Vandorist-led CGT met with no success. During 1969
labor struggles continued to escalate as well as student demonstrations and new urban guerrilla actions against the dictatorship.

A climax was reached in May 1969 with the first *Cordobazo* or
mass insurrection in the city of Córdoba, a qualitative leap far in
advance of the *Porteñazo* of 1959. Students and workers struck
together, occupying a large sector of the industrial city until they
were forcibly dislodged by the military. Although Onganía was

able to restore order, Krieger Vasena and four other cabinet members resigned. Onganía also lost his principal ally in the labor movement with the execution of Vandor by a revolutionary Peronist commando in June. Vandor was executed for scuttling the CGT(A)'s general strike in support of the *Cordobazo* and collaborating with the police in repressing the Peronist left. He was also held responsible for the shoot-out at the pizzeria "La Real" of Avellaneda on May 13, 1966, when his hired thugs took the lives of two militants. The CGT(A), which had sparked the *Cordobazo,* was intervened by the government: its offices were closed, its funds were confiscated, its leaders were jailed, and Ongaro was charged with responsibility for Vandor's death.

The *Cordobazo* was followed by a *Rosariazo* in September, but it too was crushed when martial law was imposed in Rosario and 14,000 striking railroad workers were promptly drafted into the army. In October the CGT(A) called another general strike, which was also opposed by the Vandorist CGT. Because of the limited response to the strike which was effective only in Córdoba, and because military repression had destroyed the capability of the CGT(A), the latter chose to dissolve. This action contributed to the reunification of the CGT at its Unity Congress in July 1970, when Perón intervened to impose José Rucci as the new secretary-general. Re-elected in 1972, Rucci was directly responsive to Perón. Although an official in Vandor's union, he represented a centrist leadership independent of both the Ongarist and Vandorist factions.

Although the "CGT of the Argentines" was no longer a threat, it had given birth to a new kind of unionism whose slogan "Unite from Below, Organize through Combat" was to become a basic feature of the resistance. From his prison cell, in August 1969, Ongaro reiterated its strategic line: "the permanent and generalized struggle of the people against the dictatorship, the oligarchy, and the imperialism of money" (*Confluencia,* May 1974). The objective of that struggle was nothing less than power to the people, a strategy designed "to socialize with a national character the wealth produced by the workers but appropriated by the capitalists and their servants." Such a strategy, according to Ongaro, required the CGT(A) to go underground as the only alternative to the restrictions on its political activity. After the *Cordobazo* new tactics were evidently required. These included the concealment of the persons, names, and addresses of union leaders, the refusal to comply with the labor directives of the military regime, and the rejection of all directives not proceeding from the Peronist bases in the labor movement. In addition, Ongaro called for the organization of rank and file groups (*agrupaciones de base*) for exercising effective leadership in each union; the establishment of organic links with students, revolutionary intellectuals, and rebel priests in a united front for national and social liberation; and opposition to all projects for a new military coup, whether of the left or the right, in view of their reformist illusions and contempt for the leading role of the Peronist masses.

The "CGT of the Argentines" had been nurtured on the revolutionary tendency and on Rearte's Peronist Revolutionary Movement as the successor to Cooke's National Command. By 1969, however, the highly politicized trade union sector had all but eclipsed the political sector organized in the MRP. Consequently, in December 1969 Rearte organized the Revolutionary Movement 17th of October (MR-17), designed to overcome the limitations of the MRP by developing a political vanguard rooted in the trade unions. The new organization was also to replace the defunct CGT(A) and mobilize the masses for a popular war. Rearte was searching for a new kind of organization capable of overcoming the limitations of both Ongaro's *agrupación de base* and Guevara's political-military foco, one combining both armed and semilegal forms of resistance.

Parallel with the emergence of MR-17 was a somewhat different movement of convergence on the trade union bases—the Peronist Revolutionary Front (FRP). Founded in 1970 by Armando Jaime, it included a strong dose of Marxism-Leninism. Jaime began with an intensive campaign of political education among the workers of Salta and Tucumán with the help of two small periodicals, *Cabecita Negra* and *Vocero Popular*, whose first issue appeared in January 1971. In contrast to Rearte's main concern with unity of action, Jaime stressed the importance of ideology. All efforts at unification, he believed, should be realized on the basis of ideological-programmatic agreements compatible with the historical and class interests of the workers. Furthermore, he claimed that this unity depended upon the organization of a political party of the proletariat led by its most class-conscious and combative elements. And, finally, he held that the armed struggle for

overcoming imperialism and establishing socialism could be unified
only under political, not military, leadership. Whereas MR-17
aimed at strengthening the Peronist left without regard to ideological differences, FRP worked to instill in the Peronist masses a
knowledge of Marxism-Leninism.

The emergence of the "CGT of the Argentines" had provided
the impetus not only for the *Cordobazo* of May 1969, but also for a
revival of the armed struggle and preparations for a major
confrontation with the dictatorship. Following the defeat and
imprisonment of the principal cadres of the EGP and MNR
(Tacuara) in April 1964, both the rural and urban armed resistance
virtually disappeared for a period of four years. It was not revived
until the middle of 1968 when militants of the Peronist Youth under
the leadership of Envar El Kadri organized the Peronist Armed
Forces (FAP). Its first guerrilla detachment, the "17th of October,"
was established at a camp called "El Plumerillo" in the vicinity of
Taco Ralo, Tucumán. Having returned from a long march, the
guerrillas were surprised by a large police force without being able
to offer even minimal resistance. In a declaration from prison
where they had been held incommunicado for twenty-eight days
and savagely tortured, the "17th of October" explained the motives
and objectives of its struggle.

> Convinced of the need to achieve economic independence,
> political sovereignty, and social justice in our country and of
> the impossibility of doing so by any other means than armed
> struggle, groups of young Peronists decided to organize the
> Peronist Armed Forces (FAP) and, like the gaucho Mon-
> toneros and the *descamisados* who made possible the 17th of
> October 1945, to initiate the revolutionary war as a way of
> showing the people the authentic road to their liberation . . .
> and of challenging the political power of the regime in the
> only language it understands (*Confluencia*, May 1974).

The influence of the Cuban Revolution on the FAP was openly
admitted in an interview with its commander in December 1970,
published in the English edition of the Cuban Communist Party
newspaper *Granma* (3 January 1971). Although by then the FAP
had shifted to urban guerrilla operations in conscious imitation of
Baxter's Tacuara, it did not exclude the role of rural guerrillas
—provided they were initiated from the cities. The urban armed

struggle, no less than the rural, was intended to conform to Che's international strategy of confronting imperialism on a Latin American scale—a strategy requiring as many political ties as possible with revolutionary organizations in other countries. Within Argentina a strategy of solidarity and cooperation with other underground movements was favored, including joint military actions with the Guevarist-oriented Armed Forces of Liberation (FAL), with which the FAP differed concerning the political interpretation of Argentine reality.

The FAP seems to have evolved through three principal stages. Until Perón's first return to Argentina on November 17, 1972, the guerrillas followed a strategy of *foquismo* (reliance upon mainly military operations by a vanguard without organic links to the masses). The guerrillas did not make a concerted effort to integrate themselves with the politics of Peronist mass organizations until the beginning of the electoral campaign, when they became immersed in community and neighborhood work. It was only after the electoral triumph in March 1973 that the FAP admitted to its "electoralist" and "triumphalist" errors (*Militancia,* 16 August 1973). Its neighborhood organizations had not organized workers in their shops and factories; it had also failed to develop political-military cells of support for its armed detachments. In an effort to establish ties with rank and file militants in the trade unions, the FAP then swung to the opposite extreme of a "classism without the laboring class." The resulting "ideologism," stressing the struggle for a socialist perspective in the objective interests of the proletariat, neglected to consider the workers' subjective interests and level of political development. This ultraleft strategy was as ineffective as its earlier "triumphalist" identification with the populist and polyclass character of the movement.

In direct response to the *Cordobazo* of May 1969, revolutionary cadres within the Peronist Youth gave rise to a second guerrilla organization, the Montoneros, named after the gaucho contingents of Argentina's first War of Independence in 1810 and of the civil wars that followed against the port city of Buenos Aires. Unlike the FAP, the Montoneros were an urban armed movement from the start with a pronounced adherence to Christian militancy. Fernando Abal Medina, its founder, had been a leader of Catholic Action (AC); his successor, Mario Firmenich, a leader of the Catholic Student Youth (JEC). Carlos Ramus, killed with Fernando

Abal on September 7, 1970, had also been a leader of the JEC. All had come under the direct influence of Juan García Elorrio, the editor of *Cristianismo y Revolución* and the principal Argentine interpreter of Camilism—the revolutionary theory and practice of the Colombian guerrilla-priest Camilo Torres. Thus the Montoneros represented the convergence of two different but related ideologies on the left: the revolutionary Peronism of Cooke under the general influence of Guevarism; and the revolutionary Christianity of Juan García as molded by Camilism. In effect, the Montoneros had less in common with the FAP than with Baxter's Tacuara, which had also originated in Catholic circles and had been a preeminently urban guerrilla movement.

The Montoneros were also unique in their choice of tactics, beginning with the abduction, trial, and execution of ex-President Pedro Aramburu on the first anniversary of the *Cordobazo*. In a communiqué dated May 31, 1970, the Montoneros announced the decision of its revolutionary tribunal to execute the former president for the following "crimes" against the Argentine people: for "legalizing" the execution without trial of the twenty-seven Argentines who had collaborated in the first Peronist military action of the resistance in June 1956; for formally condemning to death, in violation of the authority of the War Council, the eight military officers who led the insurrection; for proscribing the Peronist Party and the Peronist trade union organizations; and for desecrating the tomb of Evita Perón and stealing her remains. In addition he was charged with a series of delicts for which he refused to admit responsibility. The execution of Aramburu was followed on July 1 by the seizure of the town of La Calera in the province of Córdoba, where the Montoneros recuperated money and arms for the resistance. By the subsequent successful raid on the Bank of Galicia and Buenos Aires in the capital's suburb of Ramos Mejia on September 1, 1970, they gave further evidence of the viability and strength of the new organization.

Unlike the FAP, the Montoneros gave priority to spectacular actions which tended to raise the political consciousness of the nation. In almost every instance their armed operations were designed not to inflict a military defeat on the enemy, but to cultivate popular support directly through some action the masses might readily identify with. Although the Montoneros went through an early stage of *foquismo* in which they gave precedence to the work of political-military vanguards, the purely military side of their struggle always had a clear and evident political content. Since their actions could dispense with lengthy explanations and justifications, the Montoneros' communiqués were usually brief. Unlike those of the FAP, they consisted of little more than firsthand reports of the facts and motives of a particular operation; they relied mainly on the propaganda of the deed rather than on doctrinaire exhortation and verbal agitation to awaken a political response. Although the communiqués and documents of the Montoneros lacked political depth, their very simplicity made them immediately understandable to people with only the rudiments of a political education—which contributed to making the Montoneros the largest and most powerful armed movement of the Peronist resistance.

Emerging publicly about the same time as the Montoneros was a third armed organization of the resistance, the Revolutionary Armed Forces (FAR). Unlike both the FAP and Montoneros, the FAR was originally Guevarist in inspiration, although by December 1970 it had begun to converge with Peronism. Actually, its origins antedated those of both the FAP and Montoneros since its original nucleus was organized toward the end of 1966 and the beginning of 1967 in preparation for joining Che's Bolivian campaign. The original cadres of the FAR, who were then known as "Che's men," were to acquire their military experience in Bolivia after which they were expected to return to Argentina to fight under Che's orders there.

In 1969 the FAR planned to join Inti Peredo's revived Army of National Liberation (ELN) in Bolivia, until the *Cordobazo* in May convinced it that the first task of liberation was a national rather than a continental one. At the same time, the effectiveness of the Tupamaros' strategy of urban guerrilla warfare in neighboring Uruguay helped to turn it away from a rural guerrilla strategy. The FAR first attained notoriety on July 30, 1970, when it seized the town of Garín with 30,000 inhabitants, a military action deliberately modeled on the Tupamaros' occupation of the city of Pando on October 8, 1969. A FAR communiqué covering the action gave lip service to the Peronist resistance and to the independent road initiated by the Argentine masses on October 17, 1945, when they demonstrated in Plaza de Mayo for Perón's release. But it noted that the guerrillas' main allegiance was to the "revolutionary example of that other great Argentine and Latin American, fallen in Bolivia and converted by his struggle into a San Martín of the twentieth century: Comandante Che Guevara" (*Confluencia*, May 1974).

Within six months of the seizure of Garín, the FAR began to have second thoughts concerning the viability not only of Che's continental strategy, but also of any revolutionary strategy pursued independently of the Peronist movement. By the end of 1970 it had opened discussions designed to explore the bases for unity with the Montoneros. In December a leader of the FAR informed Prensa Latina, the Cuban news agency, that Che's insistence on the Bolivarian or continental character of the Latin American revolution was tantamount to putting the cart before the horse. The failure of the Bolivian campaign was attributed to Che's failure to achieve recognition by the Bolivian masses by responding to their specific needs and mandates. In effect, the FAR was the first Guevarist-type organization on the continent to learn the lessons of Che's failure in Bolivia and to adapt Guevarism to a national context. As a generator of political consciousness, the FAR's political-military vanguard was henceforth to act within the historical limits and possibilities imposed by Peronism as the dominant ideology among the Argentine masses. This called for a strategy of convergence with the Peronist movement for the purpose of uniting with its revolutionary tendency and combating its conciliatory wing. The FAR's political strategy was no longer sectarian: "Our organization considers itself to be a Peronist one. . . .If Marxism does not define our political identity, it is because Marxism is not a universal political banner" (*Cristianismo y Revolución*, April 1971).

Although in its beginnings the resistance was an exclusively Peronist affair, it became fused with a Guevarist tendency as early as 1959–60. This tendency gained further momentum with the escalation of armed resistance in 1963–64 and again in 1969–70. As the resistance developed, new Guevarist organizations also appeared independent of Peronism. The Armed Forces of Liberation (FAL), organized in 1966 by dissidents of the Communist Youth to implement Che's call for a Latin American Vietnam, launched its first armed action in April 1969 by attacking the military base at Campo de Mayo outside the nation's capital. Unlike the FAR, which had a similar origin, it never acquired a Peronist character.

At its Fifth Congress in July 1970 a Trotskyist vanguard, the Workers' Revolutionary Party (PRT), organized its own armed forces, the People's Revolutionary Army (ERP)—likewise in response to Guevarist influence. It soon became the most active guerrilla force in Argentina, outrivaling the Peronist Montoneros. Although the PRT-ERP later broke with the Fourth International (Unified Secretariat), it retained its Guevarist orientation and independence of the Peronist movement. Thus the Argentine resistance developed an increasingly influential side-current and ceased to be synonymous with Peronism.

The Onganía dictatorship had managed to survive the *Cordobazo* of May 1969, only to collapse before a joint coup by the three military chiefs of staff a year later. Confronted by mounting armed resistance to the dictatorship, the military decided to intervene when General Pedro Aramburu, responsible for the original wave of repression against the Peronist movement, was abducted by the Montoneros and then executed. After forcing the resignation of General Onganía in June 1970, the military replaced him with General Roberto Marcelo Levingston.

Under General Levingston the death penalty was decreed for kidnappings and other terrorist acts. But it did not stop the mounting popular violence in July nor dissuade a pre-Montonero commando in August from executing José Alonso, who had betrayed Perón by collaborating with Vandor against the "CGT of the Argentines." Labor unrest reached another high in November when the reunified CGT under the alleged "neutral" leadership of its new Secretary José Rucci, called a general strike that was eighty-percent effective. In November the principal political parties banned by the military regime were also successful in organizing a broad front for the purpose of pressuring the government to abdicate and to call new elections. This coalition, calling itself the "Hour of the People," included the Radical Party, the Popular Conservative Party, the Progressive Democratic Party, and the Socialist Party, in addition to the Peronist Party.

In March 1971 a second *Cordobazo* again shook up the military regime. The three chiefs of staff launched a second coup-within-a-coup by forcing Levingston's resignation and replacing him with General Alejandro Lanusse. Unlike his predecessors, Lanusse combined increased repression against the Peronist resistance with a liberalization of the dictatorship. In June he decreed new penalties for terrorism, but in July legalized political parties; in September he announced forthcoming presidential elections.

The legalization of political parties and preparations for new elections, however, did not put a lid on social discontent. In April 1972 Lanusse, like his predecessors, was confronted with mass demonstrations against the military government. In Córdoba, Rosario, San Luis, San Juan, and Mendoza the masses mobilized to protest an increase in electricity rates. The culminating point of the demonstrations occurred in Mendoza. The *Mendozazo*, which lasted four days, required the intervention of federal troops to quell it. Several deaths resulted before the government finally capitulated and reduced the rates to their former level, not only in Mendoza but in all the provinces where mass mobilizations had occurred. The *Mendozazo* was shortly followed by a *Rocazo*, an uprising in the city of General Roca in the province of Rio Negro. A provisional government was formed in that city in repudiation of the official one, and the army was again asked to intervene. During his brief administration, Lanusse had his hands full in coping with social disorders.

In 1971 Lanusse launched a plan known as the "Great National Accord" (GAN), a final desperate act by the military designed to incorporate the political opposition into a government-led electoral front. The GAN's immediate objective was to bring together in a single coalition all sectors of the population, both those which had and had not participated in political power since the outlawing of Perón's party in 1955. This front was expected to include the traditional right, the representatives of business both large and small, sectors of the labor bureaucracy, and the military. It was flatly rejected by the "Hour of the People."

At the same time that the military sought to co-opt important sectors of the Peronist movement, it also threatened to place new restrictions on the Peronist Party unless Perón denounced his movement's left wing. Perón refused and in November 1971 replaced Paladino with Héctor Cámpora, who was friendly to the Peronist left, as his personal representative in Argentina. Under Cámpora's leadership the Peronist movement then stepped up its resistance, while the Peronist armed formations put further pressure on the government.

Once the "Hour of the People" had accomplished its objective, Perón's response to the GAN was to organize his own electoral front based on a general program of national reconstruction. This program brought together organized labor, the national bourgeoisie, and a variety of political groups of the moderate right and left. First presented to the country on February 15, 1972, it became the doctrinal basis of the Civic Front of National Liberation (FRECILINA) organized in the months that followed. Later, in December, the new electoral front changed its name to the Justicialist Front of Liberation (FREJULI), a coalition of twenty-five organizations led by the Peronist Party.

Selected as his party's presidential candidate in June, however, Perón was unacceptable as a candidate to the military government. Anticipating that any popular front with Perón on its ticket would carry the elections scheduled for March 1973, Lanusse announced on July 9, 1972, the adoption of a residential clause prohibiting any person from running for public office who had not established his residence in Argentina prior to August 25, 1972. Perón was unable to comply with this new restriction. He could not return safely until Lanusse chose to annul the charge against him as a "traitor," pending before a military tribunal since 1955, nor could he return legally without the proper documents and the government's authorization.

Perón was finally authorized to return in November, which prompted speculation of a Perón-Lanusse agreement behind the scenes. However, Perón never met directly with Lanusse nor is the evidence more than circumstantial that he agreed to a negotiated settlement with the military. He endorsed instead of repudiating the Peronist Youth and chose left-leaning Héctor Cámpora to be the FREJULI's presidential candidate in his place. Thus he was unable to nullify the effect of the residential clause directed against him in his absence. After failing in this objective, he returned to Madrid in December.

Although Lanusse personally vetoed Perón's candidacy, he did not carry through his threat to ban the Peronist Party. Apparently, he counted upon Perón to pacify the tumultuous masses and to discipline the special armed formations which Perón could safely countenance from exile, but might be expected to repudiate if he returned to Argentina. But Perón had come and gone, without once denouncing the armed struggle. On the contrary, his statements tended to encourage it. The pressure of the resistance from below rather than that of the armed forces from above helped to dictate

Perón's decisions. Instead of hurting the electoral chances of the FREJULI, Perón's firmness offered the only prospect of social peace. Although the military tried to manipulate the elections to prevent a Peronist victory, Cámpora won approximately fifty percent of the vote, while six representatives of the Peronist left wing were elected governors of Buenos Aires, Córdoba, Mendoza, San Luis, Salta, and Chubut.

Perón's role during the resistance was a complex one corresponding to the heterogeneous nature of the Peronist movement. It is to be explained as a product of his responses: first, to the countervailing pressures from rival tendencies within the movement; and, second, to a variety of external pressures, notably the extent of official repression and the movement's ability to work effectively within the law. As long as the Peronist Party was banned from running its own candidates, and as long as gubernatorial and congressional elections were likely to be annulled in response to a Peronist victory, Perón favored the boycotting of elections and the mobilization of workers against the government. Although he did not exclude the possibility of a negotiated settlement, first with Frondizi and later with Lanusse, he was extremely skeptical of such a solution. This accounts for the predominantly revolutionary image of Perón throughout the resistance and the continued loyalty of the movement's left wing following his return to power.

To succeed against the military he had to mobilize the Peronist masses, which required a return to the original dynamism and revolutionary thrust of his first administration. At the same time, he had to hold his movement together and make periodic concessions to its moderate or reformist wing. Yet an extreme situation called for extreme measures which Perón did not hesitate to take once he was safely out of the country, and once the movement had recovered from its initial shock—the systematic repression launched by General Aramburu in November 1955. In any case, his original role was to launch the resistance, not to moderate the differences between opposing factions within the movement.

Later, Perón was obliged to perform a moderating role in order to preserve unity and a common front against the enemy. The Peronist movement was divided into rival and increasingly hostile tendencies. On the one hand, the "62 Organizations" constituted the principal organized support for the movement's reformist wing. On the other hand, the Peronist Youth, officially organized in 1958, provided the bulk of the cadres for the armed struggle and the revolutionary wing. Since the Peronist Party was banned, the fundamental opposition internal to the movement was that between its trade union and youth branches. Although important sectors of the CGT backed the revolutionary tendency in 1959, 1962, and again from 1968 to 1970, more often than not its leadership favored negotiation rather than confrontation.

Perón was not compelled to play a moderating role until he had successfully reorganized and rebuilt the Peronist movement. Then a revived trade union bureaucracy would begin to challenge the confrontationist tactics of the movement's left wing. Ironically, in exile he soon discovered that the role of moderator carried little weight with Peronist leaders, whether of the right or the left, who had become accustomed to directing their particular sector of the movement without him. To be effective at all, he had to align himself either with the movement's revolutionary or conciliatory wing. Throughout most of the eighteen years of the resistance, Perón sided with the popular currents which had characterized his first administration. It was only after his return to power that he began to favor again the trade union and political bureaucracies and to put a halt to the revolutionary process unleashed by the resistance.

At the beginning of the resistance, when the trade union leadership was imprisoned and Perón found himself deserted by the political leaders of the movement, his only recourse was to turn to new leaders from the militant tendency represented by John William Cooke. Later, when the trade union bureaucracy had revived and taken a position independent of Perón, he again sided with the Peronist left. Only when the left likewise threatened to become independent did he begin to adopt a more moderate position. But that transpired only after the Peronist movement returned to power in May 1973.

Perón himself relied upon the special armed formations and the *agrupaciones de base* to harass the military into calling new elections with Peronist participation. As he conceived it, the role of the Peronist left was to pressure the military to abdicate, certainly not to seize political power or to serve as the fulcrum of a popular front aimed at winning the elections. The Peronist electoral front was to consist of as broad a coalition as possible compatible with the hegemony of the Peronist Party. Once the military had abdicated, but only then, the revolutionary currents would be either disciplined or purged from the movement. Both prior to and after his return to Argentina in November 1972, Perón refused to bow to military pressures that would have him openly repudiate his movement's revolutionary wing.

Unquestionably, the resistance under the leadership of its left wing was the fundamental factor in bringing to an end the military dictatorship. A series of different strategies had been approved by the military between 1955 and 1973 for nullifying the influence of the Peronist movement. From 1955 to 1958 a military government ruled as an interim measure aimed at restoring the old political parties and the type of political system existent prior to Perón; from 1958 to 1962 a "developmentalist" economic strategy was tried; from 1963 to 1966 the military experimented with a "demoliberal" government; and from 1966 to 1973 it attempted to govern on its own. With the outbreak of the second *Cordobazo* in March 1971, it was evident to the military that all had failed. After deposing General Levingston, the leaders of the coup decided to call new elections in an effort to obtain a constitutional sanction for their rule. This decision was a response to the combined pressures of two *Cordobazos,* an explosive social situation characterized by a sustained wave of strikes with no end in sight, mounting guerrilla warfare that had mushroomed in 1970, and mass political pressures for the return of Perón.

Seen in perspective, the Argentine resistance passed through four major stages or cycles in the flow and ebb of opposition to military dictatorship and pseudoconstitutional governments. During the first stage (1955–58) the resistance had as its objective the undermining of the military regime through mass industrial unrest, sabotage, guerrilla operations, and the enlistment of support from the regular army. During the second stage (1958–62) the principal objective was the legalization of the CGT and the Peronist Party, with the expectation of returning to power through an electoral victory. During the third stage (1962–66) the objective was the creation of systematic chaos through a "Battle Plan" aimed at paralyzing the country economically and, with the help of armed resistance, at putting pressure on the government to secure Perón's return. The resistance during the fourth and final stage (1966–73) sought to end the military dictatorship through a combination of tactics including labor unrest, mass mobilizations, armed struggle, and the organization of a new electoral front. With the exception of the last stage in which the resistance succeeded in getting the military to abdicate, each one was characterized by an initial militant upsurge followed by an ebb in the revolutionary tide.

The resistance also exhibited certain overall patterns. With the exception of the first stage, when the Peronist movement experienced its greatest setback, each successive stage was accompanied by an escalation of repression and preparedness on the part of the masses for resisting it. Once the masses had recovered from their initial shock and organized themselves for a protracted struggle, the level of the resistance tended to correspond to the level of repression. Each successive flow or high tide of insurgency mobilized a larger percentage of the population in opposition, escalated the armed struggle, and was more militant than its immediate precursor. Parallel with this growth in the revolutionary tendency was a corresponding strengthening of the tendency favoring a negotiated settlement with the military. Paradoxically, the strategy that failed during the resistance was to prevail after victory. From beginning to end the Peronist left was the main impetus or driving force of the resistance, but the negotiating tendency was its principal beneficiary.

3

Contradictions in the Revolutionary Tendency

During the resistance, which may be conventionally dated from the military coup of September 1955 to the reestablishment of the Peronist Party in power on May 25, 1973, the various sectors of the resistance were unified by one common objective: overthrowing military rule. Although the revolutionary forces were divided into rival factions, their differences did not impede special armed formations from carrying out joint military actions of various kinds. In 1972, for example, the FAR engaged in joint operations with both the Trotskyist ERP and the Montoneros. In a joint communiqué with the ERP, the FAR acknowledged its role in the April 1972 execution of General Juan Carlos Sánchez, chief of the Second Army Corps in Córdoba, in retaliation for his role in the suppression of the second *Cordobazo* in March 1971. On August 15, 1972, twenty-five militants of the FAR, ERP, and Montoneros escaped from the Rawson Penitentiary in Patagonia in a joint action planned by the three organizations. Again, in June 1973, the FAR and Montoneros issued one of the first in their series of joint communiqués, calling on the people to defend the Peronist victory at the polls "through a struggle without quarter, in all terrains and by all means used by the people since 1955" (*Militancia*, 21 June 1973).

This tendency toward joint military actions was to culminate in the organizational merger of the FAR and Montoneros on October

12, 1973. In September Perón had commissioned the leaders of the FAR and Montoneros, Roberto Quieto and Mario Firmenich, to invite representatives of the various youth organizations to a top-level reunion with him to discuss the reorganization of the movement's youth sector. The purpose of the reorganization was to guarantee the representative character of the youth leadership without dissolution of their special organizations (*El Descamisado*, 11 September 1973). Although the FAP was present at the meeting on September 8, the dominant influence was that exercised by the FAR and Montoneros. Shortly afterward, these two organizations announced the fusion of their respective structures and commands and became the largest and most influential paramilitary apparatus in Argentina. Under the name of Montoneros, the new organization was intended as a contribution to the reorganization, institutionalization, and unification of the youth movement demanded by Perón. In a public speech to the Peronist Youth (JP) a week later, Quieto singled out Carlos Olmedo of the FAR and José Sabino Navarro of the Montoneros as the pioneers of the Act of Unification, whose foundations had been laid as early as 1971.

The tendency toward unification was more than offset, however, by an accentuation of the differences within the Peronist left following the return of the Peronist movement to power in May. Although originally unified by the objective of overthrowing a common enemy, the principal factions of the left began quarreling among themselves once this goal had been achieved. The "movementist" sector represented by the FAR-Montoneros and the Peronist Youth concluded that the resistance had indeed come to an end, and that a major change of strategy—aimed at working within the official Peronist movement—was needed. Henceforth the Peronist armed formations would be used to defend the popular government against efforts to subvert it. In effect, the armed struggle would be given a legal sanction and subordinated to the preeminently political effort to implement the Peronist program of national liberation. Another, or "classist," sector, led by the FAP and the Peronist Bases (PB)—remnants of the "62 on Foot" and the "CGT of the Argentines"—made common cause with the principal non-Peronist guerrilla organizations, believing that the resistance should continue until the establishment of a "Socialist Fatherland." This meant a strategy not only of independence of the Peronist movement, but also of confrontation with the Peronist political and trade union bureaucracies, the reactionary armed forces, and the multinational corporations.

The Montoneros had emerged as an armed detachment of the Peronist Youth, but it was not long before it became the head of a reorganized youth movement. Once its political-military vanguard acquired control over the JP, the latter became the principal legal as well as mass front of the Montoneros. Together they became the parent body and organizing nuclei of the Peronist University Youth (JUP), the Union of Secondary Students (UES), and the *Agrupación Evita* or youth sector corresponding to the feminine branch of the movement. Cadres of the Montoneros and JP also collaborated in 1973 to organize the Peronist Working Youth (JTP), a trade union branch, and the Movement of Peronist Urban squatters (MVP), made up of the inhabitants of the *villas miseria* or occupied lands and slum dwellings alongside the railroads, canals, and fringes of the big cities. In addition, the Montoneros could count on the support of part of the older generation of Peronists, Perón's old friends organized in the Association of Authentic Peronism (APA). This group was made up of former leaders from the National Command, the strike at Lisandro de la Torre, and the 1962 conference at Huerta Grande.

For the Montoneros the new period, beginning with the formal abdication of the military and Héctor Cámpora's inauguration as president, signified that Perón had captured the government without seizing political power. Because their strategy was to use the government to win power, they temporarily abandoned the armed struggle. However, it is important to note that the Montoneros did not lay down their arms after May 1973 and that José Rucci, the secretary-general of CGT, was executed in September without any of the rival armed organizations of the left claiming responsibility for the deed. At the time, the Montoneros could not claim credit for this action because of their policy of working within the official movement.

The strategy of the Montoneros toward the government was one of critical support or loyal opposition. As long as Perón lived, their loyalty remained unshakable. The government's shift to the right they interpreted partly as a betrayal of Perón by the political and trade union bureaucracies, partly as a response to external pressures from the cordon of military regimes established along Argentina's eastern, northern, and western frontiers. For these developments Perón could not be held responsible, although they virtually obliged him, or so it was believed, to retreat from constructing a form of national socialism in Argentina. Loyalty to Perón did not imply unquestioning acceptance of his every act, some of which were said to have been forced upon him by right-wing elements in the movement. Thus throughout this period the Montoneros tended to vacillate between the two poles of their strategy: support for Perón, and opposition to the Supreme Council of the Peronist Party which was presumably working against him.

The overall result of this strategy was an alternating succession of retreats and advances. At one moment loyalty to Perón would lead the Montoneros to endorse his acts; at another, to denounce legislation inconsistent with his earlier program of national liberation. Actually, the strategy of the Montoneros underwent the following shifts during 1973–74: first, a steady retreat before the advances of the right wing of the movement lasting from May 25, 1973, until the Olivos meeting between Perón and representatives of the youth branch on February 7, 1974; second, a temporary advance or assertion of independence that began with the boycotting of the Olivos meeting and culminated in the confrontation with Perón and the walkout from Plaza de Mayo on May 1; third, a new retreat signaled by Firmenich's speech of June 13, 1974, in response to Perón's last public appearance and threats to resign; and finally, a new advance beginning on September 6 when the Montoneros returned underground to make common cause with the FAP and the ERP against the escalation of police and military repression by the government of Isabel Perón. Although these pendular shifts in strategy were supposedly evidence of opportunism, at least according to its critics, such shifts were inevitable in view of the Montoneros' efforts to avoid a confrontation with Perón while revolutionizing the Peronist movement from within.

The strategy of retreat initiated on May 25 was reaffirmed and clarified in a communiqué by the Montoneros to the Peronist people on November 3, 1973. "Until the 25th of May we were subversives," the message declared, but "since the 25th of May we support the popular government and defend it by every means" (*Militancia*, 8 November 1973). Once the Montoneros had achieved their objective of overthrowing the military regime and paving the way for Perón's return, the communiqué explained, they adapted their strategy to the new objective of national reconstruction followed by liberation under a government of their own choice. In short, they gave up armed struggle except for the purpose of defending the popular government.

The government was to be defended not only against reactionary elements in the armed forces, but also against efforts to undermine it by a new breed of subversives working within the Peronist movement. These consisted of representatives of the trade union bureaucracy and their supporters in the political branch of the movement, who had launched an offensive against the newly elected provincial governors identified with the Peronist left wing. They were also responsible for attacks against the basic units of the JP and for harassing, kidnapping, torturing, and assassinating Peronist militants. From the moment Cámpora became president, the communiqué noted, the subversives began raising obstacles to the government's program through disruptive tactics that "coincided objectively with some of the provocations of the ultraleft." Beginning with the occupations of factories in order to prevent their occupation by militant sectors of the labor movement, they turned to direct attacks against locals belonging to the Peronist left. After pressuring Cámpora to resign prematurely in the guise of a campaign to make Perón president, they proceeded to attack the provincial governments of Buenos Aires, Córdoba, Corrientes, and Salta, followed by similar attempts against the governments of Mendoza, Tucumán, Formosa, San Luis, and Santa Fe.

There is no doubt, the communiqué continued, that these forces had tried to subvert the popular government in the course of impeding its program of national reconstruction and liberation. Objectively, they were serving the interests of imperialism, which had chosen to obstruct the Peronist movement by working within it and penetrating its trade union bureaucracy. They had also tried to push the left wing into an armed confrontation as a way of embarrassing the government, creating a climate of political violence, and provoking intervention by the armed forces: "We know that they want to inveigle us into a direct confrontation, but we are not going to fall into the trap." Thus in practice the Montoneros chose to defend the popular government by relying mainly on constitutional means. Although committed in principle to the use of violence, they regarded legal measures as the most effective instruments under the new conditions of popular rule.

The program of national liberation defended by the Montoneros was an evidently populist one, predicated on the establishment of a popular state which would control and plan the economy as a necessary condition of political and economic independence. This would be achieved through the expropriation of the property of the landed oligarchy and big foreign enterprises in Argentina, and the transformation of the professional army from an occupation force in the service of the monopolies into a force for national liberation. The liberation of the people in an immediate sense was to be accomplished through provisions regulating matters of health, housing, and employment; through the abolition of repressive laws and the granting of amnesty to political prisoners who had fought the dictatorship; and through the participation of the people in government through their political, trade union, and youth organizations. This was the Peronist program for which the people voted in the March elections—a program of revolutionary nationalism aimed at overcoming Argentina's condition of dependency.

But it was not long in being betrayed. Politically, the process of national liberation was distorted through the displacement of Peronist militants by opportunists within the movement; economically, through successive ratifications of a "social pact" between the trade unions and employers associations. The betrayal began on a government level with a conspiracy by the Vandorist vice-governors of the provinces of Buenos Aires, Mendoza, Santa Fe, and Salta. In January 1974 they were successful in ousting the left-wing Governor of Buenos Aires Oscar Bidegain, and replacing him with Vice-Governor Victorio Calabró, the ex-treasurer of the Metallurgical Workers Union (UOM), itself the principal stronghold of Vandorism in the labor movement. In other provinces the vice-governors were aided and abetted by corresponding police conspiracies disguised as a struggle for higher wages and supported by the labor bureaucracy. The efforts to oust Peronist militants from positions of political power were carried out in connection with the campaign of ideological purification launched by the Supreme Council of the Party, in response to the assassination of José Rucci, the head of the CGT, in September 1973. Under the guise of ridding the movement of Marxist subversives, Peronist militants were gradually replaced by representatives of the Vandorist bureaucracy, whose record of faithlessness to Perón had become legend during the eighteen years of the resistance.

The Social Pact freezing wages and salaries and restricting the right to strike was originally presented to the people as an alliance between labor and capital in the interest of national reconciliation. Signed by the representatives of the CGT and CGE during Cámpora's administration, its implementation had become the responsibility of the Vandorist bureaucracy and sectors of big business, who used it to serve their own interests. The Social Pact became a device for freezing not only wages and salaries, but also the class struggle. It became a generalized argument not only for maintaining the economic status quo, but also for freezing trade union political action. As enforced by the labor bureaucrats, it was used to perpetuate themselves in office and to hold back the pressures for union democracy and the efforts by labor militants to administer the pact from below. It was also used to legitimize political repression. Although the Montoneros had supported the original pact, they could not support its abuses. Accordingly, they tried to "correct" it in order to recover its original significance as an instrument for the conciliation rather than oppression of the working class.

A major break with this strategy of retreat occurred during the first week of February 1974 when, for the first time since May 1973, the Peronist left presented a solid front against the right wing of the movement. Called by Perón to meet with representatives of other youth organizations for the purpose of institutionalizing the youth branch of the movement, the Montoneros, JP, JUP, and JTP joined the FAP and PB in unanimously rejecting the invitation. Although in September the Montoneros had actively participated in such a reunion, by February a new youth group, the Peronist Youth of the Argentine Republic (JPRA), had so consolidated its position with the support of the political and trade union hierarchies that, despite its unrepresentative character, it threatened to acquire hegemony within a restructured youth organization. Moreover, the Montoneros recognized the absurdity of maintaining a united front with the right-wing paramilitary groups, which had been decimating the leadership of the JP, JTP, and kindred organizations since Perón's final return to Argentina in June 1973.

Only a few days earlier eight deputies of the Peronist Youth had resigned their seats in congress rather than vote for the repressive legislation urged in response to the ERP's January attack on the army base at Azul in the province of Buenos Aires. Furthermore, the Vandorist campaign against Oscar Bidegain contributed to his resignation as governor once Perón charged him with "culpable tolerance" in relation to the ERP and sectors of the Peronist left. In short, the escalation of repression and right-wing terrorism against all sectors of the left called for a clarification of positions and for a direct confrontation rather than artificial unification with their professed antagonists. Thus began the first serious questioning by the Montoneros, if not of the leading role they still imputed to Perón, at least of their earlier strategy of trying to influence the Peronist movement from within.

The official organ of the Peronist Youth, *JOTAPÉ*, included in its February issue two brief articles on the meeting proposed by General Perón. Among the reasons for not attending it were the following: the need to determine first the ends to be served by a reorganization of the youth branch; the lack of assurance that the bulk of the youth would be faithfully represented by the organizations claiming to represent them; and the futility of reorganizing the youth branch without also reorganizing the rest of the Peronist movement in accordance with the principle of representation. The JP was prepared to discuss and elaborate a serious project of organization with representative sectors of the right-wing JPRA, but it could not do so with the armed gangs which had been assassinating its own comrades.

The Montoneros and JP had arrived at a common front with other sectors of the Peronist left, but they had yet to change their assessment of the political situation and the theoretical basis of their strategy. The same issue of *JOTAPÉ* contained an editorial in which the fundamental question before the country continued to be presented as "Liberation or Dependency?" This question had been sidestepped by Perón, who had redefined the struggle in terms of national reconstruction as a precondition to national liberation. But as the editorial pointed out: "If we settle for reconstruction and do not liberate ourselves, we shall achieve only a reconstruction of dependency." It also noted that the seven million Argentines who voted the Peronist ticket on March 11 and September 23 did so for national liberation in the first instance. Thus the Montoneros and JP chose to remain firm behind Perón's original program. They were against his later efforts to revise it from the right, as if reconstruction were a condition of national liberation; and they were just as opposed to efforts to revise it from the left.

Theoretically, as well as programmatically, the gulf remained between the Montoneros-JP and the "classist" sector of the Peronist left. The Montoneros gave priority to an anti-imperialist front of liberation; the FAP insisted that such a front be also prosocialist. On January 30, 1974, the FAP issued a message to the laboring class and the Peronist people specifically denouncing a strategy of alliances with the national bourgeoisie as incompatible with the struggle for social liberation (*Militancia,* 21 February 1974). In contrast, the *JOTAPÉ* in its February issue reaffirmed the viability of such an alliance, if not with the big national bourgeoisie, at least with its middle sectors. Accordingly, the front of national liberation was to continue being an alliance of three classes instead of two: the working class, the petty bourgeoisie, and the middle sectors of the national bourgeoisie.

Following the temporary detention of Quieto and Firmenich and the nationwide campaign for their release, Firmenich delivered a major address at the Atlanta stadium in Buenos Aires in commemoration of the March 11 electoral victory the year before. The Supreme Council of the Party headed by Humberto Martiarena had warned that it would expel all those who concurred at the celebration. Nonetheless, some forty thousand militants were present to hear Firmenich denounce the trade union bureaucrats as traitors to the movement, and call for a new program to replace the old one of "Support, Control, and Defense of the Popular Government." As Firmenich explained, the escalation of repression had brought into question the popular character of the government, which could no longer be supported as formerly. Instead, the fundamental problem was to recover the government which had become lost to both Perón and the people. The new strategy of the Montoneros was to expose the "traitors" within the movement and return it to its original course. That strategy was continuous with the earlier one in its assumption that the government could be recaptured within the existing structures of the Peronist movement.

A major feature of Firmenich's speech was his denunciation of the Social Pact signed by the CGT and representatives of Argentine business. Since the original pact had been distorted and then institutionalized through a series of laws, it could no longer be simply "corrected" by mobilizing the workers against it. The pact was prejudicial to labor's interests; accordingly, the Montoneros were in favor of abrogating it. Firmenich called for a strategy of mass mobilizations against the wage-freeze. Unlike the old strategy of alliances with influential sectors of the official movement, the new one supported the autonomous organization of the trade union rank and file. But the differences with the Peronist Bases (PB) remained. The Montoneros still hoped to recover Perón's original program, whereas the PB was struggling to go beyond it in the belief that national liberation was impossible without the prior construction of socialism.

The new direction chartered by the Montoneros on March 8 was formalized with the publication on March 29 of its new program entitled "Rechannel the Peronist Movement as the Axis of Liberation—Reconstruct the Front under the Hegemony of the Workers—Recover the Government for the People and for Perón." This program was also adopted by the JP and its fraternal organizations, the JUP, UES, JTP, *Agrupación Evita,* and Movement of Peronist Urban Squatters (MVP). Most of it constituted a repetition of the fundamental points outlined by Firmenich on March 8. The fundamental enemy was still identified with North American imperialism, aggravated by the infiltration of reactionary and "gorilla" elements into the government and state apparatus. Instead of confronting Peronism as in the past, imperialism had shifted to a strategy of integrating it into its plans. The Vandorist labor bureaucracy had been chosen, according to the Montoneros, to accomplish imperialism's objective of displacing Peronist militants from positions of influence, after which the plan was to dispute the leadership of Perón himself.

The Montoneros' new program noted that, from the heights of the Peronist government and the Peronist or Justicialist Party, the labor bureaucracy had in fact succeeded in its task of isolating Perón from the Peronist masses. The aim of the Vandorist bureaucracy was not to share power with other sectors of the movement, but to monopolize all power for itself in a virtual "Metallurgical Fatherland"—Vandor's base of support had been the Metallurgical Workers Union (UOM)—whose real leader would be the dead Vandor rather than the living Perón. Behind all the new repressive legislation was this same Vandorist bureaucracy, which had directed its armed bands to cooperate with the police in ousting the elected governor and vice-governor of Córdoba in February. It had come to dominate not only some of the most important provincial governments, but also some of the key positions in the federal government and the Peronist Party.

Given this perspective, the immediate enemy in the struggle to recover the Peronist movement for the people and for Perón consisted of the Vandorist bureaucracy and its allies in the government, Ricardo Otero, López Rega, and Benito Llambi, respectively ministers of labor, social welfare, and the interior. So strong was the Vandorist bureaucracy that Perón's efforts to create a counterforce through the parties of the opposition and the political branch of the movement were of no avail without the parallel organization of the Peronist bases. This, then, was the strategy proposed by the new program: to mobilize mass support for Perón in order to break through the Vandorist encirclement that was isolating him from the people and crippling his original project of liberation.

The Montoneros had taken their first steps toward formulating a political strategy independent of that of the Justicialist movement and, for that matter, of Perón. Their unconditional rejection of the Social Pact marked a major advance over their earlier critical support of it. Although their new strategy continued to play up to the vacillating character of middle and lower sectors of the bourgeoisie, there could be no alliance with these sectors on terms that seemingly favored the workers. The Montoneros also began to question the effectiveness of Perón's moderating role above the several classes and factions within the Party. They questioned his alleged encirclement by hostile elements within the government over whom he supposedly had no control. They noted the fundamental agreement between his behavior in office and the project of a "Metallurgical Fatherland" favored by the Vandorist bureaucracy. Whereas earlier they had tried to guess Perón's real motives, his deeds spoke louder than words. Furthermore, his words tended to support his deeds.

The Montoneros' new strategy led directly to the May 1 Plaza de Mayo confrontation and to the massive walkout in the middle of Perón's address. Although the FAP and PB had refused to attend the May Day celebration in protest against the government's labor policies, the Montoneros-JP attended en masse for the purpose of talking with Perón and making known their differences with the government. Specifically, they hoped to convert the May Day celebration into a popular assembly and to impress upon their leader the following demands: that the "traitors" be expelled from the government and the movement; that the popular program voted by the people on March 11 and September 23 be fully implemented; and that there be an end to "gorilla" repression against Peronist militants (*JOTAPÉ*, April 1974).

Instead, the meeting degenerated into a hostile confrontation and exchange of insults. While the Montoneros chanted "What's wrong General, the popular government is filled with gorillas?", Perón retorted with remarks about the stupid and beardless youth, who pretended to have more merit than the trade union organizations which had maintained themselves intact throughout twenty years of struggle. Angrily, the Montoneros began to shout "Sawdust, saw on, the people are going!" and "Rucci was a traitor, greetings to Vandor!" Meanwhile they gave the order to retire and began their exodus from the square. This action appeared to have enraged Perón, who lost the thread of his discourse and launched into a diatribe in which the Montoneros-JP were contemptuously accused of infiltrating the movement, of betraying it, of being more dangerous than the enemies working from outside it, and of acting as mercenaries in the service of foreign interests. While approximately sixty thousand of the estimated one hundred thousand present withdrew from the Plaza, the Vandorist bureaucracy and its youth groups chanted menacingly "The Peronist police will get the Montoneros!" And, as if responding to this threat, the police joined by armed gangs of the Metallurgical Workers Union and the Peronist Trade Union Youth (JSP), the youth section of the CGT, began harassing, assaulting, and arresting some of those who were leaving.

A significant retreat from the new program formulated in March, which had pushed the Montoneros into the May Day confrontation, was initiated by Firmenich in a press interview on June 13, 1974. Responding to Perón's threats to resign and to his last public speech on June 12 in which he had denounced the maneuvers of the oligarchy and imperialism, Firmenich again called for the defense of the popular government—a return to the Montoneros' 1973 program. In a prepared document read by Firmenich entitled "We support the Organization of the People against the Oligarchy and Imperialism," the Montoneros reneged on their unconditional rejection of the Social Pact. Thus they returned to their earlier policy of "correcting" it, hoping to halt the inflationary spiral and

to reach an agreement between capital and the authentic representatives of the workers that would cease being prejudicial to the
latter.

In part, the retreat was motivated by the need for mass support
against the sinister campaign by the oligarchy and imperialism to
sabotage and create difficulties for the Peronist government. These
difficulties included the artificial creation of shortages and the
development of a black market with inflated prices designed to
wreck the Social Pact—tantamount to an economic boycott of the
regime reminiscent of the one which contributed to President
Allende's overthrow in neighboring Chile. In addition, the
newspapers of the oligarchy were creating an atmosphere of
uncertainty and tension tending to aggravate the effects of the
boycott. The new document of the Montoneros took special pains
to distinguish its opposition to the government from the campaign
of sabotage launched by the oligarchy in conjunction with foreign
interests. The new situation called for unequivocal support of
Perón, against "the agents of the oligarchy and imperialism who
are the cause of shortages and speculation on the black market, and
those who through their control of the mass media try to create
confusion and panic. . . ." (*Noticias*, 14 June 1974). Although the
Vandorist bureaucracy was assailed for placing obstacles in the way
of mass demonstrations against this conspiracy of the right, the
document made clear that the fundamental enemy was not within
the Peronist movement but outside.

This temporary retreat lasted until September 6, 1974, when, in
opposition to the repressive policies of the new government of
Isabel Perón, the Montoneros returned underground. On that day,
in a press conference, Firmenich announced that "the imperialist
and oligarchical offensive had succeeded in capturing all the key
positions in the government" in consequence of which "we will
continue our actions until these circumstances are modified" (*El
Día*, 7 September 1974). At the same time, he declared that the
Montoneros would desist from their opposition to the government
on the following conditions: first, the elimination of all forms of
repression; second, the restitution to the workers of all government-
intervened trade unions; third, the implementation of union
democracy; fourth, a general amnesty for political prisoners; and
fifth, the end of political censorship. Until these conditions were
satisfied, the Montoneros would carry forward the process of

national liberation in the only effective ways left to them, i.e., through illegal actions. This was the first time since Perón's death in July that the Montoneros had taken a decisive stand against the new government, which it accused of taking a right-wing course. Thus, once again, they reaffirmed their independence of the official movement, returning underground in anticipation of a long and hard struggle against the combined efforts of López Rega (in control of the Party and the government) and of the Vandorist bureaucracy (in control of the CGT).

In sharp contrast to the Montoneros' strategy of retaining the links with the official movement, the much smaller and increasingly uninfluential Peronist Armed Forces (FAP) gave up all hope of influencing the movement from within. Like the ERP, the FAP opted to continue the resistance by participating in armed operations against the oligarchy and the multinational corporations until the land, the factories, the hospitals, and the schools should have become the property of the people. The main difference between the FAP and the ERP was that the FAP continued to regard Perón as its leader, actively working for his election in September. Nonetheless, it relied on its own powers rather than Perón's to push the movement forward on a socialist course. The independent organization of the Peronist rank and file was believed to be the only force available for breaking through his encirclement by hostile elements within the party. Not until January 1974 did the FAP lose faith in Perón. Simultaneously it began to look upon the Peronist movement as having outlived its historic usefulness to the working class.

From May 25, 1973, to the end of January 1974, when the FAP definitely broke with Perón, the principal differences between the FAP and Montoneros did not concern their respective assessments of Perón, but rather the opportunities and prospects of working within the official movement. For the FAP the opportunities were nil and the prospects dismal; hence the masses would have to be organized independently. The movement was handicapped not only by a corrupt bureaucracy, but also by a program of liberation predicated on a broad populist coalition including sectors of the bourgeoisie. Such a program, the FAP argued, was self-defeating. The national bourgeoisie had a vested interest in maintaining the capitalist system of exploitation which was the principal institutional support of the native oligarchy and the multinational corporations in Argentina. How, then, could it be a reliable ally in a struggle against those forces if its own interest required their perpetuation?

The FAP's struggle for national liberation precluded any agreement with the national bourgeoisie and the collaborationist or conciliatory trade union leadership. On the premise that the establishment of socialism was a necessary condition to overcoming domination by the landed oligarchy in league with foreign interests, the fundamental issue for the FAP was not "Liberation or Dependency" but "Dependency or Socialism." It was not that the FAP's cadres were impatient to push ahead toward a socialist alternative. Although the Montoneros opted to move forward cautiously through separately demarcated stages, the differences between them were also based on their differing interpretations of Argentine political reality.

Apparently, the FAP's original strategy tried unsuccessfully to steer a middle course between the sectarianism of the ERP and the integrationist policies of the Montoneros. Not until the resignation of President Cámpora on July 13, 1973, did the FAP undergo a serious self-criticism of the pendular stages in its development and of the corresponding "deviations." The first such criticism appeared in its August 3 "Briefings for an Analysis of the Present Situation" (*Militancia*, 16 August 1973). There it summarized its past errors under the headings of "the policies of sects" which tended to atomize or isolate the political-military vanguard from the Peronist bases, and of "the policies of vacillation" which tended to absorb or integrate the vanguard in a Peronist movement controlled by the political and trade union bureaucracies.

In this perspective, the principal internal task of the FAP was to restructure its political-military vanguard so that it would be neither atomized nor absorbed. This task, requiring the independent organization of the trade union rank and file, was presented as a condition of overcoming the principal internal enemy, i.e., the trade union bureaucracy. Envar El Kadri, the founder of the FAP, in a speech at a convocation of the Peronist Bases (PB) on September 15, made a special point of identifying this task with that of the PB:

> In order to make a reality of Evita's slogan that Peronism will be revolutionary or it will be nothing, we propose the

> necessity of organizing the Peronism of the Bases in all places
> where there are two, three, five, twenty Peronists who share
> our principles; because only in this way, through organizing
> ourselves in factories, workshops, schools and neighborhoods,
> through creating an independent organization of the laboring
> class and the Peronist people from below, are we going to
> realize the just, free, and sovereign fatherland, the Socialist
> Fatherland, for which our comrades have given their lives and
> for which the people have been struggling for the past 27
> years (*Militancia*, 20 September 1973).

The FAP's new program adopted in response to Perón's return to
power on October 12, 1973, was set forth in an October 17
communiqué, commemorating the day in October 1945 when he
was released by the military under pressure from the first grand-
scale mobilization of the Peronist masses. A special effort was made
to distinguish the popular brand of Peronism from that of the
political and trade union bureaucracy. On the premise that there
was more than one Peronist tradition, that of October 17 and that
of July 13 when President Cámpora was pressured to resign by the
Peronist political and trade union leadership, the FAP's new
program was articulated in response to two fundamental questions.
Why did the Peronist workers vote for Perón on September 23?
Why did the bourgeoisie and the political and trade union
bureaucracies also vote for him? (*Militancia*, 8 November 1973)

The workers voted for Perón in order that they might receive a
decent wage, that their children might have access to education,
that they might control the production and sale of their own
products, that workers' democracy might be implemented in each
factory and neighborhood, that housing and medicine might
become a right for everyone, that the land might belong to those
who cultivate it, that the military might be barred from any
participation in government decisions, and that imperialism might
be expelled from Argentine soil. The communiqué also underlined
what the workers had voted against. They had said no to the
presence in the country of monopolies and capitalist exploiters, to
the political and trade union bureaucracy linked to the interests of
the bosses, to the Social Pact, to the use of the mass media to
silence popular opposition, to the military and police repression, to
the growth of right-wing parapolice organizations encouraged by

the government's campaign against the left, and to the proposed
law of professional associations aimed at perpetuating in office the
trade union bureaucrats and their stranglehold over the rank and
file.

During the eighteen years of the resistance, the communiqué
continued, Perón had proclaimed that the only road to liberation
was through the construction of a socialist fatherland and the
elimination of capitalist exploitation. However, his program was
later redefined independently of the need for socialism, which
encouraged the bourgeois to make it their own since it did not
prejudice their special interests. The bourgeoisie who voted for
Perón did so in order to develop the infrastructure of the Argentine
economy and as a condition of bargaining with the multinational
corporations from a position of strength instead of weakness. At the
same time, the political and trade union bureaucrats voted for him
in order to maintain themselves in office and to keep the Peronist
masses in a condition of dependency on the Party and the CGT.

Having made this implicit distinction between a Peronism
co-opted by the national bourgeoisie and the political and trade
union bureaucracy, on the one hand, and a Peronism of the masses
on the other, the communiqué proceeded to outline how the first
variant of Peronism might be combated. In the first place, Perón's
hand had to be strengthened by the independent and revolutionary
organization of the Peronist bases. Since the implementation of a
program of national liberation was not his responsibility alone, the
only way of guaranteeing it was through the continued mobilization of the masses against the bosses and the capitulationist
political and trade union leadership. Accordingly, the FAP
proposed the following slogan: "Perón in the government, but
without exploiters and traitors." In the second place, the resistance
had taught the workers that imperialism, the monopolies, and their
native allies were not going to resign their privileges voluntarily,
that the armed forces were still the principal protector of those
interests, and that the armed struggle ends not with an electoral
victory but with the seizure of power by the people and the
construction of socialism. Since the continuation of the resistance
was evidently not in the interests of the Peronist bureaucracy, it
called for an independent alternative for the working class.

Such an alternative required a new set of tactics leading to the
implementation of workers' democracy from "below" against the

maneuvers of the bureaucracy from "above." This required the sabotage of all plans and measures not voted by the workers themselves, mass mobilizations in repudiation of all deals and negotiations made by the trade union bureaucrats over the heads of the workers, and the replacement of the old conciliatory leadership in the trade unions by combative and authentic representatives of the rank and file. In addition to these tactics, the communiqué also recommended certain political ones: the application of "popular justice" through armed actions against the most hated figures in the political and trade union leadership; the occupation and self-management of factories and commercial enterprises in retaliation for the action of paramilitary groups and the armed gangs of the Peronist right wing; and the transformation of the basic units and neighborhood juntas of the Peronist movement into centers of popular opposition to the bureaucracy. In these ways, it was anticipated that the resistance would not lapse, but continue forward as a "people's war" against the class enemies of the workers.

The course that the FAP had charted in October was short-lived and replaced by a tougher one in January 1974. On January 5 the FAP issued a communiqué directly criticizing Perón for dissociating national from social liberation—a criticism that was also directed at the Montoneros (*Militancia*, 17 January 1974). Then on January 30 it issued a communiqué changing its assessment of Perón's role in the movement. For the first time in a FAP message to the working class, the thesis of Perón's encirclement by hostile elements within the government was silently abandoned together with the earlier slogan "For the return of the People and Perón to power!" (*Militancia*, 21 February 1974). Perón was held responsible for new repressive legislation against the left in January and for encouraging the growth of right-wing paramilitary organizations. Presumably, little was to be gained by having Perón in power with the people's backing—hence the rationale for abandoning the earlier slogan.

The definitive rupture with Perón in January was based on the conviction that it was hopeless to have a leader who was trying to restore a program viable in 1945, but no longer in 1973. Because the international situation immediately following World War II permitted a semi-independent development of the national economy, the national bourgeoisie had originally had an objective interest in joining an anti-imperialist alliance with the Peronist masses—which was no longer the case. Moreover, the Argentine working class had ceased to struggle in order to make exploitation more tolerable, in favor of abolishing it altogether. Consequently, there were no longer grounds for the cooperation of labor and capital or for a social pact between them. For these reasons the FAP chose to reject Perón's program of national liberation not only as obsolete, but also as an objective apology of imperialism and of the government's repression of the workers. Henceforth, the FAP's escalation of armed operations would be justified not by appeals to Perón, but independently of both him and the Peronist movement.

Like the Montoneros, the FAP needed a legal cover and a mass front for its operations. The FAP's front consisted not of the Peronist Youth, from which both it and the Montoneros had originally emerged as armed detachments, but of the Peronism of the Bases (PB). The Peronist Bases had been organized in 1972 independently of the FAP, but by the middle of 1973 FAP cadres, who were seeking to build their principal base of support within the factories, were taking the initiative in developing new branches throughout the country. Although a sizeable sector of the PB retained its independence of the FAP's political-military directives, by the beginning of 1974 the FAP had established itself as the political-military command of an influential part of the PB. Unlike the Montoneros, who continued to rely upon students and university youth for recruits, the FAP hoped to recruit its fighters mainly from among young workers. Organized along lines similar to those of the *agrupaciones de base* which had survived the demise of the CGT(A), the PB consisted at the beginning of 1974 of sixteen regional branches loosely coordinated through a national committee.

The principal labor support for the PB came from the "Combative CGT" of Córdoba. During the second *Cordobazo* in March 1971 the conciliatory and collaborationist trade union bureaucracy was again discredited, with the result that in April the Córdoba regional organization of the CGT voted out of office those union leaders identified with the policies of the national leadership. Its new secretary-general, Atilio López, was subsequently elected vice-governor of Córdoba, after which he was illegally removed by a provincial police coup and later assassinated by right-wing elements. Among the new leaders of the Córdoba CGT were also several professed Marxists, notably Agustín Tosco, head of the Light and Power Workers Union, and René Salamanca, secretary-general of the Córdoba branch of the Union of Mechanics and Affiliated Automotive Workers (SMATA) and of the Revolutionary Communist Party (PCR). Such figures, backed by other trade union militants, assumed control of the regional organization which became known as the "Combative CGT"—unquestionably the most militant branch of the national CGT.

Just as the Montoneros-JP became the parent body or organizing nucleus of a series of fraternal organizations focusing on special issues, so did the Peronist Bases. The industrial city of Córdoba continued to be the center of organizing activities based on the rank and file. In July 1973, the PB helped to organize the Movement of the Trade Union Bases (MSB), which formally pledged itself to a union movement that would be antibureaucratic, anticapitalist, and independent of the new popular government. In February 1974, the Combative Trade Union Movement (MSC) was organized with the support of both the MSB and Armando Jaime's "Classist CGT" of Salta. Its main objective was to mobilize workers against the Social Pact.

The Peronism of the Bases also deserves attention as the most enlightened political expression of the "classist" tendency within the labor movement. Its program, based on the proceedings of its Second Congress late in 1973, focused on the development and strengthening of a "classist" orientation (*Militancia,* January 31, 1974). The class struggle against the fundamental enemy, the ruling or capitalist class, was to take two principal forms: an economic struggle and a political-military one. As trade unionists and members of a political organization of the working class, the Peronist bases were to wage a struggle on both fronts simultaneously. The classist economic struggle was conceived mainly as a defensive one against exploitation—"the first step in the politicization of the workers." The classist political struggle was designed to destroy the capitalist system and build a new socialist society. The economic struggle was to give precedence to the organization of the masses; the political struggle, to the role of a vanguard fully conscious that a merely economic struggle is insufficient to abolish exploitation. Since it is a mistake to transform the trade union struggle into a struggle for power, the program noted, the leadership of a revolutionary movement must be assumed by

"classist" political organizations, not by the trade unions. At the
same time, the immediate task was to implant a "classist"
orientation in the trade unions as a condition of developing a
political vanguard. Hence the importance of the slogan "Trade
Union Recovery," which signified putting labor's house in order
prior to a clandestine and illegal confrontation with the system.

In this sense, the workers' struggle to regain control of their
unions—the struggle for trade union democracy—was also a political struggle. As the preliminary step toward workers' control of
production, it was bound to create difficulties with the state. Basic
to the application of such a strategy, according to the program, was
an organization politically suited to the rank and file: the *agrupación de base*. The latter was defined as a political organization
within the trade unions, a vanguard organization of Peronist
militants whose purpose was to give political content to the
economic struggle and build a revolutionary army of the people.
The *agrupación de base* was a more advanced form of organization
than the trade union: it had a political purpose and it did not have
to become legally recognized to be effective because it operated
clandestinely. In short, the *agrupación de base* was to the classist
trade union movement what the armed apparatus was to the
classist political struggle.

According to the PB's program, the strategy of isolating one's
enemies one by one was nothing short of utopian, since one could
not confront effectively the capitalist class without waging a
simultaneous struggle against the trade union bureaucracy and the
state. Although the trade union and political bureaucracies were
not the main enemy, they had to be confronted in the course of
challenging the ruling class—but through a preeminently political
struggle, not an economic one. In effect, the bureaucratic mode of
exploitation could be left unchallenged. What could not go
unchallenged was the bureaucracy's politics of capitulation, its role
as an agent of the capitalist class. Ironically, the anticapitalist
revolution would have to be made by the rank and file not only in
its own interests, but also those of the bureaucracy. Whereas Lenin
in 1905 had argued that the proletariat in a backward and
semicolonial country would have to take the initiative in liberating
the bourgeois from their status of dependency on the landed
oligarchy, by 1975 the strategical problem had shifted, at least in
Argentina, to that of liberating the political and trade union

bureaucracies from their status of dependency on the bourgeoisie.

In retrospect, it is now evident that the FAP began to evolve in a sectarian direction once it became absorbed in building the "classist" tendency of the Peronist Bases. Actually, the FAP failed to note any difference in kind between Perón's own government and that of the duo Isabel-López Rega which followed. This interpretation failed to appreciate the centrist role of Gelbard in Perón's last administration and the moderating role of Dr. Taiana, the leftist minister of education. The fact that these and other centrist ministers were dismissed shortly after Isabelita became president is an indication that a fundamental shift to the right occurred with the emergence of López Rega as the power behind the throne. This called for a different set of tactics against the new government, but not the kind that the FAP had prematurely applied against its predecessor. A popular front with other parties was still necessary to combat the official one, but the "classist" orientation tended to discourage instead of promoting it.

Whatever the purely intellectual merits of the two principal sides to this debate, it was the Montoneros and their mass fronts rather than the FAP and the Peronism of the Bases which carried the principal weight in the struggle against the trade union bureaucracy and the official sector of the movement during the period from May 1973 to September 1974. It is noteworthy, for example, that most of the victims by hired killers, by the police, and by right-wing death squads during 1973–74 were known militants of the JP, JTP, and MVP. Moreover, the practical outcome of the contradictions within the Peronist left was that the FAP virtually dissolved in October 1975, while the Peronism of the Bases likewise disappeared from the political scene. Just as the FAP's surviving militants were absorbed mainly by the Montoneros and the ERP, so one sector of the PB joined the Montoneros-JP while another broke with Peronism altogether in favor of Marxism-Leninism and the Front Against Imperialism and For Socialism (FAS). The remainder seem to have rejoined the Combative Trade Unions. Meanwhile, the Montoneros' capacity for combat continued to grow along with their support among the working class. Together these factors account for the clear and evident hegemony of the Montoneros-JP within the Peronist left, thus making them rather than the FAP-PB the principal political and military opposition to the policies of the official movement and the government.

4

Restructuring the Revolutionary Front

The restructuring of the revolutionary front came in response to new repressive legislation against the working class and sectors of the Peronist movement under the changed conditions of the Peronist Party in power. Following Perón's election as president on September 23 and the beginning of a new wave of repression in response to José Rucci's assassination on September 25, there was a growing awareness that the so-called popular government represented a sanction and continuation of the repressive policies of the former military and pseudoconstitutional regimes. The resulting disaffection first with the Justicialist Party and later with Perón himself encouraged the growth of a separatist or "classist" sector within the Peronist left and its convergence with the Guevarist opposition in Argentina.

The main impetus to this convergence was the revival of the resistance in November 1973, spearheaded by the FAP and its fraternal organizations. On the premise that Perón had been "encircled" and "betrayed" by the Peronist right wing, the partisans of an independent alternative continued to regard him as their leader until the end of January 1974, when they either expressly or tacitly broke with Perón and the official movement. Although many revolutionaries continued to regard themselves as Peronists, they identified with the Peronism of the original Labor Party and the traditions of October 17, 1945, instead of with the official wing. Peronism had ceased to be the attractive label it once was, with the result that many others disillusioned with the outcome of the Peronist government went beyond the FAP in rejecting the label altogether.

The first step in the restructuring of the political left was overcoming the doctrinal differences between revolutionary Peronism and Guevarism. This began with joint military operations made possible by convergent strategies, and ended with a series of organizational mergers. Thus the "Peronization" of the Guevarist FAR culminated in its integration with the Montoneros in October 1973, and the "Guevarization" of sectors of the FAP ended in their fusion with the ERP the following October. An important result of this process of convergence and organizational mergers was a restructuring of the left into "movementist" and "classist" sectors, with Peronists and Guevarists to be found in both camps.

One alternative in the restructuring of the left, and in the revival of the resistance, was the formal organization of a revolutionary front capable of encompassing independent Peronist and Guevarist organizations alongside mergers of the type just mentioned. By November 1973 both the Peronist Revolutionary Front (FRP) and the Revolutionary Workers Front (FTR) began appealing to workers to overcome their ideological differences and to join in a united front against the hostile Peronist forces in control of the government. These two fronts also joined the larger Front Against Imperialism and For Socialism (FAS), which distinguished itself by clarifying and expunging the populist ambiguities in the Peronist slogan of "National (anti-imperialist) and Social (socialist) Liberation." Although the FAS was created as early as 1972 on the initiative of the FRP and the combative trade unions of Córdoba, it did not acquire the proportions of a mass organization until its Fifth Congress in November 1973, when it was joined by virtually all the representatives of the "classist" sector.

Even before the abdication of the military and the return of Perón to power in September, efforts were being made to strengthen the resistance through joint actions by Peronist and Guevarist armed groups, whose convergent strategies culminated in the organizational merger of the FAR and Montoneros on October 12, 1973—the day of Perón's inauguration as president. The significance of this merger is that it rested upon a split within the Guevarist sector of the resistance parallel to that within the Peronist left. The partisans of Perón and Guevara would henceforth be fighting side by side. In effect, the parallel ruptures in both the Peronist and Guevarist left were more than compensated, and in part healed, by the convergence and eventual merger of their respective "movementist" sectors in 1973 and of their "classist" sectors in 1974.

Since the emergence of a nationalist tendency within the Guevarist FAR was a necessary condition of its future realignment with the Montoneros, it is worth considering in some detail. It began with the May 1971 polemic by cadres of the ERP against a FAR interview published in the April issue of *Cristianismo y Revolución*. The ERP's polemic, republished in *Militancia* (5 July 1973), proceeded from an analysis of the conceptual confusions in the FAR report to a consideration of the FAR's misunderstanding of Marxism and then Peronism. It concluded with a consideration of the FAR's strategical errors.

First, the FAR was nominally committed to both revolutionary nationalism and socialism, but without having distinguished the Marxist or "classist" from the non-Marxist or populist uses of these terms. Only by using such terms loosely was it able to establish a common denominator between Marxism and Peronism. The FAR's emphasis on the ideological common denominator of these separate movements had contributed, according to the ERP's analysis, to obscuring their fundamental differences. The FAR had neglected to consider, in other words, the basic incompatibility between a socialist and bourgeois ideology. In fact, its fundamental opposition was between a "clear" and a "distorted" view of historical reality—as if history could be interpreted independently of class interests.

Second, the FAR had distorted the fundamentals of Marxism in the process of adapting it to the historical experience and national traditions of the Argentine workers. It had maintained, for example, that "Marxism is not a universal political perspective." On the contrary, the ERP argued that during the present phase of imperialism, in which the most remote regions of the earth have been submitted to the capitalist mode of production, the revolutionary struggle had acquired an international dimension. A Marxist perspective on a universal scale was possible precisely because the communists on different continents were fighting a common enemy. The FAR had further claimed that Marxism consisted exclusively of a science of society and of man, in turn a theoretical instrument for bringing about a socialist revolution. Such a science was not a monopoly of Marxists, it argued, but might also be placed at the service of Peronist philosophy. The ERP's reply was that Marxism was not only a science, but also a unique philosophy or interpretation of the world. Accordingly, to place its science at the beck and call of a populist movement was to subordinate it to a different philosophy, while distorting its original Marxist significance.

Third, the FAR had no better an understanding of Peronism than it had of Marxism. The effort to present Peronism as an indigenous expression of the Argentine working class failed to weigh accurately its polyclass character. If the fundamental political antagonism of Argentine society was that between Peronism and anti-Peronism, as the FAR maintained, then why were Perón's enemies negotiating his return? Evidently, they did not take seriously his appeals to a Christian form of national socialism—nor should Marxists—an indication that the opposition between Peronists and anti-Peronists was neither fundamental nor irresolvable. Instead, the ERP argued that the basic antagonism presented by the class struggle was also evident within the Peronist movement in the coexistence of two different Peronisms, each competing for the attention of the leader. In effect, the FAR's acceptance of Perón's leadership was tantamount to accepting his pendular politics, based on the ecclecticism of a fictitious Third Position.

Finally, the FAR's efforts to formulate a realistic strategy were limited to a narrowly national context. Without an appreciation first of the international situation, then of the situation on the South American continent, and finally of the situation in the Southern Cone (Uruguay, Argentina, Chile), the ERP argued, it is impossible to acquire an accurate and comprehensive picture of conditions within Argentina. A revolutionary strategy that does not take all of these factors into account can only proceed blindly and cannot achieve the desired objective of a political and social victory for the working class. Thus political realism should not be confused with an analysis tied to the immediate situation or to the narrowly empirical without regard for the dynamic relationships between a given country and the rest of the world—conditions that define its national reality.

The FAR's reply to this criticism, published in the same issue of *Militancia,* was the work of Carlos Olmedo who died in combat on

November 3, 1971. The conditions of repression under the military dictatorship prompted him to conceal the manuscript, which was not located until 1973. Because of its timeliness and accentuation of the differences within the Guevarist tendency following Perón's return, the document was regarded as a major contribution to the discussion of the FAR's continuing discrepancies with the ERP.

Instead of a point-by-point reply, which would not have risen above the level of polemics, Olmedo chose to clarify the basic political concepts separating the two organizations. Underlying their political differences, he discovered radically different conceptions of the role that national factors play in the elaboration of a revolutionary strategy. In claiming that the Argentine working class could never seize power without the direction of a Marxist-Leninist party, the ERP had taken a negative view of the historical role of Peronism in Argentina. For the ERP, Peronist ideology served fundamentally bourgeois interests, which meant that it had to be openly combated and eradicated from the sentiments of the people. In this perspective, the fundamental issue for the ERP was not the popular issue of national liberation versus imperialism, but Marxist social liberation versus the counterrevolutionary ideology of the national bourgeoisie—with Perón as its spokesman.

On the contrary, Olmedo argued that Marxism was not an integral part of the historical experience of the Argentine masses, whereas Peronism was; and that the people, and not a self-denominated vanguard, determined the issues that were fundamental at any given moment. Subjectively considered, the basic issue for the Argentine masses revolved around the antagonism between Peronism and anti-Peronism. In effect, the differences between the FAR and the ERP stemmed from their choice of starting points: the conscious interests and sentiments of the Argentine workers (FAR) as opposed to their objective economic and political interests (ERP). If the Argentine workers were in fact confused concerning what their interests really were, then the ERP was right in believing that they stood in need of a guardian. Nonetheless, it is not enough to declare oneself a guardian of the people's interests, Olmedo noted, to become recognized as their legitimate representative.

These contrasting assessments of the importance of the people's conscious and unrecognized interests were tied to a corresponding difference in the ERP's and FAR's analyses of Argentine political reality. The ERP began with world economic conditions and the international revolutionary struggle; the national situation of the Argentine working class was analyzed only as a function of the international situation. The FAR began with an analysis of the national peculiarities of Argentina and with the concrete historical experience of Argentine workers in relation to Peronism, in the conviction that any scientific analysis of world conditions would have to be based on a prior knowledge of national conditions not only in Argentina but also in all other countries. Owing to their different theoretical starting points, the ERP focused on the ideological backwardness of Peronism as a polyclass movement, ending by condemning it mainly for what it had not done. In contrast, the FAR stressed the advanced character of Peronism in relation to the workers' immediate past, ending by accepting it mainly for what it had accomplished.

This byzantine discussion, or dialogue of the deaf, in which neither party came to grips with the problem of its adversary but argued instead at cross-purposes, Olmedo continued, might nonetheless be resolved. The crucial advantage of revolutionaries who adopt a national starting point is that they are able to identify politically with Peronism, while using the Marxist science of society as a guide to revolutionary struggle within a specifically national context. In this way they avail themselves of the chief contributions of both Marxism and Peronism. Marxists who identify with a universal political position and proceed in their analysis from the world economic situation, however, cannot discover any positive contribution in the Peronist experience. To do so would contradict their conception of its role within a global analysis. According to Olmedo, the international left has only two choices, both undesirable from a strategical perspective: to ignore or to negate the contributions of Peronism. Since on either of these options something useful has to be sacrificed, an intelligent strategy requires the assimilation of the actual political positions of the Argentine workers and a Marxist science of society. "The Peronist revolutionary movement," Olmedo concluded, "can appropriate and will appropriate everything that can be of use, such as Marxism, in order to understand reality better and to struggle for the restoration of the people in power, yet without compromising its political identity in the least."

Olmedo's reply conformed in principle to the FAR interview

which touched off the controversy. The fundamental mistake of the Marxist-Leninist groupings in Argentina had been their failure to appreciate the historical experience and level of political development of the Argentine masses. In the original FAR report, vanguardism was identified as one expression of this neglect. To serve the people in the role of a vanguard, the report noted, one cannot stand alone. There are no leaders without followers; a self-denominated vanguard without mass support is a contradiction in terms. Since the Peronist resistance lacked a revolutionary force capable of leading it beyond populist solutions, the strategical problem was to create such a vanguard: first, by establishing organic links with the masses through a process of incorporation within the Peronist movement; second, by establishing organic ties with other revolutionay movements. It was not enough to know and to represent faithfully the objective interests of the workers in order to become their vanguard. One also had to represent their subjective interests, or risk losing their respect and confidence. In effect, revolutionaries must adapt themselves to the ideological development and expectations of the masses and learn to work within those limitations.

"Ideologism" was identified as a second barrier to the appreciation of the concrete political experience of a people. It was defined as a type of analysis focusing on what people believe, mainly on their ideological conceptions, independently of the concrete circumstances which led them to adopt a particular belief or might lead them to modify it in the future. The realization that Peronist ideology was confused or that it mixed up the interests of antagonistic social classes, for example, should be understood as a necessary part of its historical role in making the Argentine workers recognize their independent interests. The discovery that Perón borrowed and incorporated elements of a fascist ideology should not be divorced from the historical circumstances of Argentina's relation to British and North American imperialism, which prompted Argentine neutrality during World War II. To dissociate the ideological expressions of Peronism from the successive stages of its development as a political movement, according to the FAR, was to give them an abstract and static content that did violence to their changing meanings. The ERP's association of the Peronist movement with a polyclass or populist ideology was tantamount to denying the movement's capacity to go beyond the formulations of Justicialism—the theory of the peaceful coexistence of labor and capital. Although Peronist ideology had become infused with a socialist content without a corresponding alteration of its conceptual foundations, the fact that the Peronist left was also part and parcel of the same movement indicated that the foundations might be changed to adapt to new circumstances.

The shift in the FAR, from a position within the international left to one of convergence with revolutionary Peronism, was made possible by the new mass politics it developed within a Guevarist framework. It also marked the beginning of a restructuring of the revolutionary movement in Argentina: the national wing of Guevarism was in conformity with the "movementist" sector of the Peronist left, in opposition to the international wing which was in conformity with the "classist" sector.

In breaking with the Trotskyist Fourth International (Unified Secretariat) in June 1973, the ERP sought to "proletarianize" itself, which signified its insertion within the historical experience of the Argentine working class and, to some extent, its nationalization. Evidently, it had learned something from its discussions with the FAR. Nonetheless, that it continued to favor a modified international strategy was evident from the regional bloc it organized in February 1974 with the Uruguayan Tupamaros, the Chilean Movement of the Revolutionary Left (MIR), and the Bolivian National Liberation Army (ELN)—a "Revolutionary Coordinating Committee" that was designed, after the manner of Che's Bolivian foco, to coordinate the revolutionary struggle in neighboring countries and to give narrowly national struggles a continental dimension.

The principal beneficiary of the ERP-FAR debate was not the ERP, but a minority which split from the ERP over the issue of support for the FREJULI in the March 1973 elections. Unlike the majority in favor of abstention, the minority advocated active support for the Peronist ticket. Calling itself the ERP-22, it served as a memorial of the Trelew massacre of sixteen comrades of the ERP, FAR, and Montoneros on August 22, 1972. Having escaped from the Rawson penitentiary in Patagonia, they surrendered at the Trelew airport, after which they were butchered in cold blood on orders of the military in an action reminiscent of the firing squads of June 1956. Although the ERP-22 favored a continuation of the links established with these comrades in arms, it had more in common with the "classist" strategy of the FAP and other fraternal organizations. Thus by May 1974, several months before the Montoneros chose to return underground, the ERP-22 began making common cause with the Peronist Bases.

The ERP and ERP-22 were not the only Guevarist groups to benefit from the FAR's new perspective. The Peronist ticket in September was also supported by the FAL and by the newly formed Popular Commandos of Liberation (CPL)—which left only the ERP as a consistent advocate of internationalism. Like the ERP-22, their interpretation of Guevarism gave precedence to a strictly national struggle for liberation. However, the ERP-22 became incorporated into the unofficial wing of the Peronist movement, whereas the FAL and CPL chose to cooperate with the Peronist left while retaining their ideological and political independence.

This convergence of Guevarist organizations on the revolutionary sectors of Peronism was attended in 1973–74 by a parallel case of convergence of the FAP on the international sector of Guevarism. The shift in the FAP's strategy became a matter of public knowledge beginning with its manifestations of solidarity with the ERP's attack on the army base of Azul in January 1974. In its January 30 communiqué, it gave special credit to the mobilizations of Peronist workers, the actions of their armed organizations, and the massive vote for the FREJULI in overcoming the military dictatorship. At the same time, it noted that the organizations and the mass of the workers responsible for this transformation had no possibility of deciding anything under the Peronist government (*Militancia*, 21 February 1974). That government, like its predecessors during eighteen years of the resistance, continued to represent the interests of the bourgeoisie—through the Social Pact signed by the bosses and the trade union bureaucrats, through new repressive laws, and through the approval of old ones which left the workers in the same plight they suffered under the dictatorship. Only this time the repression had met with Perón's approval.

The FAP's repudiation of Perón's leadership had been preceded by a communiqué issued by the Hilda Guerrero de Molina Commando of the FAP in Tucumán (*Militancia*, 7 February 1974). Although it warned against placing in Perón's lap all of the responsibility for constructing a socialist fatherland, he was accused of legalizing a system of repression more barefaced and violent than the one displaced. He was also charged with attacking comrades belonging to the movement's left wing. This critique was combined with a defense of the ERP's attack on the army's base at Azul as being in the best tradition of the resistance.

The ERP was quick to acknowledge the FAP's support and escalation of armed actions in response to the Azul operation. The statement issued by the FAP Commando in Tucumán was republished, prefaced by a brief note, in the ERP's official organ *Estrella Roja* (11 February 1974). The note commended the FAP for its military actions and solidarity on the heels of the ERP's confrontation with the regular army. In addition, it underscored the importance of the FAP's rebuttal of the government's charges that the ERP consisted of mercenaries and psychopaths, instead of comrades working to forge a socialist fatherland by building a people's army. Thus the ERP's response to these expressions of support was to reciprocate with a corresponding statement of solidarity with the FAP.

In July 1974, after Perón's death, the convergence of the FAP with the ERP was accelerated. This was prompted by the Catamarca massacre of sixteen cadres of the ERP in August, the resignation of the "soft-liner" Ber Gelbard as minister of economics in October, and the virtual take-over of the government by López Rega, the minister of social welfare and Isabel Perón's principal adviser. On October 25 a FAP commando executed Lieutenant-Colonel René Mas, in solidarity with the ERP's oath of vengeance against the armed forces for its actions in the Catamarca affair—a repeat performance of the Trelew massacre of August 1972. The next day it issued a communiqué announcing its adherence to Marxism-Leninism and its organizational merger with the ERP. "We subordinate ourselves to the project of the Workers' Revolutionary Party (PRT) and incorporate ourselves in the ranks of the People's Revolutionary Army (ERP)," declared the communiqué (*Excelsior*, 26 October 1974). Unlike the Act of Union announcing the merger of the FAR with the Montoneros, the incorporation of this FAP commando in the ERP was the first instance of the opposite process—of a Peronist armed movement becoming identified with Guevarism.

The FAP was not alone in repudiating Perón, the Peronist government, and the Justicialist movement. On February 2, 1974, the national board of the Peronist Bases held a press conference on the government's response to the Azul operation and its concessions to the non-Peronist right. These concessions included the appointment of Alberto Villar, torturer and originator of the antiguerrilla brigades under the military regime, as assistant chief of the Federal Police; and of Luis Margaride, repressor of the 1959 strike at Lisandro de la Torre, as chief of Federal Security. Among the questions put to Jorge Di Pasquale, speaking for the national board, were those asking about the position of PB with respect to the Peronist movement and Perón's leadership. In an indirect slap at the official wing of the movement and at Perón, Di Pasquale replied that the PB would continue organizing and working among the masses, as it had during the eighteen years of the resistance, in a combined struggle not only against imperialism and the monopoly bourgeoisie, but also against the political and trade union bureaucracies and the reactionary armed forces. Should there be room for this kind of struggle within the governing party, then the PB would be there; otherwise it would work for an independent alternative. The Peronist movement, Di Pasquale continued, had been totally penetrated by elements of the right, who were serving the owners and bosses more than the workers. For that reason the PB had constructed its own independent organization in the conviction that the bureaucratic structures of the Peronist movement and the Peronist Party had outlived their original purpose (*Nuevo Hombre*, 15 February 1974).

This response of the Peronist Bases was seconded on February 6 at a press conference called by the Peronist Revolutionary Front (FRP). Speaking for the FRP, Armando Jaime denounced the profascist bourgeoisie entrenched in government circles, while calling for a new coalition between the Peronist left wing and the non-Peronist left. The government's war on Marxism, he noted, had fomented a species of ideological terrorism which, combined with new repressive laws, had given encouragement to the multinational corporations and their hired assassins. Confronted with this escalating repression from the right, the FRP called upon all Peronists to observe the following: first, to return to the style of struggle for national and social liberation before May 25, 1973; second, to repudiate the bureaucratic and proimperialist clique which had usurped control over the movement; third, to avoid becoming intimidated by agents of the CIA and imperialism, by paramilitary and fascist groups hiding under the camouflage of Peronist orthodoxy; fourth, to unite all sectors of the movement's left wing for the purpose of directly confronting the combined forces of imperialism, capitalism, fascism, and the capitulationist political and trade union bureaucracies; and fifth, to extend this front to include all the popular and revolutionary forces in the country struggling for national liberation and socialism (Ibid.).

Actually, the effort to restructure the revolutionary movement through a united front of the Peronist "Independent Alternative" and the bulk of the Guevarist left did not begin with the government's response to the Azul operation, but was brought to a head by it. By November 1973 Perón's failure to reverse the political trend, which began with the Ezeiza massacre and the events following President Cámpora's resignation, prompted the questioning of a government that was not living up to popular expectations. Perón's abandonment of his earlier program of liberation gave an added impetus to efforts to restructure the revolutionary forces against the stranglehold on the movement exercised by the Party's Supreme Council. Thus on November 19, 1973, in its Act of Unification with other fraternal organizations, the FRP reaffirmed its socialist objectives while calling for the mobilization of the Peronist masses and for the creation of a united front with non-Peronist revolutionary organizations against the official Peronists in control of the government.

In the confrontation with the official leadership of the movement, the Revolutionary Workers Front (FRT) was among the first to abandon the Peronist label. The first plenary meeting of the FTR occurred in Córdoba on November 18, 1973, when representatives of its various regional organizations issued a Declaration of Principles and established the basis for a national organization. The Light and Power Workers Union of Córdoba led by Agustín Tosco played a prominent role in creating the new front, which concentrated on uniting the "classist" and combative tendencies within organized labor. The Declaration of Principles did not mince words in demanding the "violent destruction of the system and its replacement by a society without exploiters and exploited. . . , possible only through the organized and armed forces of the people" (*Militancia*, 29 November 1973). The FTR was conceived as an organization of the most politically advanced and militant sectors of the labor movement for the purpose of confronting the common enemy represented by the official wing of

Peronism in alliance with Argentine business. The Declaration concluded by welcoming within its ranks revolutionaries from both the Peronist and non-Peronist left, regardless of political origins and party affiliation.

The most important of these revolutionary fronts was the Front Against Imperialism and For Socialism (FAS). By the time of its Fifth Congress on November 24, 1973, it had already acquired the dimensions of a mass organization under the principal influence of the PRT-ERP. For over a year it had been urging a united front for overcoming the artificial divisions and sectarian differences on the left. This project was later formalized at its Sixth Congress on June 15, 1974, which proposed the creation of a "Coordinating Junta of Popular and Revolutionary Organizations" (*De Frente,* 27 June 1974). The FAS had the singular advantage of including under one roof not only Peronists, but also non-Peronists who had voted for Perón (ERP-22, FAL, CPL). It also included anti-Peronists who had abstained from the elections (PRT-ERP). The FAS had been conceived as a revolutionary alternative to the FREJULI's watered-down version of national and social liberation. Nonetheless, the majority of its constituents, Guevarists as well as Peronists, had supported the Peronist slate.

Although unable to attract the Montoneros-JP, the FAS was supported by several regional branches of the Peronist Bases (PB), the Trade Union Movement of the Bases (MSB), the Peronist Revolutionary Front (FRP), the Revolutionary Workers Front (FTR), and other representatives of the "classist" sector including the FAP. Among the Guevarist groups that participated in the Fifth Congress were the PRT-ERP, the FAL, and CPL. Although the CPL refused to become formally integrated with the FAS, it continued to share the latter's objectives (*Militancia,* 13 December 1973). Especially important to the FAS was the formal adherence of some of the principal journals and periodicals of the Peronist and Guevarist "classist" tendencies, among these *Posición, Patria Nueva, Nuevo Hombre,* the PRT's *El Combatiente,* and the ERP's *Estrella Roja.*

In addition to the "classist" Peronist and Guevarist tendencies, the FAS was integrated by the pro-Peking Communist Party (ML), the Spartacist Group, the Trotskyist "Labor Politics" (PO), and by a delegation of observers from the Socialist Workers Party (PST)

—the leading Trotskyist party in Argentina informally allied to the Fourth International (Unified Secretariat). The FAS was also supported by an alliance of four Marxist-Leninist *groupuscules* consisting of the Movement of the Revolutionary Left (MIR), the Revolutionary Organization "Labor Power," the Communist Revolutionary Organization "The Laborer," and Communist Struggle (LC). Although they eventually went the way of the CPL by formally withdrawing from the front, they continued to support it in principle (*El Obrero,* 17 April 1974).

The Montoneros-JP remained visibly aloof from these efforts to restructure the revolutionary movement independent of Peronism. Only after Perón's death on July 1 was there an indication of a rapprochement with the "classist" sector. By September 6 the Montoneros had returned underground in order to resist effectively the repressive policies of the new government. For the "classist" sector this action signified an indirect admission that the Montoneros' strategy of working within the official movement had failed and that the only intelligent response to the government's war against Marxism had been to continue the resistance.

On closer inspection what appeared to be the vacillating and conciliatory policies of the Montoneros was part of an integral but malleable strategy combining a variety of tactics adapted to different moments and circumstances. Although the Montoneros renounced the tactics of subversion in May 1973 only to revive them again in September 1974, they did so not in consequence of a change in strategy but in response to an objective change in the government. Unlike Perón's administration, whose repressive policies were designed to curb the influence of the Peronist left and to establish an equilibrium with the Peronist right wing, the policies of its successor aimed to crush the left altogether. Considering the impunity with which right-wing death squads were slowly decimating Peronist as well as Marxist militants, the government's highly publicized campaign against the "two extremisms" was evidently a cover for an all-out war of extermination against the left. Thanks to the presence of "soft-liners" and centrist ministers in Perón's government, the tactics of the Montoneros had succeeded at least partly in their objectives. But they were wholly ineffective against the Peronist right wing which, in the guise of representing the center of the movement, had usurped control of the Party and of

Isabelita's government. In this perspective, the Montoneros' earlier tactics were not so much mistaken as they were ill-adapted to the new political situation following Perón's death.

Although the Montoneros became an acknowledged part of the renewed resistance in September, they admitted to having engaged in earlier and anonymous political-military actions, including the execution of a regional leader of the right-wing Peronist Organizational Command (*El Día*, 8 September 1974). Claiming loyalty to Perón's mandate, the Montoneros and its mass fronts again opted for an independent alternative, but for tactical reasons opposed joint military actions with the ERP. Although a new resistance movement had taken shape as early as November 1973, the second Peronist resistance dates from September 6, 1974, when the principal force of the Argentine left rejoined the other groups in opposition.

In October Isabelita appealed to all sectors of the movement to join in condemning the campaign of terror waged by extremist factions of both the right and the left. In a maneuver to support this project the Intelligence Services published on October 9 a communiqué by a nonexistent group called the "Montoneros of Perón." In response to Isabelita's appeal, this group was said to have separated from the Montoneros because of an agreement which placed the Montoneros under the operational directives of the ERP (*El Día*, 10 October 1974). As an expression of good faith and its intention of returning to the official fold, it had allegedly exploded its arsenal in the Paraná River on the island of "La Paloma," located approximately thirty kilometers from Rosario. The only basis in fact for this police invention was the existence of a dissident tendency which had opposed the new tactics of returning underground and had split to form its own "Loyalty" sector. To this psychological warfare aimed at bolstering Isabelita's highly publicized and hypocritical campaign the Montoneros replied with an offensive of their own. Thus, a week later, they abducted the corpse of ex-President Aramburu, threatening to retain it until the repatriation of the remains of Evita Perón and the restitution of the combative trade unions intervened by the minister of labor (*El Día*, 17 October 1974).

The Montoneros' decision to revive the armed struggle was sealed on November 6 by the government's declaration of a state of siege. Originally contemplated in response to the Montoneros'

September 6 decision to return to clandestinity, it was actually invoked because of the assassination of the Chief of the Federal Police Alberto Villar on November 1 and the Montoneros' communiqué the next day threatening a similar action against López Rega and Minister of Labor Ricardo Otero. The communiqué explained that Villar had been executed for having organized the Argentine Anti-Communist Alliance ("Triple A") and for having tortured and ordered the assassination of members of the resistance during the military dictatorship (*El Día*, 3 November 1974). That the chief of the Federal Police was directly implicated in the wave of right-wing terrorism that was plaguing the country was evident from the fact that not one person had been arrested in connection with the score of assassinations publicly boasted by the "Triple A," whereas hundreds of leftists were being detained or indicted on lesser charges.

The state of siege was originally limited to actions by the Federal Police, in conjunction with local police forces, with the logistical support of the army. On February 9, 1975, however, the government escalated its private war against the left by calling for the full-scale intervention of the armed forces in the repression of subversion. In August 1974 the government had requested the army's participation in repressing the ERP's first rural foco in Catamarca. Thus the armed forces were again asked to intervene, this time on a national scale, after the appearance of the ERP's second rural foco in Tucumán.

The escalation of repression against all sectors of the Peronist left, and not only against Guevarist and Communist groups, contributed to the Montoneros-JP plan to organize a new political party in conjunction with other dissident sectors of the Justicialist movement. First announced on January 27, 1975, the plan for a new *Descamisado* Party in the province of Misiones was directed at uniting the Peronist resistance and other revolutionary sectors in opposition to the official party in the forthcoming provincial elections. Although the party was to be constructed on the basis of the various regional organizations of the JP, it was also expected to unite with other sectors of the Peronist left in establishing a party on a national scale.

Formally constituted on February 9, 1975, it was immediately challenged in the courts for appropriating the name *Descamisado*, allegedly the property of the FREJULI. Having changed its name to the Authentic Peronist Party (PPA), it was again challenged by the FREJULI. The charge was dropped only when the UCR, the principal opposition party, threatened to withdraw its candidates and to discredit totally the elections (*El Día*, 13 April 1975). Supported on a national scale by the entire Peronist left including the deposed governors of five important provinces, the PPA in Misiones rejected a proposed alliance with the Communist Party, the Socialist Workers Party, and the Intransigent Party on the ground that its battle was within the Justicialist movement. Thus it hoped to unify the left under a Peronist banner—in fact the only banner with a significant mass appeal.

On March 11, 1975, the new Peronist party became organized as a national party. The PPA was the joint product of the Montoneros-JP and the Authentic Peronist Association (APA) under the direction of Andrés Framini, former secretary-general of the CGT and governor-elect of Buenos Aires in 1962.

The origins of this group went back to the "Permanent Commission of Homage to the 11th of March," created at the beginning of 1974 by veteran Peronists with a long history of loyalty to the leader. This commission was reorganized as the APA on September 3, 1974. The principal political role of the APA was to bring under a single roof the Peronist "old guard," the adherents of ex-president Cámpora, and the Montoneros-JP in an effort to restore internal democracy in the official movement. Failing this, its political purpose was to give an electoral expression to the united forces of the Peronist left aimed at defeating and replacing the official party in power. It also sought the support of other parties on the left in a broad appeal aimed at overcoming imperialism and establishing a national form of socialism in Argentina.

By 1975 the political options open to the second Argentine resistance had boiled down to a choice between two revolutionary fronts: the Front Against Imperialism and For Socialism integrated by the "classist" Guevarist and Peronist sectors; and the national liberation front integrated by the Montoneros-JP, their fraternal organizations, and the PPA as their legal and electoral instrument. Although the FAS had the advantage of uniting the various splinter parties of the left, as *groupuscules* they contributed little to its overall growth. Within the FAS these parties were overshadowed by the financial resources and fire power of the PRT-ERP, which were also better organized to survive repression by the Federal Police and paramilitary forces of the right. Although the leaders of the FAS came from the "classist" and combative trade unions of Salta and Córdoba, they had adopted Marxist-Leninist policies which effectively converged with those of the PRT-ERP—its most disciplined and influential nucleus. In effect, the FAS was a preeminently Guevarist or modified Marxist-Leninist front, whose ideology was bound to appear foreign to the Peronist masses.

The choice of revolutionary fronts was basically an option between the PRT-ERP and the Montoneros-JP. Specifically, the options for armed struggle against the new government had narrowed to a choice between the ERP and Montoneros. The smaller Guevarist armed nuclei, notably the FAL and CPL, had either been smashed by the repressive forces or reduced to impotence by the state of siege and the antiguerrilla campaign launched by the army in February. In October 1974, the FAP-17 of October merged with the ERP, while the other sectors of the FAP, principally its National Command and the Buenos Aires regional branch of the FAP, chose to dissolve their various organizations. Carlos Caride, the most important leader of the FAP next to Envar El Kadri, publicly announced his decision to join the Montoneros. Other militants of the dissolved FAP commandos presumably followed him. Having pursued a strategy intermediate to those of the ERP and Montoneros, the FAP split apart at the seams when the showdown occurred with the new government in September —the bulk of its militants joining one or the other of the two principal remaining armed groups. Although the choice was between two political-military organizations each testifying to Guevarist influence, one identified with Peronism while the other rejected the Peronist mantle.

They differed over matters of strategy as well as politics. The Montoneros argued that the indiscriminate killing of army officers, in retaliation for the army's assassination of ERP militants in Catamarca, was counterproductive for the resistance since it alienated intermediate sectors of the population. Accordingly, the death sentence was reserved only for the most notorious and hated members of the government, such as López Rega and Ricardo Otero, along with recognized torturers and the heads of the principal paramilitary right-wing organizations. Although the Montoneros and the ERP were both political-military vanguards, organizationally they were quite dissimilar. Every member of the Montoneros was also a member of the JP; but not every member of the JP belonged to the Montoneros. In contrast, all members of the PRT were incorporated in the ERP, but not conversely. Organizationally broader than the Montoneros, the JP had the law formally on its side until September 1975, whereas the PRT was handicapped by having to function as an illegal political party. Thus the Montoneros were able to combine all forms of struggle, both legal and illegal, which gave them a decided advantage.

5

The Crisis of Peronism

The resistance was ultimately successful in compelling the military to give in to popular pressures so that elections were called for March 1973. These resulted in the consequent landslide victory for the Peronist ticket headed by Héctor Cámpora. But that victory, followed by Cámpora's assumption of the presidency on May 25 and Perón's final return on June 20, was a hollow one from the start. For the Peronist movement, like Salvador Allende's Popular Unity coalition in Chile, still had the reactionary armed forces to contend with. If it is true that "political power grows out of the barrel of a gun," then the armed forces continued to be a potential threat to the Peronist movement in Argentina. Although Perón had a considerable advantage over Allende in controlling not only the executive, but also the legislative and judicial branches, it was the military, after all, that had consented to his return. It is safe to say that the military never fully relinquished power in Argentina; that it continued to supervise the political process from behind the scenes with the intention of intervening again should the Peronist movement get out of hand.

The Cuban Revolution, like the Mexican and Bolivian Revolutions before it, had refused to negotiate with representatives of the old regime. To different degrees each had dismantled the regular army, while replacing it with a new rebel army and popular militias. Although the Peronist resistance also refused to negotiate with miltiary leaders, it succeeded through new elections and

105

through a political victory at the polls, rather than a military rout of the professional armed forces. Having abdicated peacefully, the Argentine military could preserve its ranks virtually intact, save for the forced retirement of some of its top-ranking officers active during the dictatorship. Thus the Peronist movement was handicapped in power by a military bureaucracy that treasured its independence and only grudgingly gave its allegiance to the new government.

Among the first to anticipate what might happen on Perón's return were the Peronist Armed Forces (FAP). In an interview with FAP commandos in December 1970, published in the English edition of *Granma* (3 January 1971), they were asked if the power structure could incorporate Perón into the system as a last-ditch effort to halt the armed struggle by Peronist organizations. The FAP's answer was that, if he returned on the basis of negotiations with the armed forces, he would have to give up his socialist demands and play ball with the military. At the same time, the FAP did not believe that Perón could be integrated into the system because, should he return on those conditions, he would be politically dead. In effect, the Peronist movement would be threatened by a split that would ultimately undermine its status as the majority party.

Although the FAP was right in the conviction that Perón would not settle for a negotiated peace, it was wrong in believing that he could not be integrated into the system. Having returned from exile, Perón renounced all talk of a "Socialist Fatherland." His repeated calls for moderation soon prompted an "Open Letter" to Perón, dated August 1973, from sectors of the movement's extreme left wing. The letter reminded him of what he had said during his eighteen years in exile: that his 1945 project for social reconstruction would not suffice for 1973; that the only viable alternative to military dictatorship was revolutionary war; that he had been mistaken in believing that a social revolution could be achieved through evolutionary means; that the political and trade union bureaucracies had betrayed the movement; that the historic mission of the working class was to destroy capitalism root and branch; that Guevarist as well as Peronist armed organizations had jointly contributed to the dictatorship's impasse; and that Perón would always do what the people wanted.

Fearing a head-on collision with the armed forces, Perón hesitated to launch a massive purge of the military hierarchy. Actually, there was little he could do to transform the political character of the professional army since its intermediate ranks were also solidly anti-Peronist. But at the same time, he failed to organize an adequate counterforce of his own. It was not enough to gain control over the Federal Police. The development of popular militias was also indispensable to offset the monopoly of force by the professional military—a strategy proposed in April 1973 by Rodolfo Galimberti, the head of the Peronist Youth. However, that too would have evoked a military response. Moreover, the Radical Party denounced the proposal, while the trade union bureaucracy did not publicly support it. Galimberti was called to Madrid for top-level talks with Perón and on his return resigned from the leadership of the JP, presumably at Perón's bidding.

Perón's failure to dominate the military signified that the Argentine resistance, unlike the Cuban, heralded little hope of a decisive transfer of power from its reformist to its revolutionary sectors. From the beginning of the resistance the objective of its reformist wing was to use the armed struggle as a means of political bargaining and to overcome through negotiations the military barriers to the free functioning of the Peronist Party and the Peronist-controlled CGT. In sharp contrast, its revolutionary wing aspired to a social as well as political revolution. Throughout the resistance Perón performed a moderating role in the effort to hold together the two wings of the movement, while using its revolutionary wing as a counterforce to the comparatively stronger and semiautonomous political and trade union bureaucracies. It was only after his return in June 1973 that he regained undisputed control over the Peronist movement, although at the price of accommodation to its right wing and alienation of the left. If he then sided with the bureaucracy it was because the revolutionary tendency had become a liability rather than an asset. Under conditions in which his overwhelming victory at the polls and his cooperation with the opposition Radical Civic Union made him comparatively sure of retaining power, the armed sectors of the movement became increasingly superfluous. Besides, they were damaging his relations with the military. Once his preoccupation shifted from seizing power to using it toward national reconstruction in which there would be neither victors nor vanquished, the movement's left wing was almost bound to be purged in the interest of pacifying the armed forces.

Peronism had gone through many internal crises before, but this one was unquestionably the worst. Following the military coup in September 1955 the movement was faced with mass desertions by representatives of its right wing. Later, during the emergence of Vandor as the strong man in control of the "62 Organizations," the trade union bureaucracy threatened to take over the movement if Perón did not accede to its demands including the purging of the Peronist Revolutionary Movement (MRP). Even so, the revolutionary tendency continued to be fostered by Perón as an unofficial sector of the Justicialist movement. Not until his election to the presidency and the assassination of José Rucci in September 1973 did he publicly chastise his movement's left wing and warn it to mend its ways. On assuming the presidency in October he then took the initiative in purging representatives of the Peronist left from important positions in the party and the government. In short, the crisis in the movement which began with Perón's repudiation of its left wing in September 1973 ended not only in a split that promised to be irrevocable, but also in one whose long-term effect was to damage, weaken, and discredit the Peronist government.

The Peronist electoral victories of 1973, the amnesty for political prisoners, the legal recognition of the outlawed Peronist armed vanguards and the non-Peronist People's Revolutionary Army, the diplomatic recognition of Cuba, and the fraternal relations with Allende's government of Popular Unity encouraged a triumphalist posture in the conviction that these achievements would lead to other similar ones and that the eighteen years of struggle would shortly lead to social as well as national liberation. These hopes were abruptly shattered beginning with Perón's return. The Ezeiza massacre, the turn to the right on the heels of President Cámpora's resignation, Perón's declared war on Marxism, the emergence of group terrorism against the Peronist and non-Peronist left, the armed gangs encouraged by the Ministry of Social Welfare and successive chiefs of the Federal Police, the continuity (*continuismo*) in high government positions of former servants of the military dictatorship, the unrepresentative character of the Peronist high command or Supreme Council, the Social Pact freezing wages and salaries, the enactment of new repressive laws, the use of the national guard to protect the plant, offices, and executive personnel of U.S. and European corporations, and the campaign of ideological purification designed to weed out revolutionary currents within Peronism—all these came as unexpected blows to the Peronist left.

In contrast to Perón's first and second administrations, his third government began with a series of repressive laws. The Law of Professional Associations, dating from November 1973, gave to each national organization the right to intervene in the affairs of its subordinate regional and local bodies, which effectively eliminated their independence or any opposition from popular leaders elected by the rank and file. It also extended the mandate of elected officers from two to four years, and the obligation to convoke national congresses or assemblies from one to two years, which gave the bureaucracy a free hand to act and to perpetuate itself in power. Beginning in 1974, the Law of Redundancy gave all organizations, including universities, the right to fire excess personnel—a law used to get rid of political militants and trade union activists. The Law of Compulsory Arbitration made all strikes for higher wages illegal, thereby placing labor entirely at the mercy of the government. This law, originally decreed under the military regime of General Onganía, was given continuity and sanctioned by the Peronist Congress. The Law of the University guaranteed that the universities would be "non-political" in turning out only professionals and specialists. The Reform of the Penal Code, consisting of twenty-one amendments to the old law, increased the maximum terms of imprisonment for political crimes. The penalties were raised to life imprisonment for homicide through premeditated collective action, to fifteen years for armed assault, to ten years for extortion, to fifteen years for kidnapping with the intent of ransom, to fifteen years for the possession of arms or the manufacture of explosives, to ten years for the leaders or organizers of subversive organizations, to ten years for acts of public intimidation, and to six years for inciting to collective violence against persons or institutions. The Act of Obligation to the National Security gave the federal government the right to intervene in the internal affairs of the provinces in the interest of national security. Once signed into law by the provincial governors, this act gave the minister of the interior the right to remove elected officials and representatives identified with or friendly to the Peronist left wing, who could be legally deposed despite their popular mandate.

The escalation of police terror and actions by paramilitary right-wing groups, as a counterterror to that of the various Peronist and non-Peronist armed organizations, also became a typical and continuing feature of Argentine political life. On the day Perón returned, marching contingents of the JP, JTP, and JUP, flying Montoneros' banners, were fired upon at the Ezeiza Airport to prevent them from assembling in front of the platform where Perón was expected to speak. The shooting began when a JP column from La Plata, headed by the Montoneros, FAR, and ERP-22, approached the central stage. Armed bands of the Peronist right had occupied the Ezeiza Hospital and stationed themselves at the windows of the airport's International Hotel forty-eight hours before the event, apparently to prevent the movement's left wing from gaining access to Perón. The hospital and its ambulances were seized by members of the Organizational Command (C de O) wearing white armbands, while the hotel was occupied by armed workers of the JSP wearing green armbands and by professional bodyguards on the UOM payroll. These forces were supported by armed cadres of the University National Concentration (CNU), a parapolice organization whose specific objective was to rid the universities of student militants. All of these groups were under the command of Colonel Jorge Osinde, the chief of Perón's security guard, who had privately circulated the rumor that he had been personally charged by Perón with sweeping the "bolshies" from the movement. The marching contingents with their Montoneros banners were caught in a cross fire from the hotel and the central platform where the security guard was armed with heavy weapons including rifles, carbines, and machine guns. Although the Montoneros had come armed with pistols in self-defense, they were no match for Osinde's armed thugs. The resulting massacre, which left more than thirty dead and several hundred wounded according to official reports, was actually an ambush rather than a spontaneous skirmish between the Peronist left and right wings.

The original actions attributed to the C de O and CNU were subsequently overshadowed by those of the Argentine Anti-Communist Alliance (AAA). The "Triple A" acquired notoriety in January 1974 when it announced its first death list—a long one including political and trade union leaders, a bishop in the Catholic Church, and a colonel in the regular army (*Militancia*, 7 February 1974). This came in response to the January attack by heavily armed contingents of the ERP on the army base at Azul. Although the AAA's death lists were not taken seriously at first, after Perón's death in July it began in earnest to hunt down "Marxist subversives" both inside and outside the Peronist movement, including "sympathizers" from all walks of life—the theater, the cinema, the sports world, the press, and the universities. Even congress was not exempt, as demonstrated by the attempts on the lives of representatives of the opposition Radical Civic Union and threats to blow up its national headquarters. The resulting flood of political refugees to Mexico included two former rectors of the University of Buenos Aires, the ex-minister of the interior in the government of President Cámpora, and Ricardo Obregón Cano, the former governor of Córdoba who was deposed by a police-sponsored coup in February 1974. Among the scores of death victims attributed to the AAA, calculated at more than seventy between July and December 1974, were the historian Rodolfo Ortega Peña, co-editor of *Militancia*, Atilio López, the vice-governor of Córdoba, the lawyer Alfredo Curuchet, the priest Carlos Mújica, the hero of the resistance Julio Troxler, and Professor Silvio Frondizi, an outstanding Marxist political scientist and the brother of ex-President Arturo Frondizi.

The assassination of Frondizi came in response to a press conference in August in which he, along with three other lawyers, publicly denounced the mass murders and tortures by the armed forces in Catamarca Province. The military was specifically charged with having assassinated sixteen members of a rural guerrilla column of the ERP, *after* they had surrendered. A fifth colleague, Alfredo Curuchet, was intercepted by the AAA and executed on his way to the conference. In an AAA communiqué dated September 17, 1974, Frondizi was condemned to death along with ex-President Cámpora and the congressman Héctor Sandler. A second communiqué, affirming the AAA's responsibility for Frondizi's death on September 27, read:

> Under the mandate of his brother, he was responsible for infiltrating communist ideas among our youth. . . .As our beloved and patriotic Argentine people observe, we have been keeping our word slowly but steadily. We are not identified with the "left-handed" mercenaries of death, but with Peronist and Argentine patriots who want the present tribulations of our fatherland to have an Argentine future and

not a communist one. . . .Long live the armed forces! Death
to the "bolshie" assassins! (*Excelsior,* 28 September 1974)

In another communiqué published the same day the AAA also
assumed responsibility for three other deaths, including those of
two actors for corrupting the minds of the youth: "As our people
can see, we are eliminating the 'bolshies' from our country, in
which we will have peace only after liquidating the very last one of
them. No matter how clandestine they are, we will catch the
'bolshie assassins' of our military patriots" (Ibid.).

The escalation of political murders by the "Triple A," which
bears a marked resemblance to Brazil's infamous "Death Squadron" and "Commando for Hunting Communists" (CCC), was a
direct reply to the ERP's announcement that it would avenge the
murders of its sixteen comrades in Catamarca by the indiscriminate
killing of as many officers of the regular army. Thus began a duel
between the ERP and the AAA to see how many corpses each
could pile up in the developing civil war between them. In this
unequal duel, however, the AAA had the advantage of government
protection. It was well known that López Rega, a former police-
man, had subsidized the Organizational Command with funds from
his ministry of social welfare, and that Alberto Villar, the chief of
the Federal Police, had been his protégé. That the AAA operated
with complete impunity and with the complicity of the Federal
Police was evident from the number of kidnappings that were
transformed into police arrests in response to immediate pressures
by the opposition political parties, and efforts to implicate the
government in these activities. In effect, the AAA did the work of
the repressive forces for them, by hunting down "subversives" and
otherwise compelling them to flee the country.

The new repressive legislation and the escalation of paramilitary
terrorism against the left paved the way for increasing concessions
to the right wing of the Justicialist movement. Once the military
had formally abdicated, Perón was confronted with the double task
of holding his movement together and also of moderating the
differences between Peronists and anti-Peronists that all might
work together toward the reconstruction of the country. This was a
complex and difficult assignment, if only because the solution to
either one of these problems effectively barred a solution to the
other. The two horns of the dilemma were the following: to

proceed directly to social liberation and the establishment of a Socialist Fatherland, at the risk of alienating the military and provoking a new civil war; or to develop Argentina into a great power and to postpone indefinitely the objective of national socialism, at the risk of alienating the Peronist left.

The issue hinged on a choice of allies. Should Perón align his movement with the main party of the opposition, the Radical Civic Union, or should he try to cement the unity of all Peronists? To whom should he make concessions: to the few who wielded military and economic power or to the many committed to a socialist transformation against an enemy that could easily wreck all hope of social reconstruction? That Perón decided from the day of his return to cast his lot with the stronger of these forces, even at the risk of splitting the Peronist movement, is evident from his response to the Ezeiza massacre.

In a speech to the nation delivered the day after the massacre, he outlined the priorities of the new 1973 post–civil war period in which national reconstruction was supposedly a condition of national liberation (*El Descamisado*, 26 June 1973). First, the deplorable economic situation of the country was such that the struggle for national reconstruction was hopeless unless everyone participated and collaborated in the common endeavor. Hence the need for a great national agreement concerning fundamentals—a project which also had the support of the armed forces. Second, the crusade for national reconstruction would be guided by the structure of established values and the best interests of the country. A revolution was necessary, but it would have to take place peacefully and constructively, without sacrificing the life of a single Argentine. Only hard work, Perón insisted, could redeem the country from its past follies. One had to choose the best men, whatever their political origins, for the job that had to be done; each man should be judged by his services to his country, regardless of his political predilections. Third, as the only guarantee of liberty and justice, a legal and constitutional order was necessary. Each Argentine had the inalienable right to live in peace and security, which the government had the obligation to secure. The only enemies of the people were those who violated the public order established by a legitimate and popular government. Fourth, Peronists had to return to the foundations of the movement in the effort to neutralize those who would deform it from below and

from above. Those who ingenuously believed they could infiltrate
and capture the movement through duplicity were mistaken and
would be dealt with accordingly. Finally, the goal of reconstruction
was the creation of a great power (*Argentina potencia*), in which
the citizens would enjoy the highest standard of living of which the
nation was capable. Everyone should work for the future and put
aside old rancors in the common effort to achieve this goal.

Perón's address constituted an appeal to concentrate on
preeminently economic objectives. Political considerations were
deemphasized, which suggested that the struggle for social liberation was no longer on the political agenda. As in 1955, under the
pressure of the armed forces on one side and the Peronist bases
clamoring for the organization of a workers' milita on the other,
the general had taken the path of least resistance by declaring in
effect: "I have ceased to be the leader of the National Revolution
in order to become President of all the Argentines."

The grounds for national unity were further clarified in a private
interview with representatives of the Peronist youth organizations
on September 8, 1973 (*El Descamisado*, 11 September 1973). The
ingredients of a revolution, Perón declared, were twofold: blood
and time. "If much blood is spent, time is saved; if it takes a lot of
time, blood is spared." Which option should one choose? Perón
noted that it was not enough to try to change the world, but to do
so intelligently. "One must realize that on the other side there is an
opposed will which also has force, and that it is pointless to break
one's skull in a head-on collision, which is what is happening in
Chile." What is the point, he continued, of workers occupying
factories and putting their organizations in jeopardy? What was
well organized should be conserved and not placed at the mercy of
a renewed military intervention. During the resistance the trade
union organizations were unjustly criticized by representatives of
the Peronist Youth for their alleged lack of militancy, although it
was Perón himself who had ordered them to desist from dangerous
actions. The youth sector had been ordered to proceed in a
different manner only because it had less to lose. In the guidance of
a popular movement, Perón observed, one has to orchestrate
different kinds of action suited to different kinds of men. At the
present time, the youth sector was fragmented and desperately
needed to be unified. Some were to the right of the ideology and

doctrine of the movement, others to the left—but they were all
equally Peronists. "I don't know which side has more reason for
protesting," Perón remarked. "What interests me is that there is a
movement that is multifaceted and that includes all the facets
which such a movement needs." In politics one has to accumulate
the largest number of people possible in pursuit of a given
objective. Consequently, the fundamental consideration was to
establish unity rather than to decide who was right: "I am here to
lead all, the good and the bad, because if I only want to lead the
good I shall be left with only a few, and in politics one cannot do
much with them."

The price of so-called national unity, however, was disunity
within the Peronist movement. In the effort to achieve the former,
Perón unwittingly promoted the latter. As in 1955, the Peronist
Party sought to forge a union of incompatibles. Only this time its
official sector no longer enjoyed the confidence of militants in the
movement. Once the internal struggle against the left had become
an obsession of the "popular government," the party's shift to the
right was a matter of course.

Perón misinterpreted the radicalization of the Peronist left as an
occasional or passing phenomenon, as a direct response to military
repression which would presumably dissipate under a popular
government. Instead of a wave of the future, Marxist socialism was
treated in terms of a cold war mentality, as a political perversion
with no more future than capitalist imperialism. For Perón the
persistence of the revolutionary current after power had been won
indicated a pathological inability to adapt to the new social reality.
Evidently, he lacked an historical perspective of the changes in the
balance of social forces which had contributed to transforming the
character of both the Peronist movement and the working class
during the eighteen years of the resistance.

Like the pacification policy of 1955, the new Social Pact of 1973
brought together organized labor and a bourgeoisie whose economic interests had become increasingly identified with the multinational corporations. Perón's mistake was to have believed in the
possibility of reviving the original alliance of 1945–55, when the
national bourgeoisie still had an interest in economic protectionism
and a policy of vast social and labor reforms. If such an alliance was
no longer feasible, it was because the national bourgeoisie had

since cast its lot with the international or imperialist bourgeoisie. In effect, the Peronist movement in 1973 was at best a pale replica of that during Perón's first and second administrations.

Perón also failed to recognize the long-range effects upon the movement of Argentina's changed status as a dependent country. During his first and second governments the laboring class experienced the benefits of a genuine redistribution of the national wealth promoted not only by the armed forces, but also by sectors of the national bourgeoisie. Since these sectors benefited from the development of the internal market spurred by higher wages and the increased consumption of the masses, they too had a vested interest in Perón's national revolution and struggle against imperialism. By the time of his ouster in 1955, however, economic independence had ceased to be a fighting issue because of the internationalization of capital and the changed strategy of foreign corporations. From having sought to destroy local enterprises as possible competitors, the multinationals had turned to absorbing or integrating them through interlocking directorships and the exchange of securities. In that way native capitalists were able to trade off their independent ownership for the advantages of holding stock in the multinationals, while continuing to manage their former enterprises in dependence on foreign interests.

Between 1955 and 1973 the Argentine national bourgeoisie actively cooperated with foreign interests in extending the scope of imperialist economic penetration in Argentina. As a result, the share of this sector of the bourgeoisie, producing mainly for the domestic market, was reduced to a small fraction of what it had been under Perón. In a study by the North American Congress on Latin America (NACLA), *Argentina in the Hour of the Furnaces,* the participation of foreign corporations in industrial production was reported to have grown during this period from eight to forty percent. Competition with the superior technology represented by foreign interests struck hard at the small and medium manufacturers. Bankruptcies mounted while restrictions on the transfer of profits abroad, combined with successive devaluations by the government, encouraged the use of foreign reserves to buy up local companies.

By the end of the resistance more than sixty percent of the total production of goods and services had come under the control of the multinational corporations. According to a FAP report dated

August 3, 1973, "Briefings for an Analysis of the Present Situation," this figure was compared to twenty-five percent for the state sector and only fifteen percent for the native private sector. At the same time, the most successful representatives of the national bourgeoisie were endeavoring to negotiate their dependence in order to become junior partners of the international bourgeoisie—a sad commentary on Perón's earlier projection of an independent capitalist development for Argentina.

The crisis of Peronism may be attributed in part to the political pressures on the Supreme Council of the Party by these least favored sectors of the national bourgeoisie. Seeking an accommodation with imperialism that might benefit them as well, they favored an anti-imperialist front with the working class for the purpose of renegotiating their dependence from a position of strength. But precisely because this front was conceived as mainly an instrument to such negotiations, they could no longer support, as during 1945–55, the full-scale confrontation with imperialism demanded by the Peronist rank and file. In effect, they could no longer count on the bulk of the labor movement to conform to their economic projects—a circumstance that virtually obliged them to woo the trade union bureaucracy. Thus the anti-imperialist front or Justicialist Front of Liberation (FREJULI) was never the organization it was imagined to be by sectors of the Peronist left. Far from striving for either national or social liberation, it sought to improve the fortunes of the national bourgeoisie together with those of the Peronist political and trade union bureaucracies, at the expense of organized labor.

The official Peronist Party had survived more than one crisis during the past three decades and there was reason to believe that it would also survive the present one. Merely to survive a crisis, however, is not to recover from it. Throughout all earlier crises the Peronist Party had retained its status as the majoritarian party in Argentina. In sharp contrast, the present crisis threatened to transform it into the party of a minority.

During the eighteen years of the resistance the Peronist movement was confronted with a mainly military crisis. A military coup had forcibly ousted the Peronist Party from power, after which the armed forces intervened in successive elections to nullify the Peronist majority at the polls. The first Peronist resistance was aimed at military and pseudoconstitutional governments designed to prevent the majoritarian party from ever reaching the government. During those years the Peronist movement was faced by crises external to its own organization. Although the movement also had to face internal divisions including a major split in the CGT between 1968 and 1970, these tended to be overcome through a united front against the common enemy.

With the return of the Peronist movement to power, the military crisis gave way to a political one. From having been a secondary source of difficulties, the internal divisions in the movement became the principal source. Beginning in January 1974, the movement began to disintegrate in consequence of a new wave of repressive legislation and paramilitary terrorism, which led to a fundamental and irreparable split between its left and right wings. A year later, in March 1975, a second Peronist Party was founded for the purpose of contesting the hegemony of the official party at the polls. Led by Andrés Framini, the Authentic Peronist Party (PPA) anticipated running its own presidential candidate in the national elections. Thus there was reason to believe that the division of the Peronist vote would put an end to the majoritarian status of the FREJULI. In short, the most serious challenge ever to be faced by the official movement was not a military but a political one: the erosion of its popular support to the point that its historic invincibility at the polls could no longer be taken for granted.

The premonitions of a major electoral crisis were first evident in the gubernatorial and congressional elections held in the province of Misiones on April 13, 1975. There the principal beneficiary of the decomposition of the Peronist movement was the old Radical Civic Union. The FREJULI won with forty-six percent of the vote, as against thirty-eight percent for the UCR and fifteen percent for a coalition of the PPA and the Third Position—a local left-wing Peronist party. The distribution of seats was somewhat less favorable for the victor: sixteen congressmen for the FREJULI, thirteen for the UCR, and three for the coalition of the PPA and the Third Position. More revealing than these absolute figures were the comparative ones. Thus the FREJULI vote was approximately twenty percent less than in September 1973, whereas the UCR vote had increased by more than sixty percent.

In March 1973 the Third Position had received 29,000 votes compared to 51,000 for the FREJULI; two years later it and the PPA won only 15,000 votes between them, tantamount to a loss of almost fifty percent. That the Peronist left had suffered an electoral reversal was understandable in view of the conditions under which it had to wage its political campaign. In March 1973 it was heralded as the vanguard of the popular forces which had compelled the military to abdicate; two years later it was publicly discredited and persecuted by the Peronist government and the Federal Police. With the Montoneros waging a war against the government, it was extremely difficult and also hazardous for representatives of the Peronist left to build a new party. At the same time, the ministry of social welfare mounted the most expensive electoral campaign in the history of Misiones, including the massive distribution of free refrigerators and sewing machines in an effort to win votes. Despite these efforts and the repression, the PPA amassed more than double the votes of all the other opposition parties with the exception of the UCR. Even in defeat, the PPA emerged as one of the three principal political parties in the country and as the most important single party on the left. Moreover, the Misiones elections were hardly typical of the country as a whole. With an urban population of only forty percent compared to the national average of eighty percent, with virtually no industry and an insignificant working class—the principal support of the new party—the results of the elections were an unreliable index of national trends.

That the Authentic Peronist Party was a force to be feared was evident from the government's response to its showing in the elections. On April 18 the police in Buenos Aires announced the arrest of the head of the JP, Juan Carlos Dante Gullo, and of Dardo Cabo, a leader of the PPA, after an armed encounter in which both were accused of directing the Montoneros. This action was followed on April 22 by the formal expulsion of ex-President Cámpora from the Justicialist Party for "treason and disloyalty." Specifically, Cámpora was expelled for not having denounced the guerrillas, the new movement of resistance to the government of Isabel Perón, and the Peronist Youth reorganized under the banners of "Authentic Peronism"—evidence of his disrespect for the principle of verticality and directives of the official party. The following day Cámpora replied in a "Message to the Argentine People" in which he astutely denounced his accusers as persons without political merit and as having only circumstantial authority to judge his case. Appealing over their heads to the Argentine people, he asked it to judge whether he was at fault or whether the fault lay with his accusers.

In addition to organizing a new party, the disaffected left wing of the movement had entered into an informal alliance with other left-of-center parties to set up a rival to the FREJULI in the forthcoming presidential elections. The initial move in that direction had been made by the Peronist Youth in a press conference on November 24, 1974, in which, after denouncing the government of Isabel Perón as "illegitimate," it called upon all the national and popular sectors to form a new front of national and social liberation to replace the old one. One of the first steps was the organization of a rival Peronist party, which contested the legitimacy of the FREJULI in the provincial elections in Misiones in April.

A month later and in response to the showing of the PPA in Misiones, the Intransigent Party (PI) of Oscar Alende announced on May 9 its support for a broad front similar to that in Uruguay in 1971. The Intransigent Party consisted of the remnants of the former Intransigent Radical Civic Union, after ex-President Frondizi had split with it in 1963 to organize his own Movement of Integration and Development (MID) committed to a front with the official Peronist movement. Alende hoped to participate in a center-left coalition that would overcome the forced option at the polls between the official Peronist Party and the Radical Party (UCR), the former Popular Radical Civic Union, of Ricardo Balbín. In an effort to organize a new coalition, contacts were made with the Authentic Peronist Party, the Communist Party, the Christian Revolutionary Party (PRC), and the Progressive Democratic Party (PDP). Later, the Front Against Imperialism and For Socialism (FAS) was to add its support to the new front.

The urgency of a new front was reiterated at the First National Congress of the PPA, held in Córdoba at the end of November. Besides clarifying the party's revolutionary program and its role as the political and legal arm of the Montoneros, the congress discussed ways and means of constituting an electoral front. Alliances were to be established mainly with the Intransigent Party and with ex-President Cámpora representing a sector of loyal Peronists still included within the official Party. Following the congress the principal leaders of the PPA, Andrés Framini and former governor Oscar Bidegain, met with Cámpora and Alende in an effort to reach an agreement in which it was anticipated that

Cámpora would head the front's presidential ticket with Alende as vice-president. In a lengthy message to the National Convention of the PI on December 13, likewise meeting in Córdoba, Alende reiterated his own party's call for an electoral front based on the Peronist masses, the Yrigoyenist radicals, and other democratic sectors striving for "authentic social and economic change." It was the imminent formation of such a front that prompted the government on Christmas Eve 1975 to outlaw the PPA, precisely for serving as a legal front of the Montoneros, and to ban the publication and circulation of its fortnightly *El Auténtico.*

On the model of a kind of left-wing FREJULI, the PPA was successful in establishing the embryo of such a front with a group of left-of-center parties committed to implementing the program voted by the people on March 11, 1973, but subsequently abandoned or betrayed by the government. Among the smaller parties supporting such a front were the Christian Revolutionary Party (PRC), the Christian Popular Party (PPC), the Yrigoyenist National Movement (MNY), and the Vanguard Socialist Party (PSV). This list has a certain interest because only a few hours before the coup against Isabel Perón on March 23, 1976, these smaller parties joined with representatives of the Intransigent and Authentic Peronist Parties to found a new weekly, *Información,* whose purpose was to arrive at common solutions to the political and economic crises ravaging the country.

During the resistance the Peronist movement continued to present a common front against its enemies. After the March 1973 elections and during the fifty days of euphoria under the leftist government of Héctor Cámpora, however, it became increasingly evident that the competition between the two Peronisms was rapidly eroding the unity of the movement. It also became obvious that the revolutionary current rather than the opposition political parties and the reactionary armed forces had become the principal threat to the Peronist political and trade union bureaucracies. Since peaceful competition was attracting the majority of the Peronist rank and file to the side of the Peronist left, the Peronist right wing was pushed into launching a cold war against the "Marxist infiltrators" who were allegedly subverting the movement. These measures were apparently insufficient to halt the growth of the "Marxist insectifying tendency." Accordingly, the cold war was escalated into a hot one in which police terrorism was reinforced by the actions of paramilitary gangs bent on physically liquidating the Argentine left. Once again the history of Argentina was being written with the blood of revolutionaries, which cannot be negotiated.

Hitherto the struggle between the reformist and revolutionary tendencies in the movement stopped short of a decisive rupture because of the urgency to join forces against the military. Yet within less than a year of Perón's return from exile, his original alliance had virtually collapsed to be replaced by another one. Government figures sympathetic to the Peronist left wing were pressured to resign, beginning with Oscar Bidegain, the governor of Buenos Aires. The self-styled orthodox tendency had prevailed upon Perón and then Isabelita to depose the elected governors of six provinces—Córdoba, Mendoza, Santa Cruz, Formosa, Salta, and Misiones. Regional offices of the major trade unions were intervened by the rightist trade union bureaucracy in control of the CGT, followed by the government's seizure and "normalization" of recalcitrant unions, the Graphic Workers Union led by Raimundo Ongaro and Agustín Tosco's Light and Power Workers Union of Córdoba. With warrants for the arrest of union leaders and the assassination of key spokesmen of revolutionary Peronism, the Peronist left had ceased in 1975 to represent the same effective force for social change that it had a year earlier. Nonetheless, the emergence of the Authentic Peronist Party on a national scale amounted to the left's resurgence within the area of electoral politics. Since the conditions which had originally engendered the Peronist left showed no signs of disappearing, a longer view of history indicated that the reformist tendency had entered upon a phase of continuing crisis from which it was unlikely to recover.

Evidently, the effort of the Justicialist movement to "Mexicanize" the Argentine revolution had partly failed in its objective. The FREJULI had fallen short of receiving an absolute majority in the Misiones elections and was likely to fall even shorter in the elections scheduled in other provinces. Clearly, it was in no condition to repeat the example of Mexico's Institutional Revolutionary Party (PRI) by converting the government into its private possession, at least not through constitutional means. Unlike the Mexican virtual one-party system, Argentina had two viable political parties contending for a simple majority—with the prospect of still a third.

In other respects, the Argentine revolution seemed to be

traversing the same stages as the Mexican Revolution. Following the leftist administration of President Lázaro Cárdenas during the 1930s, the ruling party abandoned its radical populist orientation for a policy of dependent capitalist development with the help of large doses of foreign capital. If Perón's first and second administrations are in many ways comparable to that of Cárdenas, his third government is a reminder of the shift to the right under Cárdenas' immediate successor, Avila Camacho. In this perspective the government of Isabel Perón corresponds to the institutionalization or freezing of the Mexican Revolution under President Miguel Alemán, combined with the escalation of political repression under President Gustavo Díaz Ordaz in 1968. Historical analogies, however, are misleading. Thus there is reason to question whether Argentina in the 1970s was capable of repeating the experience of the Mexican Revolution during the 1940s, much less the repudiation of President Díaz Ordaz' repressive policies by the new President Luis Echeverría.

Were the repressive policies of Isabelita's government really comparable to those under Alemán or Díaz Ordaz? Or had the Peronist movement been so polarized by the events of 1974–75 that there was no longer hope of recovering its original balance? In view of the far greater strength of the Peronist left compared to the Mexican, it was understandable and predictable that the Peronist right wing would go to much greater lengths in its struggle against the left. To the Ezeiza massacre in June 1973 were to be added the exploits of the "Triple A," which had been both subsidized and protected by government agencies. In April 1975 the Montoneros released a document entitled "What is the AAA?" which described in detail López Rega's complicity and that of the Federal Police in the wave of right-wing assassinations of Peronist militants. The substance of the indictment was confirmed a year later, in February 1976, by an investigatory commission of the Chamber of Deputies on the basis of a confession by Salvador Paino, one of the founders of the "Triple A." Repression of the political left was worse under Isabelita than it had been in Mexico under any of Cárdenas' successors. To add to the climate of repression, Argentina was completely encircled by hostile military regimes. Thus foreign, as well as domestic, pressures contributed to the shift toward the right and to the continuing political crisis that foreshadowed the collapse of both the Peronist Party and the government—first of López Rega and then of Isabel Perón.

6

The Peronist Enigma

If few political analysts have reached an accurate understanding of Peronism, it is because of its extreme complexity compounded by a mass of demagogical appeals and ideological compromises. As Perón noted in a March 1973 interview in *Oui* magazine, nobody had yet been able to fathom its fundamentals nor had he been willing to help for political reasons. Its enigmatic character is to be found precisely in its ambivalence and defiance of traditional categories and efforts to classify it. Because Peronism is a pragmatic social and political philosophy, it has shown an extraordinary capacity to adapt to the most varied historical circumstances. This has earned for it the reputation of opportunism. Peronism, as we shall see, has several faces. Actually, its interpreters have judged it to be attractive or repulsive depending on when and which of its many profiles it has chosen to present to the public.

In this perspective it is understandable that, after almost three decades of open or repressed hostility to Perón and Peronism, the U.S. State Department should have suddenly reversed itself following the Peronist landslide in the March 1973 elections. The foreign policy of the new government installed in May threatened to break the U.S. blockade of Cuba, but its domestic policy promised a new era of social peace and political stability with an end to guerrilla operations against U.S.-based corporations in Argentina. The State Department was on friendly terms with comparable populist and nationalist regimes in Mexico and Peru, which also had diplomatic ties with Cuba. Since an accommodation to such regimes was apparently worth the price of domestic stability in those countries, a similar logic seems to have dictated the State Department's accommodation to Peronism.

The liberal establishment in the U.S. also took an active interest in the success of the new Peronist government. In view of the rash of right-wing coups against democratic regimes in Brazil, Bolivia, Chile, and Uruguay, not to mention the military dictatorship in Argentina from 1966 to 1973, the fascist character of Peronism had evidently been exaggerated. At the same time, the monopoly of political power by a populist party tended to be reappraised as at least a viable form of democracy south of the Rio Grande. Since Peronism represented the most persistent effort on the continent to repeat the experience of Mexican one-party rule based on periodic elections, liberals in the U.S. began reassessing its authoritarian features in favor of its democratic facade.

This, however, was only one of the many faces presented by Peronism. Representing an alleged middle road between capitalism and communism, Peronism constitutes a complex tissue of ideas congenial alike to authoritarian nationalists and to non-Marxist, self-styled socialists. During the late 1940s and early 1950s Perón claimed that his philosophy of Justicialism represented the only viable alternative to social unrest and communist subversion provoked by the then prevailing liberal-democratic governments in Latin America, dominated for the most part by landowning and plutocratic interests. Subsequently, he claimed that it was the only viable alternative to the corporate military dictatorships in Brazil, Bolivia, Chile, and Uruguay as well as to the Fidelist and Guevarist movements on the continent. In the effort to reconcile the claims of capital and labor through the massive organization of the working class and its participation in political power, Justicialism became the Argentine equivalent of a similar philosophy of social justice first institutionalized by the Mexican Revolution under President Lázaro Cárdenas—a pragmatic and flexible social philosophy aimed at reconciling political opposites.

As late as 1968 Perón reaffirmed the continuity of his "Third Position" with the struggle of pre–World War II Italian fascism and German national socialism to steer a middle course between the demoliberal plutocracies of the West and Soviet totalitarianism. Historically considered, fascism and communism were regarded by

Perón not as polar opposites, but as rival aspects of the same redemptive movement of the twentieth century: the struggle against capitalist-imperialism and its political counterpart, liberal democracy. Ethically, however, communism was interpreted as barbaric and inhumane, and its promotion of class struggle instead of class peace as detrimental to civilized society. Thus the official wing of Peronism made common cause with the Third World in opposition to the "two imperialisms," a struggle against the same unholy alliance of international finance capital and international subversion waged by the fascist powers during World War II.

The fascist elements in Peronism are evident not only in its populist appeal to a fictitious "Third Position" intermediate to capitalism and communism, but also in its demagogic efforts to win over the working class through the nominal acceptance of a socialist ideology. There are at least two historic instances in Latin America of the defeat of a revolutionary tendency through the adoption of its banners by a political and military bureaucracy. The first occurred during the Mexican Revolution when Carranza, following General Álvaro Obregón's advice, accepted popular demands for an agrarian reform as a condition of acquiring mass support, after which he proceeded to smash the peasant armies of Pancho Villa and Emiliano Zapata. The second occurred during the Peronist resistance when, on the advice of John William Cooke, Perón gave free reign to the pro-Guevarist tendencies within his movement—a strategy of guerrilla warfare which directly contributed to the abdication of the military and to his eventual return to power—after which he proceeded to purge the movement of "Marxist infiltrators" and the Peronist revolutionary tendency.

Years earlier, in preparation for the presidential elections of 1946, Perón had also made demagogic use of leftist tendencies by running as the Labor Party's candidate. Then, after becoming president, he forcibly dissolved the party and imprisoned its independent leaders. This seemingly ambivalent strategy of stealing the thunder of the left and then proceeding to crush independent movements of the masses is to be distinguished from that of other "Young Turks" within the military who, following a successful campaign against guerrilla movements, have embraced the revolutionary banners of anti-imperialism, economic independence, and social justice in order to overcome the causes of social unrest. Thus the Peruvian military coup of October 1968 and the

Bolivian military coup by General Juan José Torres in October 1970 contrast strikingly with the comparable Mexican and Argentine experiences, in which a systematic war against the left followed rather than preceded the conquest of political power.

Actually, the Peronist movement harbored a lion which could not be tamed. Under the impact of John William Cooke and the Cuban Revolution, the Peronist resistance developed a Guevarist tendency. The influence of the Cuban Revolution was also evident in the program of the Peronist left wing, reorganized by Gustavo Rearte in 1964 as the Peronist Revolutionary Movement (MRP). Calling for armed struggle against the elected government of Arturo Illia, the program anticipated a protracted struggle that would continue even after the conquest of power. Thus it is not surprising that both Cooke and Rearte were delegates to the Cuban-sponsored Organization for Latin American Solidarity (OLAS) in 1967 and that their group dominated the Argentine delegation. That they could still be identified with Peronism was made possible by Perón's encouragement of the revolutionary tendency as a counterforce to the collaborationist Peronist political and trade union bureaucracies, and by his concerted efforts to moderate the differences between his movement's left and right wings.

Peronism pretended to reconcile political opposites. But what are we to make of its alleged synthesis of capitalism, communism, and fascism? That capitalist and communist tendencies can coexist in peaceful competition is no longer cause for skepticism. That capitalism and fascism are compatible is even less perplexing, as the historical record of European politics between the two world wars indicates. But that revolutionary Marxist and counterrevolutionary fascist currents can exist side by side within the same political movement—that is surely cause for surprise. In fact, the central enigma of Peronism is precisely how to account for the coexistence of these hitherto irreconcilable and contradictory political tendencies.

The doctrine of Justicialism, formally presented to the Argentine public in 1949, was the philosophic expression of a polyclass movement that had deliberately incorporated fascist as well as capitalist and communist features. Each of these political-economic syndromes was conceived as a response to two sets of antinomies, which Peronism sought to reconcile in a higher synthesis or "Third Position" intermediate to the extremes: first, the opposition between individualist and collectivist tendencies; second, the opposition between materialism and idealism. Communism, for example, was interpreted as a synthesis of collectivism and philosophical materialism; capitalism, as a composite of individualism and materialism; fascism, as a combination of collectivism and philosophical idealism.

These principal political combinations of the twentieth century had the advantage, according to Justicialist doctrine, of overcoming the extremes represented by each of their special poles in isolation. Thus the unviable political options were anarchism (individualism), totalitarianism (collectivism), egoism (materialism), and theism (idealism). Perón's objection to communism, capitalism, and fascism was that they, too, were mutually exclusive. Accordingly, Justicialism was conceived as an effort to harmonize these major political and economic tendencies through a system of ideological checks and balances permitting their coexistence. By its self-identification with a form of Christian national socialism, moreover, Justicialist doctrine also gave prominence to the theocratic element overshadowed or ignored by these other combinations.

What is the relationship between these ideological components of Justicialism and the division of the Peronist movement into left and right wings? Under the impact of the Cuban Revolution, the left wing has increasingly favored a socialist solution to Argentina's social problems. In contrast, the right wing supports the capitalist system without the leadership of the capitalist class. Since fascism has historically represented a last-ditch defense of capitalism through a political transfer of power from the traditional parties of the bourgeoisie to a professional bureaucracy ruling in its own interests, the Peronist right wing shares the political objectives of fascism, if not its methods. Agreeing with elements of the fascist syndrome in opposition both to the political sovereignty of the bourgeoisie and to a social revolution from below, the Peronist right has stood for a "Third Position" allegedly intermediate to both capitalism and communism, but in fact partial to capitalism. In this respect, Peronism has served and continues to serve as the representative of specifically bourgeois economic interests.

The fascist sources of Peronism may be traced to Perón's direct experience of Italian fascism and his efforts to assimilate its lessons.

During his two-year stint from 1939 to 1941 as a military attaché of the Argentine Embassy in Rome, he had ample opportunity to study Italian fascism and was evidently influenced by Mussolini's example. "Mussolini was the greatest man of the twentieth century, although he made a few mistakes," Perón quipped. Presumably, Mussolini's greatest mistake was to have misjudged the military strength of the allied powers and the continued viability of representative political institutions in the West. Although the Group of United Officers (GOU), the military lodge created by Perón, was a pro-Axis and intensely nationalistic organization dedicated to displacing the corrupt electoral system in Argentina with a military one, Perón adapted after World War II to the ways of the victors. Thus the Peronist movement acquired a democratic character, but with a strong dose of authoritarianism institutionalized in the person of the leader and the so-called "principle of verticality"—the transmission of authority from the top down. It was civilian rather than military in composition and opted for electoral avenues rather than armed violence as a means of achieving political power. Accordingly, many interpreters tend to rule out the fascist features of the movement. However, just as one can speak of a revolutionary tendency within Peronism, so the movement was broad enough and sufficiently complex to include a fascist current.

That fascist currents continued to be an important and integral part of Peronism was evident from Perón's decision in May 1974 to return to the fundamentals of the movement by reaffirming the centrality of Justicialist doctrine. In an address to the Congress of the Justicialist Party at the end of May, he redefined the conditions for membership in the movement in terms of unconditional acceptance of the Peronist ideology contained in the following works: *The Organized Community, Peronist Doctrine,* and *Peronist Leadership.* This meant that the essence of the movement was to be determined by those works dating from the period when Peronism was in office, as opposed to those which sanctioned the policies of the Peronist Youth and the revolutionary wing of the resistance, such as *Latin America: Now or Never.* It was abundantly clear from Perón's speech that, although he had relied on the revolutionary tendency during the critical years when the movement was outside the law, the politics and strategy of a "Socialist Fatherland" were no longer acceptable after his return to power.

In retrospect, all of Perón's declarations concerning an Argentine form of socialism were to be interpreted within the context of his "Third Position," i.e., a mixed economy governed by capitalist relations of production but including a strong public sector. Socialism in the strict or Marxist sense of a new social formation dominated by noncapitalist relations of production was out of the question—a distortion of Justicialist doctrine. Prior to his speech Peronism could be nominally conceived as embracing the politics and strategy of social as well as national liberation. After his speech it was clear that the deviations from Peronist orthodoxy, which had characterized the resistance during his involuntary exile, were to be finally exorcised from the movement. Accordingly, Perón's simultaneous attacks on both the left and the right were not intended as a repudiation of the Peronist right wing. On the contrary, they were directed against the Marxist-Leninist left allied to the revolutionary tendency *within* the Peronist movement, and against the native oligarchy allied to imperialist interests *outside* the movement.

The enigma of Peronism during the past twenty years was thus partly clarified. The Peronist left was never more than an instrumentality, never the finality of the movement. Having established the conditions of orthodoxy, Perón declared that those elements and tendencies which would not or could not accept the ideology crystallized in the above works constituted pathological germs. Since these germs were contagious, they had to be eliminated from the movement before the infection could spread. Hence Perón's recommendations for combating the infection: first, the election of a new leadership capable of returning the movement to its ideological foundations in Justicialist doctrine; second, the elimination from the movement of the subversive or pathological tendency represented mainly by the Peronist Youth.

The aftermath of Perón's speech was that the Supreme Council of the Party excluded the left-wing Peronist Working Youth (JTP) from the trade union branch, which was officially limited to the CGT and to the right-wing Peronist Trade Union Youth (JSP). At the same time, the Supreme Council was restructured because of Perón's decision to replace the representative of the youth branch by a representative of the pro-fascist Peronist Revolutionary Legion. The provisional Supreme Council, created by Perón in July 1973 for the purpose of making the movement more representative, had consisted of delegates from the four principal branches of the movement: Humberto Martiarena, president of the Justicialist Party bloc in the senate, representing its political branch; José Rucci, secretary-general of the CGT, as the representative of the trade union branch; Silvana Roth, representing the women's branch; and Julio Yessi, leader of the right-wing Peronist Youth of the Argentine Republic (JPRA), as the representative of the youth branch. By replacing Yessi, Perón did not make the movement any more representative, since the Legion had been part of the JPRA from which it had only recently separated.

Following the lines of the fascist corporative state in Italy, the Revolutionary Legion proposed to establish a national syndicalist state in Argentina, a project documented in *Primicia Argentina* in June and July 1974. In conformity with this project, business enterprises would be compelled to "give possession or, better still, the ownership of commodities and the means of production to the workers." This would eliminate the role of absentee owners, mostly foreigners or agents of foreign interests, who attach little importance to the greatness of Argentina and to the well-being of its people (*Primicia*, 2–8 July 1974). This piece of demagogy was far from identifying workers with organized labor. On the contrary, the category of "workers" was conceived in the broadest sense, including the managers of corporations and, by implication, capitalist entrepreneurs and partnerships as opposed to anonymous stockholders.

Ideally, the Peronist movement was to prevent this current from acquiring independence by subordinating it to a broad coalition or complex political synthesis that included the Peronist left wing. The fascist current was to become an instrument of the party and the government in securing an equilibrium of forces allegedly beneficial to the country as a whole. In practice, however, neither the party nor the government established an equilibrium between their left and right wings, but dedicated themselves to the defense of the existing economic system through the repression of revolutionary tendencies both inside and outside the movement. Matters were aggravated after Perón's death, when the sinister features of Argentine fascism were encouraged through paramilitary organizations secretly financed by sectors within the party and the government. Once the bourgeoisie had been removed from power through a Peronist landslide at the polls, the principal threat no longer stemmed from it but from sectors intent on abolishing capitalism and establishing a "Socialist Fatherland." Although prior to achieving political power Peronism represented an uneasy truce between its anticapitalist and anticommunist sectors, after power had been won and the bourgeoisie had been tamed the only serious enemy internal to the movement became its revolutionary wing. In displacing the bourgeoisie from power, Peronism was politically revolutionary; but in suppressing the struggle for socialism, it was economically reactionary.

Unquestionably, there is a family resemblance between fascism and Peronism; but that Italian fascism was the first in a series representing a new twentieth-century political syndrome did not make it the ideological parent of Peronism. The difficulty with those characterizations of Peronism as a "left-wing fascism," "fascism of the lower classes" or "labor fascism" is that they mistake a sibling relationship for a parent-child one. Although Peronism owes more to Italian fascism than to any other single source, its relationship to the latter can be more accurately designated by the metaphor of a political younger brother than by that of an intellectual brain child or ideological progeny. Perhaps the outstanding difference between Peronism and Italian fascism, to which one might add German national socialism and Franco's "military fascist" regime in Spain, is that Peronism stopped short of being totalitarian. For one thing, the armed forces were never successfully subordinated to the Peronist Party. If there were no mass concentration camps in Argentina, if the jails were not overflowing with political prisoners, if police tortures and assassinations were isolated rather than everyday events, if civilian life was not militarized, it was because Peronism never had to face—at least not until Perón's third government—a systematic and powerful Marxist opposition capable of paralyzing the government and the country. The conditions of social unrest that Mussolini faced in 1920–21, Hitler during the Great Depression, and Franco during the Civil War, Perón was not obliged to confront until his third administration, and then only from January to July 1974.

There is another salient difference between Peronism and fascism. The Latin American governments that most resemble the totalitarian dictatorships of Fascist Italy, Nazi Germany, and Franco's Spain are the military regimes in Brazil, Bolivia, Chile, and Uruguay—governments which are anti-Peronist as well as anticommunist. In Chile, where a socialist-communist coalition controlled the government from 1970 to 1973, a totalitarian political order was established with massive concentration camps and a government-backed campaign aimed at the physical extermination of the entire Chilean left. The Chilean military junta and the comparable military regimes in Brazil, Bolivia, and Uruguay share with Spanish *Franquismo* the additional feature of having fashioned a political alliance with the most reactionary sectors of monopoly capital and the big bourgeoisie without the countervailing force of organized labor. Since the Latin American bourgeois were dependent for the most part on the interests of North American imperialism, such an alliance was tantamount to dependence on the international bourgeoisie. Thus, if the military regimes in Chile and Brazil became a pliable instrument of North American imperialism, it was because the bourgeois in those countries were neither autonomous, as they were in Western Europe, nor countervailed by a powerful and nationalistic labor movement as in Argentina.

A distinction has been made between the independent and aggressively expansionist fascism of the developed countries and dependent or so-called "colonial fascism" in the underdeveloped ones. The question is whether Argentina under Peronist domination fits either one of these descriptions. Unlike the pro-U.S. military regimes in Chile and Brazil, Peronism continues to favor a policy of alignment with the Third World, including efforts to overcome the U.S. political and economic blockade of Cuba. From the beginning Peronism represented a social pact with the nationalist sectors of the bourgeoisie in alliance with organized labor, not as in Chile and Brazil with a bourgeoisie intent on destroying the labor movement through an alliance with imperialism. Accordingly, Peronism shares far more in common with the Mexican model of authoritative democracy than with the military repressive regimes in Latin America. Rather than a form of fascism suited to underdeveloped countries, it is an alternative to the fascist model.

All of these regimes, whether military-repressive or militantly antifascist as in the case of the Mexican model, are instances of the same broad and relentless twentieth-century tendency toward the displacement of the bourgeoisie from power through a political revolution, but without a corresponding economic or social revolution—a current briefly described as politically antibourgeois and economically antisocialist. This is what these governments have in common rather than a common parentage in European fascism. As for their common denominator, it is so far nameless, although Perón roughly characterized it in terms of a "Third Position." In fact, these governments share features common to both the capitalist and socialist orders, notably the political sovereignty of a bureaucratic class and the economic sovereignty of the bourgeoisie.

Having undergone a common bureaucratic political revolution, these regimes differ mainly in the sectors of the bureaucracy which have assumed the lion's share of political power. In Western Europe the differences were limited to the two principal variants of fascism, applying this term in its broad usage: the classical political variant in Italy and Germany, where the Fascist and National Socialist parties were the supreme organs of power; and the *Franquista* variant in Spain, where the Falange was subordinated to the military bureaucracy—the origin of so-called "military fascism." Thus in Italy and Germany the political sector of the bureaucracy played a dominating role; in Spain, the military sector.

In Latin America the bureaucratic political revolution has taken nonfascist as well as seemingly fascist forms, which accounts for its varied outcomes. I say seemingly fascist because it is hardly possible to have "military fascism" without not only military rule, but also a fascist party and ideology in a subordinate role as in Franco's Spain. But in Latin America such parties and ideologies are virtually nonexistent with the exception of Bolivia, where the Bolivian Socialist Falange actively shared, after the manner of the Spanish Falange, in the military regime which overthrew the popular front government that preceded it. In November 1974, however, that party too was outlawed in a ban proscribing all political parties under the military regime. Among the new military regimes, Brazil stands alone in condoning political parties; but these have been remodeled into a two-party system in which fascist currents are conspicuously absent. Considering that these regimes, in every case except Brazil, have adopted a liberal economic policy relying on the free play of market forces instead of a regulated capitalism, they also fall short of the economic common denominator of both political and military fascism.

In addition to the repressive, if nonfascist, variants of the bureaucratic political revolution, there are several outstanding populist models. One model is presented by Mexico, unique in having achieved the participation of all sectors of the bureaucracy in power during the period when Lázaro Cárdenas was president (1934–40). Although the Mexican Revolution continues to be the most stable and viable form of the "Third Position," the political bureaucracy has since acquired hegemony over the other sectors. Peronism offers a different model in which the trade union bureaucracy has a privileged role. Such a labor variant of the bureaucratic political revolution is unique to Latin America. The Peruvian national revolution offers still another model in which the military sector of the bureaucracy is clearly in the ascendancy, but without taking the form of the military repressive regimes in neighboring Chile, Bolivia, and Brazil.

Each of these bureaucratic revolutions—Mexican, Argentine, and Peruvian—has been characterized by strong authoritarian and corporativist tendencies. Nonetheless, the corporativist tradition in social and political philosophy has a Roman Catholic rather than a narrowly fascist derivation. Its origins are to be found in early nineteenth century Christian socialism and in the papal encyclicals of Popes Leo XII and Pius XI. Thus the existence of a corporativist common denominator of the Mexican, Argentine, and Peruvian models and military repression in Chile, Brazil, Bolivia, and Uruguay is not an argument for either a common fascist parentage or the existence of fascist political institutions common to these different countries.

In Latin America the struggle for power by rival sectors of the bureaucracy has been shaped by four principal strategies: first, an alliance with native capitalists and representatives of the multinational corporations against the forces of organized labor and the political movements of the left; second, an alliance with the multinationals at the expense of native small and medium capitalists as well as organized labor; third, an alliance with the working class and the political left against the bourgeois oligarchy and the multinational corporations; and fourth, an alliance with both organized labor and the native capitalists aimed at limiting the role of the multinationals and at securing an independent role for the intermediate forces in society, i.e., the self-styled "Third Position."

The first strategy was followed by the military bureaucracy and techno-bureaucratic elites in Argentina between 1966 and 1973 and by most of the military repressive regimes on its frontiers—with the exception of Brazil. The second was applied in Brazil through a strategy that effectively denationalized part of the private sector in the interest of the multinationals, while at the same time it expanded the scope of the public sector and the economic powers of the state. The third was adopted by Fidel's July 26 Movement, by the principal Guevarist organizations on the continent, by the Peronist left, and by the Popular Unity coalition of President Salvador Allende in Chile. The fourth was institutionalized with success by the Mexican Revolution and subsequently tried by the Peronist government and by the Peruvian military junta. What distinguishes the history of the Peronist movement in the contemporary struggle for a new political and social order is its evident tendency to broaden the political bases of the bureaucracy in power after the manner of the Mexican Revolution, while its left wing has simultaneously opted for the strategy of the Cuban Revolution.

Historically, only the Cuban option is consistent with the economic as well as political hegemony of the "new class." Although the "Third Position" has been successful in raising the bureaucracy to a position of control over the government, it has yet to issue in a major transfer of the economic surplus from the proprietary to the professional elites. In contemporary Argentina and Peru, as in Mexico after almost sixty years in power, those elites continue to play second fiddle to the bourgeoisie in economic matters. The economic surplus still takes the form predominantly of profit, interest, dividends, and capitalized rents rather than salaries for professional services. Consequently, the bourgeoisie continues to be the principal beneficiary of the economic system. Only in Cuba has a political revolution been the successful prelude to a corresponding economic revolution. Far from inaugurating an era of self-styled national socialism, the "Third Position" represents at best a half-way station on the road to a new economic order. In contrast, the Peronist left wing promises to complete the political revolution by also revolutionizing existing relations of production.

Within the context of the new governments in Latin America which have emerged in reaction to the Cuban Revolution, the instability of reformist governments rivals that of economically reactionary regimes. A curious feature of governments representing the "Third Position" is their propensity to be self-defeating. They tend, for example, to strengthen not only the industrial bourgeoisie in relation to the large landowners and commercial bourgeoisie, but also organized labor and its potential for a future showdown with the proprietary classes. In this respect, Christian Democracy in Chile engendered the conditions for the revolutionary victory at the polls by the forces of Popular Unity—a factor considered by the Chilean armed forces in proscribing reformist as well as Marxist political parties in that country. One may anticipate a similar fate for the Peronist left in Argentina, once it begins to participate in national elections. In fact, the only alternative to the displacement of a reformist by a revolutionary government in Latin America has become its displacement by a military repressive one.

In *Perón and Justicialism,* Alberto Ciria classifies the different interpretations of Peronism into three principal groups: the nazi-fascist model; the Bonapartist or neo-Bismarckian model; and the populist model. By fascism is understood the totalitarian and repressive common denominator of Italian fascism and German national socialism, a usage that excludes such concepts as a "left-wing fascism" or "fascism of the working class." By Bonapartist or neo-Bismarckian regimes are meant those in which the executive branch of government rules independently of the legislative branch and also of the principal social classes and corresponding political parties. And by populist regimes are understood those representing a coalition of several classes on the basis of a common program aimed at reconciling opposing class interests. In developing this classification, Ciria relied on the most exhaustive compilation of sources available, Carlos S. Fayt's *The Nature of Peronism.* In his judgment, however, only the third model reflects Peronism as it really is.

A somewhat different classification is afforded by Ernesto Laclau's article "Argentina: Peronism and Revolution" in the *Latin American Review of Books* (Spring 1973). Laclau does not pretend to survey the entire literature on Peronism, but only that since 1969. He distinguishes the following interpretations: the liberal view, also shared by the Argentine Communist Party, which discovered in Peronism a peculiarly Argentine brand of fascism; the Third-World view which interprets it either as a bourgeois national revolution or as a bourgeois democratic revolution typical of a semicolonial country; the view of the national left, according to which Peronism is a frustrated bourgeois national revolution capable of achieving its goal of national liberation only through the independent organization of the working class; and the ultraleft view which interprets the conflict between Peronism and the imperialist bourgeoisie as an interbourgeois struggle without special significance for the working class. All of these interpretations are mistaken in Laclau's judgment. Instead, he offers a fifth interpretation of Peronism as an antibourgeois, anti-imperialist tendency within organized labor, tantamount to a nationalist labor movement committed to the defense of national against foreign interests in Argentina.

None of these interpretations taken separately, however, constitutes an accurate account of the many-sided and complex character of Peronism. It is a mistake to liken Peronism to a form of fascism, if only because it stopped short of imposing a totalitarian state and destroying the political parties in opposition. Its repressive legislation against the left likewise stopped short—at least during Perón's first and second administrations—of the concentration camps, mass murders, and police terrorism typical of fascist regimes. It is a mistake to identify Peronism with Bonapartist or neo-Bismarckian regimes because, even though the executive dominated the legislative branch, it did so as the instrument of the Peronist Party and the trade union bureaucracy. Although Peronism exhibited an equilibrium of classes between the bourgeoisie and proletariat, it was itself the vehicle of a special class consisting of the military, political, and trade union bureaucracies. It is a mistake to reduce Peronism to a form of populism because, as a catchall for a polyclass movement, this term does not contain information concerning which class enjoyed a hegemonic position within the government and the nation. Although Peronism was originally a polyclass movement, it developed during the resistance into a nationalist labor movement backed by special armed formations of the Peronist Youth. It is a mistake to equate Peronism with a bourgeois national revolution because the principal beneficiaries of political power were the Peronist political and trade union bureaucracies rather than the national bourgeoisie. Nor did it include a bourgeois democratic revolution because it did not aim at the participation of all sectors of the bourgeoisie and petty bourgeoisie in political power, but at an authoritarian state in place of the existing liberal one. Finally, it is a mistake to reduce Peronism to a nationalist labor movement, because it consisted originally and continues to consist of a much broader populist-type coalition.

Although within such a coalition labor nationalism has had an important and even predominant place, it is not the only face of Peronism.

Efforts to reduce Peronism to any one of these interpretations mistakenly assume that it was somehow a monolithic movement, which failed to develop through specific stages or failed to change its underlying character as it developed. Actually, there is no fixed "essence" of Peronism common to the principal stages of its development: the formative stage when it most clearly exhibited the influence of "military fascism" and was manifestly on the side of the Axis powers during World War II (1943–45); the classical stage when it was a broadly polyclass and populist movement with strong Bonapartist or neo-Bismarckian features, a nationalist movement without the leadership of the national bourgeoisie, that was corporativist, if not fascist, in ideology (1946–55); the postclassical stage when it decomposed into two opposed movements, a national labor movement championed by the Vandorist trade union bureaucracy in control of the CGT and a movement for national and social liberation led by the revolutionary tendency within the unions and the Peronist youth (1956–73); and the critical stage when the official wing of the movement resorted to increasingly repressive measures in its declared war against Marxism and the movement's left wing (1974–76). It would be difficult indeed to discover any basis for continuity within Peronism other than the figure of Perón himself.

7

Lessons of the Argentine Resistance

The Argentine resistance made three fundamental contributions to the strategy of mass resistance to military dictatorship and pseudoconstitutional regimes in Latin America: (1) the effectiveness of a political-military vanguard depends on its integration with the politics of a mass movement; (2) the main enemy must be isolated, not the revolutionaries; this calls for a new historic bloc of the proletariat, workers on their own account, and the petty bureaucracy; (3) the political-military struggle must be an essentially defensive one linked to national traditions of patriotism; it should be designed to save the country from impending disaster, arbitrary rule, or dependency on special and foreign interests.

These contributions were not unique to the Argentine experience. In retrospect these lessons, and not those listed by Che Guevara in his book on *Guerrilla Warfare*, were also fundamental to the Cuban resistance. Fidel Castro's July 26 Movement successfully integrated a political-military foco with the politics of the Cuban People's Party (PPC) of which it was originally the armed fist. It effectively isolated the main enemy, the military dictatorship and the ensuing pseudoconstitutional regime, from the intermediate forces in society, the national bourgeoisie, petty bourgeoisie, and so-called intelligentsia. Finally, its expressed aim was to restore the Constitution of 1940, to call new elections, and to put an end to the illegal repression mounted by the Batista tyranny. Thus it was conceived as a national-patriotic movement in the tradition of José Martí and Cuba's original struggle for independence.

The generalizations culled by Che from the Cuban guerrilla experience provide a distorted and misleading picture of the strategy against Batista. Besides the overly abstract manner in which they were presented, they failed to distinguish a strategy of the possible from one offering at least a reasonable prospect of success. Whatever the case in Cuba, Che's strategy proved to be a dismal and tragic failure elsewhere. Although it is possible for the popular forces to defeat the regular army, it is highly improbable that they will do so on the field of battle; Batista's army was not defeated militarily, but refused to fight from lack of political conviction and because of internal corruption and demoralization. Again, it is possible for an insurrectionary foco to create the conditions of a revolutionary situation when these are only partly present; but to foment a political crisis without having mobilized the masses, or assured the conditions of victory in advance of a major confrontation, is tantamount to anarchist irresponsibility and revolutionary adventurism. Finally, in newly industrializing societies where the bulk of the population has shifted to the cities it is possible, but unlikely, for the principal terrain of armed struggle to be in the countryside; moreover, a suitable environment for waging an armed struggle is determined less by purely military or geographical factors than by a politically favorable population.

The setbacks to urban guerrilla movements in Brazil, Uruguay, and Chile during the early 1970s were followed in November 1974 by a state of siege in Argentina modeled on the Uruguayan "internal war" against the Tupamaros. These reversals may be explained by the vast wave of repression throughout Latin America in response to the insurrectionary tide unloosed by the Cuban Revolution. But they were also the consequence of a faulty revolutionary strategy.

Before the Cuban Revolution the Marxist and Leninist left in Latin America accepted the strategy of peaceful coexistence and the so-called "peaceful road to socialism" adopted and disseminated by the Twentieth Congress of the Communist Party of the Soviet Union. After the Cuban Revolution and in an apparent effort to overcompensate for the opportunist and "revisionist" errors of the 1950s, the left swung to the opposite extreme of voluntarism or "revolutionary adventurism." Before the Cuban Revolution the emphasis of the left was on structural economic reforms, with little or no thought to the organization of an armed vanguard. After the revolution the emphasis shifted to military-tactical problems of the insurrectional foco or center to the comparative neglect of the day-to-day struggles of the proletariat and the building of a mass movement. Thus a lack of balance between alternative forms of struggle has been a constant feature of Marxist and Leninist movements in Latin America—a strategical defect responsible in part for the impotence of the left followed during the 1960s by a rapid succession of political-military defeats.

The coordination of the actions of military vanguards and of the political organizations of the working class has been the exception rather than the rule. Only in Cuba and more recently in Argentina was such a strategy followed systematically: first against the Batista regime, and then against a series of overt and covert military dictatorships in Argentina. The role attributed by Che to the political-military foco during the Cuban Revolution is known to have been exaggerated. The secret of the success of the July 26 Movement is to be found rather in the close ties it established between the armed struggle in the countryside and the politics of mass resistance in the cities. Under Fidel's leadership all forms of struggle were pursued simultaneously and in combination.

In Argentina, the resistance followed a similar strategy guided by Perón from exile. However, after victory Perón favored his party's right wing, whereas Fidel cultivated the left wing of the July 26 Movement. This divergence in the outcomes of the Argentine and Cuban resistance is to be explained not only by their different origins and political ideologies, but also by the comparative strength of their respective armed detachments. The Argentine military retained its autonomy through calling new elections and peacefully surrendering power, whereas Batista's mercenary forces were successfully confronted, dismantled, and replaced by the new Rebel Army.

The active union of Peronist and Guevarist tendencies during the resistance contributed to the emergence of the first political-military focos in Argentina. Initially, the Argentine resistance favored the establishment of rural focos in imitation of the Cuban model. Even before the organization of guerrilla training centers with Perón's support, Peronist cadres under Cooke's influence had launched the *Uturuncos*, a rural foco in northwest Argentina. This aborted effort was followed by the organization with Cuban arms and money of the People's Guerrilla Army (EGP) in 1963, followed by a third rural foco in 1968 organized by the Peronist Armed Forces (FAP). Although this experiment was also a disaster, the FAP was subsequently reorganized to emerge as one of the most influential urban guerrilla movements until 1971 when it was superseded by the FAR and Montoneros.

Just as the rural foco in organic connection with the peasantry was a major strategic contribution of the Cuban Revolution, so the organization of urban guerrillas closely linked to a youth movement and to the trade union rank and file was one of the principal contributions of the Peronist resistance. Parallel with the efforts to found rural focos was the attempt early in 1963 to organize the first Peronist urban guerrillas. The first such instance in Latin America was not the Tupamaros, but rather the Revolutionary Nationalist Movement (Tacuara) under the notorious "Joe" Baxter, whose successful assault on the *Policlínico Bancario* of Buenos Aires in August 1963 became the prototype for subsequent bank "expropriations" not only by the Tupamaros, but also by the FAP and Montoneros.

These Peronist armed nuclei were the first urban organizations in Latin America to have successfully integrated the armed struggle with the politics of a mass movement. Thus the Montoneros became the directing nucleus of the Peronist Youth, while the FAP aligned itself with the Peronist *agrupaciones de base* in the trade unions. The Montoneros helped to move the Peronist Youth and working class in a revolutionary direction, while the FAP contributed to organizing the Peronist Bases. In charting a revolutionary course of its own, the Peronist Youth became the largest youth formation on the continent to constitute a Marxist-Leninist tendency independently of the established Communist and Trotskyist parties. The left has much to learn from this experience of convergence of guerrilla nuclei with mass organizations—the most important sequel to the *foquista* decade in Latin America and to the misguided ventures of Weathermen and the Symbionese Liberation Army in the United States.

The ties linking the Peronist left to the politics of the Peronist rank and file distinguish it from the vanguardist tendencies prevalent during the 1960s. Although revolutionary Peronism has yet to build a majoritarian political party, a mass movement is distinguished not only by the size of its following through the demagogic cultivation of a so-called "mass line," but also by its effectiveness in mobilizing large numbers of people around concrete political issues. Despite the minoritarian character of the Authentic Peronist Party (PPA), that party was second to none in mobilizing political activists during the Misiones elections in April.

Even under conditions of illegality, the revolutionary left qualified as a mass movement. Guevarist sectors, such as the FAR, benefited from the example of the Peronist armed formations by merging organizationally with the Montoneros. Later, the Trotskyist ERP was encouraged to develop a mass basis by breaking with the Fourth International (Unified Secretariat) and by joining in a united front with the Peronist "Independent Alternative." An indispensable condition of the merger of a sector of the FAP with the ERP in October 1974 was precisely this transformation of the ERP from a narrowly vanguardist organization into a movement of the masses.

It may not be premature to venture that what Guevarism represented for the Latin American left during the past decade, the Peronist left may come to represent during the 1970s. The heroic stage when revolutionary theory could be identified with the works of a handful of revolutionary leaders—Fidel, Che, Bravo, Marighela—or with their unofficial spokesmen, such as Debray, is now a matter of history. Revolutionary theory as well as practice is currently the responsibility of the collective leadership of mass organizations and their armed vanguards. The anonymous development of the politics of mass movements has replaced the work of a few gifted individuals.

With the eclipse of *foquismo*, Latin American revolutionaries shifted from a concern with military-tactical problems to a preoccupation with the strategies of mass political movements and their trade union bases. The Debrayist controversy over the comparative advantages of a vanguard party or a political-military foco was ultimately resolved in favor of their combination. By the middle 1970s this debate had been displaced by a new one concerning the merits of the alleged solution. Was a foco-party synthesis representing a revolutionary minority, for example, as consequential as a strategy integrating the revolutionary minority with the politics of a mass movement? The evidence indicated that it was less effective. Although the PRT-ERP initiated a major breakthrough by overcoming the party/foco dichotomy, the Montoneros-JP had the additional advantage of combining the organizational features of both Peronism and Guevarism: a Peronist movement or party of the masses with a Guevarist political-military vanguard led by professional revolutionaries.

Ironically, it was not the professed Marxist-Leninist parties but the revolutionary wing of Peronism that offered a Marxist-Leninist alternative to the traditional Marxist socialist parties on the one hand, and to the new Leninist political-military vanguards on the other. The combination of the politics of a mass movement with a political-military apparatus was first developed by Fidel's July 26 Movement and then imitated by the left wings of the Peruvian Aprista Party and of Democratic Action in Venezuela—organizations all testifying to Haya de la Torre's Latin American revision of Marxism. The first instance of a non-Marxist political movement achieving a similar synthesis was that of the revolutionary tendency within the Peronist movement.

A successful resistance struggle depends upon other factors besides the union of a political-military vanguard and a political organization of the masses. A movement of the masses can be isolated and rendered impotent. To avoid becoming isolated, it needs to be integrated into a broad front with other oppressed classes. A new historic bloc is necessary with the intermediate forces in society: independent peasants, the self-supporting petty bourgeoisie, and the petty bureaucracy or intermediate stratum of salaried employees. In underdeveloped Latin America the proletariat is likely to be outnumbered either by the peasants or the petty bourgeoisie, and almost certainly by both together. Consequently, it needs their support, if only to dissuade them from backing special interests. To isolate the enemy or to be isolated—that is the question.

Both the Argentine and Cuban resistance consisted of broad fronts that included sectors of the national bourgeoisie. In effect, they were populist movements directed not at transforming the social system but at removing a political cancer. Fidel's populism and lack of ideological coherence were not appreciably different from Perón's. The absence of sectarian objectives permitted them to unify the people and to isolate the main enemy. In volume one of *The Critique of Arms*, Régis Debray recounts the secret of Fidel's success in the Sierra Maestra through an interview between Fidel

and Carlos Rafael Rodríguez in 1958. Fidel noted that the mistake
of the Communists was to have clearly defined both their revolutionary objectives and their class adversaries, which contributed to
alerting their enemies and to frustrating a broad strategy of
alliances. Such political ingenuousness was avoided in Argentina, as
it was in Cuba. Yet it was repeated on the mainland with the result
that, instead of isolating the main enemy, it contributed to isolating
the revolutionaries.

Beginning with the Cuban turn toward socialism Che's strategy
of armed struggle became directed not only at military dictatorships, but also at populist or so-called pseudodemocratic regimes,
which included the governments of Democratic Action (AD) in
Venezuela and of Popular Action (AP) in Peru. However, the
Venezuelan and Peruvian masses were unable to keep pace either
with the development of the Cuban Revolution or with the
Guevarist leadership of the revolutionary movements in their own
countries. As a result, the armed strategy in imitation of the
foquismo of the Cuban leaders, which had replaced Fidel's earlier
strategy against Batista, ended with the political and logistical
isolation of the guerrillas. At least in Argentina the leaders of the
revolutionary wing did not dissociate themselves from Peronism
after being repudiated by the official movement, but continued to
maintain close ties with the Peronist masses.

The isolation of the political-military vanguards on the mainland
was in part responsible for their strategy of "polarization," which
actually increased their distance from the workers. Its classic
formulation was given by the Brazilian revolutionary Carlos
Marighela, in an elaboration of Che's second lesson of the Cuban
revolutionary war: "It is not necessary to wait for all the conditions
of revolution to be given; the insurrectionary foco can create
them." Once a political crisis is created, Marighela argued in
"Problems and Principles of Strategy," the next step is to
unleash such a volume of revolutionary activity in urban and rural
areas that the political crisis is transformed into a military one. In
effect, the political regime must be so discredited that the armed
forces are prompted to intervene. Presumably, the population
would then be forced to take sides in a struggle against the clear
and evident tyranny of a military dictatorship. This strategy
contrasted sharply with the strategy of the Peronist resistance, in

which the fundamental objective was to force the military to abandon politics.

Implicit in this strategy was the conviction that representative political institutions under capitalism were only a facade of an underlying social and economic dictatorship guaranteeing the exploitation of the workers. Certainly, capitalism gave no opportunity for economic democracy, but sanctioned a form of despotism within the factory or enterprise reminiscent of the absolute monarchies of the seventeenth and eighteenth centuries. Accordingly, the strategical problem was to unmask the character of democratic institutions in the political arena as fundamentally escape- or safety-valves for the pressures built up within the economic sphere. The strategy of polarization was designed to educate the workers in the underlying significance of these institutions. Every so-called democratic or populist regime, so the argument went, was at bottom a tyrannical one. The essential nature of capitalist democracy was thus revealed only during a political crisis. This was a far cry from the theses of the Peronist left, which insisted on the fundamental differences between capitalist democracy and dictatorship.

The Guevarist thesis was an evidently metaphysical one. Predicated as it was on a philosophical distinction between the underlying essence and superficial appearance of political institutions, it failed to appreciate both the immediate and long-run advantages of liberal-democratic reforms recognizing the right of workers to organize and to build a political movement of their own. One of the conditions of building a mass movement is the right to organize, both economically and politically, in opposition to the dominant classes. Although the oligarchies prefer to govern within the laws and without a show of force, it was a questionable strategy to make them abandon their disguise by showing their teeth. In effect, Che failed to distinguish between the different political superstructures resting upon the same capitalist base, not to mention their comparative advantages and disadvantages for the working class. He cavalierly dismissed the antagonisms between opposed sectors of the bourgeoisie, as if rule by the proimperialist monopoly bourgeoisie were equivalent to rule by the national and petty bourgeoisie. What mistakenly passed as a strategy revealing the underlying essence of dependent capitalism in Latin America was more often than not a strategy of hostility toward the moderate wing of the bourgeoisie in power. The result was that reactionary sectors of the bourgeoisie in alliance with foreign interests were able to take advantage of the ensuing political crises by pressuring the armed forces to impose a state of siege.

As a consequence of this indifference to opposed strata within the bourgeoisie, the strategy of polarization confused the conditions making for a political crisis with those contributing to a revolutionary situation. The assassination of a president or prime minister may suffice to launch a political crisis, but it is hardly enough to mobilize the masses in pursuit of revolutionary objectives. The problem is not to create a political crisis, but to benefit from one. First, the workers must be prepared in advance to transform a political crisis into a revolutionary situation; and second, they must be strongly enough allied with other sectors of the population to transform a revolutionary situation into a popular victory. Otherwise, the triumph of the reaction would tend to make the people worse off than before. As Perón cautioned in an interview with leaders of the Peronist Youth, one should not push for a head-on collision with the enemy unless one is sure of breaking his head and conserving one's own.

In practice, the strategy of polarization applied by Marighela in Brazil, by the Uruguayan Tupamaros, the Chilean MIR, the Bolivian ELN, and the ERP in Argentina was a costly failure in isolating revolutionaries from their potential allies in other classes. At the same time, the principal alternative to this strategy—that applied by the FAR and Montoneros—threatened to swallow up the vanguard in the politics of a populist movement. Granted this dilemma of revolutionary movements and the virtual impossibility of escaping between the horns—which makes every revolution a hazardous undertaking against almost insuperable odds—are the chances of victory improved by choosing one option rather than the other?

The ERP's position was unquestionably doctrinaire. Although the only successful socialist revolutions had been achieved under Marxist-Leninist leadership, the struggle for a uniquely Argentine and national road to socialism could not be effectively presented in these terms. Even in Cuba the transition to socialism had been preceded by a struggle to overthrow a Caribbean-type dictator and to restore the constitutional order. In contrast, the ERP sought to telescope two stages into one, thus running ahead of other popular sectors intent on more modest objectives. The ERP seemingly forgot that the July 26 Movement did not have a socialist orientation and that the Cuban resistance succeeded without a Marxist-Leninist leadership. Only later, owing to the incapacity of the July 26 cadres to make the transition to socialism, was the Movement formally dissolved and replaced by the Integrated Revolutionary Organizations (ORI), to be followed by the United Party of the Socialist Revolution (PURS).

The ERP misinterpreted not only the Cuban road to socialism, but also the Russian. Unlike the political revolutions in Eastern Europe and Southeast Asia, which had the support of a socialist neighbor and the advantage of a sanctuary, the Cuban and Russian revolutions lacked these special advantages. Instead of a single stage political revolution, they developed through two separate stages: first, a political revolution under populist leadership against an unpopular and tyrannical government; second, a political revolution under Marxist-Leninist leadership against the ensuing populist regime, whose new repressive legislation aimed at bringing the revolutionary process to a halt. In both Russia and Cuba revolutionaries of a socialist persuasion bided their time, thus keeping abreast of the political development of the various oppressed sectors pursuing a common goal. Moreover, following their respective political revolutions, they continued their broad alliance with other classes. In Russia they championed a soviet form of government through workers, peasants and soldiers councils, and in Cuba they organized a popular coalition of revolutionary organizations in which the official Communists played a subordinate but increasingly important role. Since the Marxist-Leninist parties in Latin America lack the advantages of their counterparts in Eastern Europe and Southeast Asia, the Russian and Cuban models are correspondingly more relevant in this part of the world.

The question is whether the Montoneros-JP represented the other extreme of opportunism. Actually, they were far more prone to sectarian errors. The feud between the JP and the Vandorist labor bureaucracy, dating back to the middle 1960s, effectively prevented the Montoneros from reaching an agreement with the leaders of organized labor against the party's ultraright wing in control of the government. A series of assassinations of labor leaders—Vandor, Alonso, Rucci—by Peronist commandos who later joined the Montoneros, made any such agreement impossible. At the same time the Montoneros-JP failed to establish an independent base of their own within the working class comparable to the Peronism of the Bases or the Combative Trade Unions. They commenced hostilities against the government for reasons that were not readily understandable by the masses of Peronist workers and in the absence of a major governmental crisis. When they returned underground in September 1974 they did so without adequate preparation, under conditions in which the JP had ceased to function clandestinely and was an easy target for the paramilitary formations of the right. The Montoneros also showed signs of revolutionary impatience by not waiting for the revolutionary occasion to engage in armed operations, as in June 1975 when they could have counted on support from sectors of the official movement to repudiate the policies of López Rega. Moreover, the role of the Montoneros through their representatives at the First National Congress of the PPA in November 1975 exposed the party to unnecessary legal repression as the evident political front for an underground organization.

Owing to their insistence on preserving the original polyclass character of the movement, the Montoneros have been criticized for a policy of vacillations tantamount to a loss of initiative. But was Argentina as yet ripe for a more militant strategy? A revolutionary movement may reach a level of political awareness which no other revolutionary tendency achieves, but if its distinctions elude the masses then its political sophistication amounts to a practical zero. Since the raison d'être of a revolutionary movement is to change the world, history is the ultimate judge of whether the Montoneros' strategy of working within the official movement was realistic or simply unprincipled.

Still another lesson of the Argentine resistance is that it is easier to mobilize the masses in defense of arbitrarily annulled rights than in pursuit of structural reforms whose alleged benefits have yet to be experienced. The masses are more inclined to take risks in self-defense and in defense of national interests which have the character of necessities, than in pursuit of an elusive social change which may appear to many as superfluous. An assault on the established order designed to establish a new one is too ambitious a project for workers with only a limited political understanding of modern societies. Indignation and resentment are powerful motors only in recovering what a people has lost, not in propelling them forward in a struggle for what they have never known. In any event, there is more ground for hope in recovering what has been lost or stolen than in charting a new course in strange or unfamiliar territory.

In *Revolution in the Revolution?* Debray made a special point of criticizing the Trotskyist and Maoist reliance on workers and peasants militias, on the ground that their defense of a fixed terrain or so-called liberated territory could never be a match for a regular army. However, a strategy of self-defense need not be tied to a definite space, but is fully consistent with the mobile tactics of a guerrilla foco. Fundamental to such a strategy is not the defense of occupied lands, mines, and factories, but the preservation or recovery of the elementary rights of a people. A resistance movement differs from the stereotype of Marxist subversion by "professional terrorists" precisely in its defense of urgent national as well as class interests.

The defensive posture of the Peronist movement during the resistance was evident in its objectives: the restoration of the political rights of the majoritarian Peronist Party and the calling of new elections. Its program of national and social liberation, which had been an integral part of the Justicialist movement in power, was directed at recovering the Argentine nation for the people. As we have seen, the fundamental issue for the "movementist" sector of the Peronist left was "Liberation or Dependency?"; for the "classist" sector, "Dependency or Socialism?" In both instances, the struggle against dependency had for its target the special interests of the monopoly bourgeoisie linked to economic imperialism. Thus the struggle was presented as an anti-imperialist one and as the only viable alternative to the structural disabilities of a dependent capitalism.

At the same time, socialism was taken to be a condition of economic independence as well as national greatness. Far from a sectarian goal of the working class for establishing a dictatorship of the proletariat, it was the banner of a popular front including the petty bourgeoisie and entrepreneurial sectors of the national bourgeoisie. Its aim was to secure the economic and political interests not only of the workers, but also of other productive sectors against the parasitic and functionless elements in society.

An underdeveloped country aspiring to greatness, Argentina could not afford the luxury of absentee proprietors whose divided allegiance made them unfit to guide their nation's destiny. In this perspective, the struggle for socialism was neither foolish nor presumptive, but a basic necessity for the nation as a whole.

Peronist appeals to a socialist solution to Argentine problems of dependency were summarized in the slogan of a "Socialist Fatherland." This slogan contrasted sharply with the appeals of the Guevarist and Marxist-Leninist parties in Argentina, which made a fetish of "proletarian internationalism," "the continental revolution," "solidarity with the socialist camp," and so on—traditions having little in common with Argentine nationalism. The internationalist tradition within modern socialism had been responsible during World War II for efforts to align Argentina with the Anglo-French alliance against the Axis powers, in disregard of her own struggle against British imperialism. The international alliance between Russian communism and Anglo-French imperialism was repeated on a national scale in the electoral bloc between the Argentine CP and the established Conservative and Radical parties against the mass of workers organized in the Peronist movement. In effect, the FAR was right that the only viable form of socialism in Argentina had to focus on the defense of national interests. Although Marxism was a useful scientific instrument of revolutions, it was politically unsuitable for mobilizing the Argentine masses against the military dictatorship.

In response to the wave of repression launched by Perón's new government, the Peronist left applied a strategy of self-defense in calling for the abrogation or "correction" of the Social Pact, a renewed amnesty for political prisoners, effective democracy within the unions, and the suppression of parapolice and paramilitary right-wing gangs. The last item acquired increasing importance in view of the escalated terrorism by the "Triple A" and the popular horror against the rising tide of violence in Argentina. In January 1974 the AAA issued a statement in the Argentine press indicating its intention of wiping out not only all "Marxist infiltrators" within the Peronist movement, but also other revolutionaries as well. Once it began carrying out its threat directed at every last leftist in the country including fellow travelers or so-called "sympathizers," hundreds of thousands of citizens must have felt menaced by it. In addition to this informal death list there were forty thousand Chilean exiles and several thousand Uruguayan emigrés, whom the "Triple A" had also resolved to "exterminate." By April 1975 it had surpassed its earlier record of savagery by eliminating a daily average of five Argentine, Chilean, and Uruguayan leftists, with the apparent complicity of a special division of the Federal Police known as the Direction of Foreign Affairs (DAE). Under these conditions, a strategy of self-defense became more urgent than ever.

This life-and-death struggle was to give a tremendous impetus to the new resistance. In most cases, the only practical response was to go underground in self-defense. Although many feared this alternative, preferring to seek individual asylum in some foreign embassy, the consulates were overcrowded with potential exiles for whom there were not enough visas to meet the demand. Unquestionably, the most viable alternative was collective self-defense, which involved a choice between joining the ERP or Montoneros as the best form of protection.

The struggle against the AAA was both a personal affair and a matter of national concern. First, the AAA was a paramilitary arm of the government. Second, it was financed by special interests connected with the oligarchy and presumably the multinational corporations, which were replying in kind to the escalation of leftist terrorism against their executive personnel in 1972 and 1973. Third, the CIA was also suspected of intervening in Argentina's national affairs, since it was known to have subsidized similar right-wing groups in Chile. According to NACLA's *Argentina in the Hour of the Furnaces*, a gunshop owner kidnapped by the FAL confessed to providing $120,000 worth of arms to a right-wing group, which had another $3 million for ordering more of the same. Where did the money come from? It did not come from bank robberies and abductions of wealthy members of the oligarchy and foreign executives—sources of upkeep peculiar to left-wing guerrillas. Presumably, it took the form of voluntary contributions by those sectors, which gave the struggle against the AAA a definitely patriotic character.

One of the questions considered by the left was whether to reply in kind to the provocations by the "Triple A." There were evidently many fewer representatives of the oligarchy and foreign interests in Argentina than there were leftists and leftist-sympathizers. Should the ERP and Montoneros adopt, then, a tactic of reprisals by executing a member of the establishment for every leftist assassinated? A similar tactic had been applied by the ERP in response to the Catamarca massacre in August 1974, but to no apparent advantage. On the contrary, the ERP lost in popularity because of its indiscriminate killing of army officers, which was both militarily pointless and politically ineffective in mobilizing support for the resistance. Nor was anything to be gained by waging a vendetta or private war against the AAA. It was costly enough to maintain an organization of urban guerrillas—estimated by Debray in *The Critique of Arms* at $1,000 monthly for each guerrilla or $50,000 for a team of fifty in 1974—without wasting their energies on unearthing an equally clandestine and elusive organization of the right. Actually, the "Triple A" was scarcely a threat to the ERP, whose cadres were generally invisible both to the police and its paramilitary formations. The greatest danger was to leftists active in the trade unions and to other visible opponents of the regime. And their best means of defense was not to resort to the same terrorist methods, but to win popular support for the resistance from intermediate sectors of the population.

These principal lessons of the resistance have a bearing on similar resistance movements in neighboring Chile, Bolivia, Brazil, and Uruguay. Precisely because the professional military enjoys a monopoly of political power in those countries, it can be combated effectively only through a popular front of all the discontented classes and politically disfranchised parties. At the same time, it is a mistake to enter into a headlong confrontation with the military. As Lenin noted in 1917, the socialist revolution can be made without the armed forces, but only if the military is divided or neutralized. It cannot be made against a highly motivated and united professional army.

Against military repressive regimes the most effective strategy is one that frankly recognizes their ambivalent character. Despite their repressive and barbaric features, the transfer of both legislative and executive powers from the bourgeoisie to a military bureaucracy is tantamount to a political revolution. A discriminating assessment of those regimes provides the basis for a double-edged strategy of both resisting military repression against the popular sectors and supporting the military for breaking the political back of the bourgeoisie. It is virtually impossible to divide and neutralize sectors of the military without acknowledging their revolutionary contributions. At the same time the nationalist wing of the military must be persuaded that the best defense of the revolution is to broaden its base of support. In Argentina from 1966 to 1973, repression of the revolutionary forces did more to undermine than strengthen the military in power. Only under pressure from the Peronist resistance did it eventually admit to the wisdom of sharing political power with other sectors of the bureaucracy. Ironically, the return of the Peronist Party to power in May 1973 was continuous rather than discontinuous with the self-styled "Argentine Revolution" of June 1966.

Once that goal was achieved, the most effective revolutionary strategy was to democratize the trade unions and to increase the weight of popular sectors in the government rather than to push forward prematurely to the establishment of a "Socialist Fatherland." In view of the offensive by sectors of the government loyal to López Rega, it was foolish to escalate the objectives of the left by focusing on the fundamental issue of "Socialism or Dependency?" To provide a revolutionary opening on the left it was enough to recover the program of the first resistance and to revive Perón's original mandate. Although national liberation is impossible without the prior establishment of socialism, the best guarantee of socialism is a struggle for national liberation pursued to its ultimate consequences. In this perspective, the bath of purity advocated by the "classist" sector of Peronism was ill adapted to the realities of Argentine politics.

These are the most important general lessons to be derived from the resistance. But there are also a number of special lessons directly relevant to the conduct of the armed struggle in Latin America. First, armed struggle is viable provided that the guerrilla nucleus is able to reproduce itself on an expanded scale, which requires that its cadres be continuously recruited from the ranks of a mass political organization. Second, in order to reproduce itself on an expanded scale the guerrilla nucleus must be able to persuade people by its example, which it cannot do without appealing to their subjective or personal interests even more than to their objective interests. Third, for the guerrilla nucleus to reproduce itself on an expanded scale it must serve the people in ways immediately evident to all; actions that require post mortem justifications or explanations, or can be readily distorted through the established media, should be rejected as politically unwise.

Fourth, to acquire popular support the guerrillas must apply fire power in defense of the immediate demands of the workers in situations where the masses are already mobilized, e.g., during strikes, demonstrations, and occupations of factories and work places. Fifth, there is a distinct advantage in waging an armed struggle in defense of the constitution and the democratic traditions of a people. Sixth, popular support also depends on defending the elementary rules of justice and morality which have become ingrained in the mores of a people; this implies resistance to repressive legislation, police terrorism, and the use of torture by the armed forces. Seventh, vendettas between the guerrillas and the police or armed forces have been invariably counterproductive for the guerrillas. Eighth, the guerrillas must do everything in their power to prevent the physical decimation of the vanguard by the repressive forces and paramilitary right-wing groups; although there can be no vanguard without a mass following, the masses are impotent without specially trained cadres to lead them. Ninth, since the guerrillas must arm themselves and secure the logistics for their survival, there is no alternative to periodic bank "expropriations" and other assaults for that purpose; at the same time, the guerrillas must avoid the appearance of being self-serving by giving a full public account of their expenditures. Finally, granted that the struggle for national and social liberation must be directed against the military, political, and trade union bureaucracies in addition to the economically dominant classes, it does not follow that certain sectors of the bureaucracy cannot be "neutralized" or that other sectors must be confronted with the same strategy used against the oligarchy; on the contrary, the principal target should be the fundamental enemy—imperialism and the native oligarchy.

8

International Significance of the Resistance

With the onset of a new era of military repressive regimes in Latin America, the systematic repression of the left and the imposition of military rule over virtually all areas of society, the Peronist resistance acquired an international dimension. Beginning with General Onganía's coup in Argentina in June 1966 followed by the coup-within-a-coup in Brazil in December 1968, and then by similar coups in Bolivia (1971), Uruguay (1973), and Chile (1973), the Argentine and earlier Brazilian models of quasi-liberal military dictatorships were replaced by regimes which reorganized their societies along bureaucratic lines. Unlike the earlier Argentine and Brazilian models limiting mass participation in politics through restrictions on populist as well as communist parties, the new military regimes of the 1970s favored the abolition of liberal-democratic institutions altogether and their replacement by a repressive "new order."

Without question, the Peronist resistance is the most important example of a successful struggle to overcome the proscription of a majoritarian and populist party by the armed forces in Latin America. The only other examples of its kind are the Mexican Revolution, the Bolivian Revolution, and the Cuban Revolution against Batista. However, these movements of resistance were directed not so much against collegiate rule by the professional military as against personal dictators and ambitious semicriminal cliques in power who had turned their countries into private fiefs.

Such dictatorships were maintained in power through personal favors, nepotism, fraud, and large-scale corruption, to the advantage of *caciques* or local bosses combining economic and political power. Whereas the Cuban resistance was directed against a hated individual and his gangster-like associates, the Peronist resistance defined the enemy in much broader terms—that included the collective leadership of the various armed services. If the Cuban resistance stopped short of being a protracted one, it was because it attracted the support of virtually all social classes against crime in high places, thus precluding negotiations with the criminals to be brought to justice. With respect to its outcome, the Argentine resistance resembled the Mexican and Bolivian revolutions in the victory of their reformist wings. But as the immediate successor to the Cuban Revolution, it too developed a revolutionary perspective that included a socialist transformation.

Peronism was a living example of the integration of an armed resistance with the politics of a mass movement. After six years of uninterrupted dictatorship in Argentina, the military junta was pressured to abdicate under the threat of new *Cordobazos* and *Rosariazos* combined with the escalation of military operations by Peronist and Guevarist urban guerrillas. In view of the success of the Peronist resistance, it was to be expected that resistance movements in neighboring countries would avail themselves of the Argentine experience.

Among the first resistance movements in Latin America to apply directly the lessons of the Peronist resistance were the Bolivian and Chilean. A sector of the Bolivian resistance led by ex-President Juan José Torres and Major Rubén Sánchez shifted in 1973 from a united front strategy, involving a coalition with the established Communist, Trotskyist, and Marxist-Leninist parties, to a popular front strategy under the immediate influence of the Peronist movement. This development took place even before Allende's downfall and was accompanied by a relocation of Bolivian exiles from Santiago to Buenos Aires in the aftermath of the Peronist electoral victory of March 1973. The lessons of Peronism were also evident in Chile in the months following the military coup against Allende, mainly in the form of local Committees of Resistance and the organization in 1974 of a nationwide Movement of Popular Resistance. Meanwhile, the Chilean MIR had shifted from a basically *foquista* line of armed confrontation with the military junta to a strategy of mass political resistance involving the tactics employed by Peronist workers in Argentina. That Uruguayan militants had also begun to downgrade the role of military tactics in favor of mass political and economic resistance was evident from a September 1973 statement to the Argentine press by members of the Central Committee of the Movement of National Liberation (Tupamaros). And in Brazil the physical extinction of the main forces of the urban guerrillas during 1970 and 1971 led to a similar reassessment of *foquismo* and its replacement by a new strategy subordinating military actions to the day-by-day struggles of the masses. Most of these movements are still weak, if not stillborn. Nonetheless, after eighteen years of resistance to the Argentine military, the revolutionary lessons of Peronism afford new hope and are of more than merely national interest.

Testimony to the influence of Peronism on the Bolivian resistance is not hard to find. Until roughly the middle of 1973 the Bolivian resistance represented a continuation of the Popular Assembly inaugurated on May Day 1971, later declared illegal by the military forces that overthrew the popular government of General Juan José Torres in August. In exile in Chile, the leaders of the principal parties and organizations active in the Popular Assembly organized the Anti-Imperialist Revolutionary Front (FRA) for the purpose of resisting the military dictatorship. This front included the established Communist Party, the Communist Party (Marxist-Leninist) of a Maoist persuasion, the independent Trotskyist Revolutionary Labor Party (POR) of Guillermo Lora, a second Trotskyist Revolutionary Labor Party (POR) affiliated to the Fourth International (Unified Secretariat), the principal Guevarist and Camilist insurrectionary groups organized in the Army of National Liberation (ELN) and in the Movement of the Revolutionary Left (MIR), the Revolutionary Party of the National Left (PRIN) led by Juan Lechín, the powerful and influential Bolivian Labor Central (COB) also headed by Lechín, the newly founded Socialist Party which coincided with the politics of the deposed president, and Major Rubén Sánchez' Revolutionary Armed Forces loyal to the ex-president. Although the left-populist COB had dominated the Popular Assembly, the meetings of the FRA executive committee in exile were hampered by factional squabbles between representatives of rival Marxist and Leninist groups. In effect, the mass character of the Popular Assembly had all but vanished, to be replaced by a predominantly sectarian leadership.

In an effort to reintegrate the Bolivian resistance with the concrete struggles of the Bolivian masses, ex-President Torres and Major Rubén Sánchez, with the support of the COB, organized a new movement of national resistance patterned on the Argentine experience. With its headquarters in Buenos Aires rather than Santiago, this new movement or Alliance of the National Left (ALIN) reached an agreement in January 1974 with the powerful National Confederation of Peasant Workers (CNTCB). The ALIN promised to give the peasants a greater role in the management of Bolivia's economic and political affairs, in return for peasant support of the ALIN's program of national liberation and peasant recognition of ex-President Torres as the supreme conductor of the Bolivian resistance.

Parallel with the formation of the ALIN a new national democratic front was in the process of gestation as a result of the informal accords between Lechín, ex-President Hernán Siles Suazo, representing a dissident sector within the MNR, Marcelo Quiroga Santa Cruz, founder of the Socialist Party (PSB) and former minister of mines in General Alfredo Ovando's government, and Ovando himself who had traveled to Buenos Aires at Perón's personal request. General Ovando was evidently Perón's choice to head a new popular and nationalist government in Bolivia corresponding to those in power in Argentina, Chile, and Peru. Although Perón dissociated himself from the Bolivian resistance beginning with Allende's fall in September 1973, this new and broad front was tantamount to a Bolivian version of Argentina's "Hour of the People," which had pressured General Lanusse to abdicate in May 1973.

The resistance received a shot in the arm in 1974 with the February peasant rebellion in the Valley of Cochabamba followed by the abortive military putsch by young nationalist officers in June. In a "Message to the Bolivian People" by the self-styled Nationalist Armed Forces, representing 1,500 officials and cadets, the alternative to General Hugo Banzer's dictatorship was identified with a national democratic revolution opposed equally to capitalism and communism. Republished in *Chasqui* (September-October 1974) by the Mexican branch of the Bolivian Peace

Committee, the document declared in favor of a socialism that would be both Christian and humanist. In effect, it opted for a Peruvian-style revolution and for a new form of social property —the direct ownership and management of the means of production by the workers—alongside the traditional public and private sectors. This objective was to be achieved under the leadership of nationalist officers organized as the revolutionary vanguard of the people, through the mobilization of the masses and an alliance with the popular sectors: peasants, workers, students, and so-called "middle class." Although there was little evidence of any direct Peronist influence, the commitment to a "Third Force" was a decidedly Peronist legacy.

In Chile the principal parties constituting the Popular Unity coalition under the late Salvador Allende agreed in July 1974 to constitute a broad alliance based on the Communist and Socialist parties, but including the United Movement of Popular Action (MAPU), the MAPU of Workers and Peasants, and the Movement of the Revolutionary Left (MIR). Following a secret interview with Lautaro Rojas, leader of the MAPU of Workers and Peasants, it was reported that these organizations had agreed to reject guerrilla warfare as an effective strategy against the Chilean military junta, in favor of a mass resistance movement of workers and peasants (*Excelsior*, 11 August 1974). Experience had shown that guerrilla actions were the work of a revolutionary minority without organic links to the masses, and that in a highly politicized country like Chile the workers should be regarded as the principal force of resistance to the military repressive regime. This report was confirmed in an interview with Hortensia Allende, widow of the ex-president, who declared that from Arica to Magallanes there had been a reactivation of the organizations of the Chilean masses in the form principally of slowdowns, industrial sabotage, civil disobedience, and the editing of a clandestine press—the kind of opposition applied with success by the Argentine resistance (*Excelsior*, 24 September 1974).

In response to the military coup of September 1973 the Chilean MIR also underwent a change of strategy, reminiscent of the FAR's convergence on the Peronist resistance. In a major political document prepared by the MIR's Political Commission in December 1973, a new strategy of alliances was proposed aimed at incorporating the masses in a broad front of popular resistance

(*Correo de la Resistencia,* September 1974). This revolutionary front was to be constructed on the basis of clandestine committees of popular resistance supported by a formal alliance of all the political parties and movements on the left, including the petty-bourgeois Radical Party and the left wing of the Christian Democratic Party. Whereas the MIR had not belonged to Allende's coalition of Popular Unity in power, it suddenly proposed to establish formal ties with the Socialist and Communist parties.

The MIR's former objective of workers' self-government corresponded to a period of advance in the workers' movement from roughly 1967 to 1973, when its military actions had been effective in mobilizing mass support for increasingly radical goals. In contrast, the period beginning in September 1973 was characterized as a period of retreat before the repressive forces, which rendered the earlier strategy obsolete. "This is not the moment to give a decisive battle or to pose to the workers unrealizable objectives," declared the document. "The forms of struggle, however heroic and attractive to sectors of the vanguard, must be adapted to the level of political awareness, determination, and receptivity of the masses." The conditions of repression imposed by the Pinochet regime called for a strategy of collective self-defense directed at restoring civil liberties and the workers' standard of living. Although the MIR reaffirmed its decision to build a revolutionary army of the people, it acknowledged that guerrilla actions should be undertaken no longer for primarily military objectives, but in defense of the elementary rights of the workers.

In Uruguay a Peronist-type resistance was organized on the heels of the military coup which dissolved congress on June 27, 1973. The Communist-dominated National Confederation of Workers (CNT) replied with an immediate political general strike that completely paralyzed the economy. The general strike was supported by the Broad Front (FA), a coalition of Communists, Socialists, Christian Democrats, and Independents which had supported the candidacy of General Liber Seregni in the presidential elections of November 1971. The Broad Front issued an appeal to all national and democratic organizations for effective and sustained popular actions against the dictatorship. This was the prelude to the organization of a Resistance Front which included, besides the Broad Front, the National Party (the principal party of the opposition), the Movement for Unity and Reform (a faction of

President Bordaberry's own Colorado Party), the CNT, and student associations. On July 5, the Resistance Front issued its program for resolving the military crisis. The program consisted of six basic points: (1) reestablishment of constitutional freedoms and guarantees; (2) reestablishment of the rights of political parties and trade union organizations; (3) restoration of the purchasing power of wages; (4) agreement on a minimum platform for economic and social change; (5) establishment of a provisional government; and (6) provision for an immediate popular referendum. The military regime responded by arresting General Seregni, head of the Broad Front, the presidents of the National and Socialist parties, and members of the dissolved congress who supported the resistance. In an effort to smash the general strike, the military had already proscribed the CNT on June 30, 1973.

The Tupamaros also responded to the coup with an effective change in strategy. At issue was the question whether armed actions constituted the only viable response to military dictatorship. Within a month of the coup the Tupamaros issued a declaration outlining their new strategy of resistance. Several tactical mistakes in the use of violence were noted: first, an underestimation of the military capacity of the enemy in view of U.S. technical aid contributing to the modernization of the armed forces; second, an underestimation of the capacity of the masses to resist repression, combined with an exaggerated estimate of the role of a political-military vanguard. Not just military actions were required to overcome the dictatorship, but a combination of all forms of struggle in factories, schools, neighborhoods, villages, and farms—a thesis reiterated in a press conference by representatives of the Tupamaros' Central Committee in Argentina (*Militancia,* 20 September 1973). At the same time, the Tupamaros stressed the urgency of linking armed actions with the daily struggles of the masses toward maintaining real wages, restoring civil liberties, achieving amnesty for political prisoners, abolishing physical tortures, and rehiring fired workers. Although armed struggle was conceived as the only force capable of toppling a military regime, it was admittedly insufficient for that purpose without "the participation and leadership of the working class"—a theme of the Peronist resistance.

In Brazil the strategy of resistance practiced during the 1960s relied mainly on guerrilla warfare by Guevarist or Debrayist political-military focos. This strategy was abandoned in 1970–71 owing to a succession of defeats and an intensification of the repression that physically liquidated most of the vanguard. A slow process of recomposition and reorganization of the left followed on the heels of these disasters, converging on a new strategy giving preeminence to the organization and mobilization of the masses in which armed resistance was to perform an auxiliary role. Political-military cadres were restructured to assist the workers in their day-to-day struggles, to defend their standard of living through partial strikes, industrial sabotage, and the boycotting of overtime work. Thus the fundamental problem of the Brazilian left was to revive the mass struggle within the limits imposed by the dictatorship. This strategy, originally applied by the Peronist resistance, was the only realistic one in view of the nationwide repression.

The shift in strategy toward mass involvement had been anticipated by five years of clandestine organizing among the peasants in the Marabá region of the state of Pará in northeastern Brazil. This project, supported by militants from a number of different revolutionary organizations, was aimed at integrating a revolutionary vanguard with the struggles of the rural population and building a mass basis of resistance to the military regime. Although in April 1972 the repressive forces discovered the existence of this work and launched a gigantic operation to destroy it, a nucleus of militants backed by several scores of peasants sought refuge in the jungles of the Amazon with the intent of continuing the resistance. Precariously armed, but counting on the support of peasants in the area, the peasants-in-arms were able to inflict severe losses on the occupying troops. Reorganized as the "Guerrilla Forces of Araguaia," they subsequently launched offensive actions against military posts where they seized modern weapons and ammunition. The Brazilian military was compelled to renounce its original objective of destroying the guerrillas in short order, in favor of a strategic encirclement of the region and the imposition of a fierce repression in neighboring areas to prevent the epidemic from spreading. The armed resistance in the southern part of Pará continues to this day. Although geographically isolated from the principal political and economic centers of decision making, this first successful guerrilla movement against the dictatorship illustrates a new approach to mass resistance which is also being tried in the cities.

The international significance of the Peronist resistance stems not only from its having an influence on other resistance movements, but also from its being a point of convergence for resistance struggles independently of the Argentine experience. In Mexico, for example, the resistance against the repressive policies of the PRI-controlled government and trade unions, brought to a head by the massacre in the Plaza of Three Cultures in October 1968, tended to develop along lines that anticipated the second Peronist resistance. The crisis of Mexican populism corresponded in many ways to the crisis of Peronism in Argentina: first, the disillusionment with the ruling party and its political bureaucracy for failing to carry out long-promised and much needed reforms; second, the insubordination of the trade union bases in opposition to a labor bureaucracy committed to manipulating the workers in the interests of state policy; and third, the rebellion of the urban poor in search of decent housing and the satisfaction of elementary needs, frustrated by the failure of industrial growth to keep pace with demographic change and the process of urbanization.

In Mexico, as in Argentina, the populism of the ruling party aimed to satisfy the immediate demands of the masses, but on condition that they accept control by the political and trade union bureaucracies and refrain from creating obstacles to the development of the capitalist sector. This arrangement worked during the 1930s when President Cárdenas curbed the powers of the bourgeoisie by means of extensive labor and agrarian reforms, and encouraged the unionization of workers and peasants as a countervailing force under government control. Under subsequent administrations, however, the native bourgeoisie and the multinational corporations increased their share of the gross national product at the expense of the masses, with an erosion of popular support for the ruling party. At the same time, the rising tide of labor and peasant militancy, combined with the demands of the urban poor, spurred the government to rely on police repression and gangster methods to suffocate all expressions of popular discontent.

These "weak links" in the chain of repression provided the objective conditions for a strategy of political-military resistance, which emerged simultaneously with that of the Peronist left in Argentina. This strategy, summarized in a major editorial in *Punto Crítico* entitled "Notes for the Study of the Mexican Conjuncture" (August 1973), recommended the following: first, the struggle for union democracy and for a labor movement independent of the ruling party; second, the mobilization of poor neighborhoods to secure their elementary needs for water, sanitation, etc; third, the organization of a political and electoral opposition to the PRI. The organization of a "revolutionary tendency," the editors concluded, is possible only through the close coordination of each of these opposition movements, with precedence given to the struggle within the trade unions as the weakest link in the system. Since the struggle for an independent labor movement is possible only through a direct confrontation with the ruling party and the government, this strategy of the Mexican left paralleled that of the Peronist left in identifying the immediate enemy with the trade union and political bureaucracies.

That resistance movements have tended to converge on the Peronist model, whether or not they have been shaped by it, testifies to its importance and to its potential significance for future resistance struggles. The international significance of the Peronist resistance may be attributed in no small part to the fact that the Uruguayan and Brazilian resistance movements, independently of the Peronist example, abandoned their former exclusive reliance on armed struggle in favor of subordinating it to the politics of a mass movement. Furthermore, the Argentine model is relevant not only to resistance movements against military dictatorship and pseudo-constitutional regimes, but also against freely elected governments including those with a populist cast. The Peronist resistance did not end with the calling of elections and the formal abdication of the armed forces, but continued even after the election of General Perón. Although this model of a Peronist resistance without Perón is a new phenomenon in resistance politics, it is paralleled by the Mexican experience of opposition to a ruling party likewise accused of betraying its revolutionary legacy.

Epilogue
The Fall of Isabel Perón

The basic conditions underlying Isabelita's fall from power are to be found, first, in the political crisis and divisions within Peronism and, second, in the Peronist mismanagement of the economy which became evident in the runaway inflation and negative rate of growth during 1975. The economic crisis compounded the political crisis, thus resulting in Isabelita's inability to rule. Confronted with a weak and unstable government and a rapidly deteriorating economy, the military felt compelled to intervene. It did so not all at once, but piecemeal. Like the series of minidevaluations of the peso in late 1975 and the beginning of 1976, the military *golpe* that overthrew Isabelita's government on March 23, 1976, followed a series of small interventions that were hardly frightening at the time. The intervention in March was simply the final act in a coup by quotas.

One of the motives behind the coup was the escalation of guerrilla warfare against the armed forces. The Peronist government was blamed for a deteriorating political situation that was providing sustenance not only to the guerrillas, but also to a generalized climate of mass subversion. The question was how to intervene successfully against a government which had received more than sixty percent of the national vote in the elections of September 1973 and represented the first clear-cut majority in eighteen years of past interventions that had ended in a blind alley for the military. With good reason the armed forces believed that the Justicialist movement and the FREJULI could not be effectively opposed short of an internal crisis and decomposition. Accordingly, they chose to intervene by quotas and to wait for a political crisis to develop before making a decisive move.

Although the political crisis of Peronism did not reach staggering proportions until after Perón's death on July 1, 1974, the movement

167

had already begun to decompose prior to that date. By February 1974 a split had occurred between the ultraleft FAP-PB, supported by the ERP-22, and the rest of the Peronist movement. This division came in response to the escalation of repression because of the ERP's attack on the army base at Azul, and Perón's efforts to compel the governor of Buenos Aires to resign because of alleged sympathies for the guerrillas. A far more consequential schism followed between the right-wing labor bureaucracy, supported by the political branch of the movement, and other left-of-center governors. Beginning with the federal intervention in the province of Córdoba in February, the government then deposed the governors in the provinces of Mendoza and Santa Cruz who were also closely identified with ex-President Cámpora. Thus the movement ceased to represent an unstable balance between its left and right wings to become increasingly dominated by the Vandorist labor bureaucracy.

Shortly after Perón's death another major cleavage occurred when the moderate left, led by the Montoneros, followed in the footsteps of the FAP by denouncing the "illegitimacy" of Isabelita's "inner circle" and then returning underground in September to wage war on the government. The virtual elimination of the left from the official movement contributed to sharpening the tensions between the two remaining factions. Thus in June and July 1975 a new split emerged between the moderate right in control of the CGT and the extreme right in control of the government. Once again the relation of social forces within the movement was upset, this time at the expense of Isabelita's "inner circle."

In December 1975 the final split occurred between the "verticalists" in the CGT bureaucracy, backed by labor supporters in congress, and an emerging force of "antiverticalists" within both the labor and political branches of the movement. The "verticalists" supported Isabelita as head of the government, whereas the "antiverticalists" accepted only her role as head of the Party and the movement. (The difference between "verticalists" and "ultraverticalists" was that the former demanded representation within the president's "entourage" or "inner circle" of advisers, whereas the latter allowed her complete freedom in this matter.) Concurrently, a score or so of congressmen broke with the FREJULI on December 12 to form the self-styled "Work Group," whose "antiverticalism" deprived the government of its majority in the lower house. The "Work Group" entered into discussions with an "antiverticalist" faction led by Victorio Calabró, the Vandorist Governor of Buenos Aires, who had recently been expelled from the Party for insubordination. Tensions mounted within the "62 Organizations" as its head, Lorenzo Miguel, called for the appointment of a federal intervenor to remove Calabró as governor.

This schism became more pronounced in February 1976 as a result of corresponding cleavages within both the "62 Organizations" and the National or Supreme Council of the Justicialist Party. Both Angel Robledo, first vice-president of the Party, and José Báez, its second vice-president, had formed a bloc with Italo Luder, the president of the Senate, to secure Isabelita's resignation or at least another extended leave of absence. As secretary-general of the Insurance Workers Union, Báez also played a key role in the "62 Organizations." However, he was opposed by Miguel on the ground that, far from averting a military coup, Isabelita's resignation would so weaken the executive as to encourage military intervention. In his dual capacity as a leader of both the political and labor branches, Báez could count on strong support from the membership. But at the Party's National Congress on March 6, which was packed by delegates loyal to Isabelita, a renewed coalition of "verticalists" and "ultraverticalists" gave a resounding victory to the president.

By then all legal and constitutional avenues aimed at displacing Isabelita had been closed. But the apparent unity achieved at the congress could not conceal the division within the Party and between it and the government. The fissure between "verticalists" and "ultraverticalists" had not been healed, and the question of democratizing the Party and the movement was still an unsettled issue. It is noteworthy that the military waited until the divisions between "antiverticalists," "verticalists," and "ultraverticalists" had widened before risking a confrontation with the president. Only when the "vertebral column" or strongest single support of the Party, the "62 Organizations," showed signs of weakness did the military feel strong enough politically to hazard a coup. And, even at that, the top army command balked at the first attempt in December in favor of letting the divisions within the movement fester.

The political crisis that brought on the military crisis was in turn aggravated by the economic crisis. Peronist mismanagement of the economy was held responsible for the runaway inflation, the worst that the country had experienced during the past quarter century. The rate of inflation—nearly three hundred and fifty percent in 1975—was attributed to the government's policy of encouraging mass consumption through concessions to organized labor, combined with an increasing fiscal deficit from subsidizing social services and welfare of various kinds. The budget of the then infamous Ministry of Social Welfare, for example, rose to approximately thirty percent of the public revenues, whereas taxes accounted for only twenty-five percent. To pay for these services the government had to borrow or print new money.

Premonitions of the coming economic disaster were expressed as early as October 1974. In a document dated October 25 distributed by ex-President Frondizi's Movement of Integration and Development (MID), the state was said to be on the border of insolvency for having increased the money supply by eighty percent during the past month, the short-term advances of the Central Bank by one hundred percent, and the amount of government indebtedness by more than four hundred percent. The fiscal deficit was used to provide not only much needed social services, but also cheap credit for small and medium enterprises. Such credit seldom found its way into increased production, but swelled instead unnecessary selling costs or was used to speculate with foreign currency.

The Peronist program of high wages and subsidized social welfare tended to generate inflation through a combination of factors that included Argentina's dependence on the international market. High wages contributed not only to disinvestment, but also to the flight of capital in search of improved investment opportunities abroad. The increase in effective demand was thus frustrated by a decrease in the volume of domestic production. High wages also tended to cut into agricultural exports, as the increase in effective demand domestically could only be satisfied in the short run by a deteriorating balance of foreign trade. The result was increased foreign indebtedness, pressures by international monetary agencies to devalue the peso as a means of covering those debts, and consequently higher import costs passed on to domestic products. By a roundabout process the prices of many goods were being determined not by the free play of domestic supply and demand, but by fluctuations in the rate of exchange and by international monetary policies. Such policies were responsible for the successive devaluations of Argentina's currency. Here was another source of inflation as fewer goods had to compete for more money.

There is little doubt that inflation under conditions of stagnation, which had led the Argentine economy into its worst disaster since the Great Depression, was the rock upon which the Peronist ship of state foundered. Isabelita had, in a contradictory way, followed the policies shaped by Perón during his first and second administrations, revived by President Cámpora in May 1973, continued by his "ultraverticalist" successor Raúl Lastiri in July, and then by Perón again in October. The principal differences between her economic policies and those of her late husband arose from her efforts to meet the demands of the multinational corporations and the international monetary agencies, demands resisted by the Peronist-controlled congress and by the labor branch of the movement. Isabelita's marches and countermarches played havoc with the economy and she was justifiably criticized on that score. Yet Perón's own economic policies and alleged solution to the problems of labor and development in an underdeveloped country had also contributed to the deterioration and mismanagement of the Argentine economy.

Perón boasted of having discovered the most humane solution to the contradiction between the economic and political objectives of a populist regime: the economic objective of increasing investment through subsidies to production; and the political objective of subsidizing consumption as a condition of maintaining mass support. To his credit, experience has shown that an underdeveloped country cannot pursue both objectives simultaneously without increasing effective demand in relation to supply, thus contributing to inflation and generating social tensions that tend to explode and disrupt the coalition supporting a populist program. One or another class has had to pay the burden of the social costs of a development strategy, and inflation has been an indirect way of making the working class and petty bourgeoisie foot most of the bill. The populist premise of a community of interest between these two classes and the small and medium bourgeoisie collapses in the face of the realities of underdevelopment. Hence the dilemma: either a strategy of development undermines a populist coalition by encouraging profits under conditions of lagging wages, or a strategy of mass consumption undermines it by cutting into profits.

Historically, there have been three main types of populist program. First, priority has been given to developing production through subsidies and special incentives for both the public and private sectors. This policy depends for its success on curtailing the consumption of the masses, tantamount to intensified political repression. It is ultimately incompatible with populist politics because labor is the principal victim. The promise of a higher standard of living projected into an uncertain future has been insufficient to retain mass support in view of present sacrifices. Second, priority has been given to developing production under conditions in which the capitalist class is expropriated and the bulk of the economic surplus is absorbed by the state. Although consumption is curtailed, the bourgeoisie is the principal loser. Political repression during the transition to a socialist economy is directed mainly at propertied interests. At least organized labor is compensated for its sacrifices by the increased stake it acquires in an economy which has come under public ownership and control. Third, priority has been given to increasing mass consumption as a condition of stimulating private investment and preparing the workers for a later stage of intensified capital accumulation. This was Perón's option in 1946 and again in 1973. As the "Third Position" in economics, it strives to harmonize the political and economic objectives of a populist coalition in the only way feasible short of a major socialist transformation. Thus, after favoring labor's demands for increased consumption, Perón shifted during his second administration to giving priority to production.

Was his strategy successful? With the advantage of hindsight one can safely say that it was doomed to failure, and that ex-President Frondizi was right in his repeated criticisms of that policy. At most it succeeded in maintaining a populist coalition alive, which cannot be said of Frondizi's own policy of giving priority to production. A strategy similar to Frondizi's had been adopted by other populist coalitions on the continent after their first disastrous experiments of trying to combine increased production and consumption. But the new strategy was only slightly less damaging than the old. As applied in Bolivia by Paz Estenssoro's Revolutionary Nationalist Movement (MNR), it ended by dividing and ultimately destroying the populist coalition that supported him. Although Mexico is a presumptive example of the success of such a policy, it is a far better example of Perón's own strategy for development. Thus the first two decades of the revolutionary regime saw increasing concessions to the labor and peasant movements, followed after 1940 by a policy of giving priority to capital accumulation to the benefit mainly of Mexico's new national bourgeoisie. Not until the 1970s did a kind of balance emerge between production and consumption, and only after Mexico had already experimented with an economic model that was to anticipate Perón's own policies.

On March 28, 1974, in a meeting of the representatives of the political parties belonging to FREJULI, Frondizi had warned Perón of the tendency toward decapitalization and generalized scarcity consequent upon decreased margins of profitability. Today, he said, there is no investment; where there is no investment there can be no economic development; and where there is no economic development there can be no social justice. Perón's response was that a program of successful development hinged on a prior effort to restructure the state and to readjust its tax mechanisms as a means of generating the indispensable funds. That was being accomplished in the process of satisfying the most urgent demands of the masses. As for the next stage giving priority to investment, that would be launched toward the middle of 1975.

The shift from a consumerist to an investment strategy actually began in October 1974. Ber Gelbard was removed as minister of economics and replaced by the former president of the Central Bank, Dr. Alfredo Gómez Morales, who had resigned in protest against government policy that was exhausting the bank's reserves. The first austerity plan imposed by Gómez Morales became bogged down, however, owing to resistance from organized labor. With Perón's death there was literally nobody within the official sector of the movement with the authority to impose on its labor branch the type of austerity plan launched by him in 1952. Only Perón could do that because only he, by virtue of his deeds, had earned the confidence of organized labor.

As the crisis of Peronism went from bad to worse the military became bolder and began to intervene in government affairs. Determined not to launch a premature coup, it opted for partial interventions until the government had thoroughly discredited itself through ineptitude and mismanagement, economic and political gangsterism, internal bickering, and the alienation of its support among the labor movement. For two years, from May 1973 to May 1975, the armed forces adopted a posture of political neutrality and stuck strictly to professional business. But in May 1975 the government, under the instigation of López Rega, replaced the liberal Commander in Chief of the Army, General Leandro Anaya, with a Peronist general, Alberto Numa Laplane, in an effort to Peronize the armed forces. Top army brass deeply resented this patently political interference designed to reduce the military to a willing rather than reluctant instrument of Peronist policy.

As long as López Rega dominated the political branch of the movement and the government, the armed forces continued to play second fiddle. The government, not the military, took the initiative in declaring a state of siege in November 1974, which gave a free hand to the Federal Police in combating the guerrillas. Again, it was the government that called for direct military intervention against the guerrillas in February 1975. Then General Anaya was replaced for reportedly resisting the government's efforts to send troops against the 25,000 striking workers at Villa Constitución, the country's principal steelworks. The eight-week-old strike, the general insisted, was a political and not a military matter. If the government was jittery, it was because it anticipated further strike outbreaks as 400 collective contracts came up for renewal in May.

At the beginning of June another López Rega appointee, Celestino Rodrigo, assumed the office of minister of economics. A week later Rodrigo's devaluation of the peso by a hundred percent resulted in a price explosion that aggravated already existing labor tensions. On June 8 the CGT and its affiliates declared a "state of alert" in response to the austerity measures imposed by the new minister of economics. López Rega then tried to persuade Casildo Herreras, the secretary-general of the CGT, to resign in favor of one of his own appointees. At the same time he reportedly threatened Lorenzo Miguel, head of the "62 Organizations," with a settlement of accounts by the Triple A. Pressures were also being mounted within the Supreme Council of the Justicialist Party to dissolve the "62 Organizations" as part of a general plan nominally aimed at reorganizing the movement, but really designed to undermine the independence of the labor sector. During the first part of June it seemed as if López Rega might get his way, thus virtually compelling Miguel to seek the support of the rank and file.

On June 28 Isabelita rejected a request by the CGT for a hundred percent across-the-board wage increase. The president not only remained firm at fifty percent, but also ordered the cancellation of all earlier collective bargaining agreements exceeding that amount, such as the hundred-and-twenty-percent increase obtained by Miguel's own union (UOM). In retaliation the CGT bureaucracy threatened a general strike, while Minister of Labor Ricardo Otero resigned in indignation from the cabinet. A mammoth but unofficially declared strike began paralyzing the country on July 1st in protest against the government's labor policy. Then, under pressure from the rank and file, the CGT declared an official general strike of forty-eight hours scheduled for July 7 and 8—the first of its kind against a Peronist government.

On the eve of the strike the entire cabinet resigned. Concurrently, against the president's wishes, the Justicialist bloc in the Senate rebelled by electing Italo Luder, a Peronist moderate or "centrist," as its provisional president. Isabelita had hoped to keep this post vacant so that her legal successor in office might be Raúl Lastiri, president of the Chamber of Deputies and López Rega's son-in-law. Instead, she was confronted by a potential successor alien to the group of ultraright Peronists constituting her "inner circle."

The military waited until the first general strike ever called against a Peronist government to make its first move. Confronted by a combined rebellion by the trade union and political sectors of the movement, Isabelita was forced to comply with some of the CGT's demands. Far from remaining neutral during this confrontation, the army joined with the opposition in routing López Rega and his friends. Thus he was not reappointed to the new cabinet formed on July 11 and also felt compelled to resign as private secretary to the president. However, the positions abandoned by him were filled by his close collaborators, while the controversial Celestino Rodrigo continued as minister of economics.

This reshuffling of the cabinet failed to satisfy either the CGT bureaucracy or the military. Spurred by the rank and file which had been staging its own general strike since July 1, the Union of Automotive Transport Workers (UTA) on July 15 declared a thirty-six-hour national strike in repudiation of Rodrigo's reappointment. Two days later the CGT again threatened the government with a general strike if it did not sack the minister of economics and respond favorably to labor's demand for an alternative economic plan. The government complied by accepting Rodrigo's resignation on July 19 and, on the same day, under pressure from the military, López Rega was forced into an ignominious, if gilded, exile. On July 21 his successor in the influential Ministry of Social Welfare resigned. The CGT then presented its "emergency plan" for the nationalization of the banks, heavy industry, and foreign commerce, price controls, and periodic wage adjustments to deal with inflation. Although this plan was never accepted, it marked the beginning of labor's efforts to fill the power vacuum left by the ultraright.

By a vote of the Peronist-controlled congress on July 23, Raúl Lastiri was removed as president of the Chamber of Deputies, following which he was also obliged to resign as first vice-president of the Justicialist Party. In fact, Lastiri came under suspicion of participating in a projected palace coup, which would have physically eliminated the enemies of López Rega within the movement and called for his return. Documentation of the proposed coup was presented to the minister of the interior by no less a personage than Italo Luder, the new president of the Senate. Finally, on August 11, a new cabinet, the seventh during the thirteen months of Isabelita's government, replaced the remaining officials associated with López Rega's rule.

In retrospect, it was this major split between the Peronist right wing represented mainly by the CGT and "62 Organizations," and the ultraright led by López Rega with Isabelita's support, that encouraged the military to impose its own terms on the government. Although in May López Rega had prevailed in his first confrontation with the army, in July the tables were turned as the army, for the first time, got the upper hand in opposing his reappointment and then forcing him to quit the country. At the same time the armed forces were in no mood to allow the CGT bureaucrats to fill the shoes abandoned by his close collaborators. Although initially sympathetic to the CGT's efforts to check the advance of López Rega in his bid for total power, the military was to show still greater hostility toward the subsequent "advance of labor" within the Justicialist Party and the government.

This first major crisis, prompting the end of two years of political neutrality by the armed forces, led to an escalating of military involvement in political affairs that culminated less than a year later in the overthrow of Isabel Perón. Following its first military intervention in July the army intervened again on August 26 to strip the newly appointed Minister of the Interior, Colonel Vicente Damasco, of his military post. Damasco was the first military officer to have joined the cabinet since the Peronists came to power in March 1973. He was faced with the dilemma of either keeping his cabinet position or resigning his military commission when the top anti-Peronist generals insisted on maintaining their distance from the regime and refused to allow a military man to participate in the government. Since Army Commander in Chief Numa Laplane had pushed for Damasco's appointment, on August 27 the army's top brass also forced his replacement by Army Chief of Staff Jorge Videla. In a dispatch from Buenos Aires to *The New York Times* (August 28), Jonathan Kandell described the action by the army as one of "virtual insubordination" that had brought the country "to the brink of a military coup."

On September 8 the government finally decreed the banning of the Montoneros and its many allied fronts, which included the Peronist Youth. An agency to centralize efforts by all the intelligence services and to plan an overall antiguerrilla campaign was also set up. These gestures apparently encouraged General Videla, the army's new commander in chief, to announce before Congress on September 10 that he was completing the draft of another antisubversive act to be called the National Defense Law—at the initiative of the military. The draft of the new law, which later met with considerable resistance from the Peronist-dominated congress, contained provisions for organizing military tribunals to try "subversives." Some charges were to carry the death penalty.

The military intervened for the third time during the forty-day interval from September 13 to October 23, when Isabelita took an extended sick leave. Isabelita was succeeded by Italo Luder, who became the fifth president of the Republic in less than three years. (Cámpora, it may be recalled, was followed in office by a provisional president, Raúl Lastiri, rather than directly by Perón.) In the tug-of-war that ensued, former army colonel and Interior Minister Damasco led the ultraverticalist forces in trying to circumscribe Luder's powers and to restrain him from making any changes in top administration personnel. However, on September 15 Luder removed Damasco, as well as Defense Minister Jorge

Garrido and Press Secretary Cesáreo González, in a move that counted on the support of the military. Damasco was replaced by the "centrist" Angel Robledo, who also took over the foreign ministry and, as first vice-president of the Justicialist Party, became its de facto head in Isabelita's absence.

During this interregnum and in response to the Montoneros' attack on an army base in Formosa on October 5, 1975, the Argentine army demanded a bigger role. It pressured interim President Luder to approve its proposal for a National Council of Internal Security and a National Defense Council. According to a report by Kandell in *The New York Times* (9 October 1975), the Internal Security Council would serve as a rubber stamp for all antisubversive actions deemed advisable by the military. Its policies were to be enforced by the Defense Council. Repression would be carried out in all places where subversion was present, in the trade unions, factories, and universities as well as against rural guerrillas in the mountains of Tucumán. The two councils would give the armed forces the power to coordinate and centralize all of the country's repressive forces including control over the Federal Police. Thus Luder was used by the military to step up the war against leftist elements and to lay the groundwork for intervention against the combative trade unions and so-called "factory guerrillas."

The fourth instance of military intervention occurred in December in the form of a military rebellion by disaffected sectors of the air force. By then Isabelita's government had gone through ten cabinet changes and four aborted economic plans under four different ministers of economics—Ber Gelbard's Act of National Compromise (Social Pact), Gómez Morales' monetarism, the shock treatment recommended by the International Monetary Fund ingenuously applied by Celestino Rodrigo, and the modified monetarism and revived social pact of Antonio Cafiero. With no end in sight to inflation, mounting labor tensions, and financial corruption within the government, the ultraright or Pinochetist wing of the air force finally responded to calls from discontented sectors of the bourgeoisie by launching the first coup.

The rebellion began early on December 18 with the detention and removal from office of the commander of the air force by units under the command of Brigadier General Orlando Capellini. It ended on December 22, but only after General Videla had decided to intervene against the insurgents by bombing and strafing their headquarters. From its principal base in the 7th Airborne Division of Morón, the self-denominated "Argentine Air Force in Operations" began transmitting communiqués from radio stations occupied by the rebels. The first communiqué underlined the moral crisis of Peronism and its political and economic misgovernment, while Argentina's neighbors (Brazil, Chile, Uruguay) "prospered in peace and work." It disavowed the authority of the national government and called upon General Videla to assume control of the country in the name of the armed forces.

Almost immediately the rebellion received support from the head of the Federal Party, Francisco Manrique, and from ex-President Onganía who had joined the rebels in their headquarters in Morón. The 7th Brigade also received support from the 5th Airborne Brigade of Villa Reynolds in San Luis, and from the 4th Brigade in Mendoza. Although the bulk of the armed forces were sympathetic to the rebellion, the top command had been taken by surprise and hesitated to seize power without more careful preparation. The "Air Force in Operations" also hesitated to bomb the government house and the Plaza de Mayo as rebel air force planes had done in June 1955. As for Peronist resistance to the coup, it was not until the evening of December 21 that the CGT decreed a general strike to begin on the next and final day of the insurrection. Rank and file workers were also slow in responding to the crisis. They did not mobilize in the Plaza de Mayo nor did they ask for arms to defend the government.

On the heels of this rebellion the armed forces intervened a fifth time, also in December, in an effort to achieve the objectives of the rebels by legal and constitutional means. Supported by the opposition parties in the lower house, by the "Work Group" of dissident Peronists, and by the governor of Buenos Aires and his antiverticalist followers, the three commanders in chief called upon the president either to resign or to take a second and extended leave of absence. Since Isabelita refused, they turned to the only remaining institutional solution: the encouragement of impeachment proceedings for the Watergate-style administrative and financial corruption of her entourage. What has been called the "Argentine Watergate" mushroomed in June 1975. It covered oil deals with Libya, missing funds for public construction projects, financial manipulations between the Ministry of Social Welfare and a transport company, and the misuse of funds by the Crusade of Justicialist Solidarity. There was also the matter of a check signed by the president and transferring 740,000 dollars from the Crusade, a social welfare fund formerly administered by López Rega, to the estate of her late husband Juan Domingo Perón.

A sixth intervention by the armed forces came on February 2, 1976, when the commanders in chief succeeded in imposing an army tank commander, General Albano Harguindeguy, as chief of the Federal Police. A few days later a new minister of economics was appointed, Emilio Mondelli, whose plan of economic austerity had been previously approved by the heads of the army, navy, and air force. Although Mondelli had to face the same irreconcilable opposition from the CGT and the "62 Organizations" that Rodrigo had to face in June 1975, it was his support by the armed forces that encouraged the president to resist popular demands for his resignation.

During the summer months of January and February 1976 the climate of social tension mounted. Hardly a week passed without rumors of a new military coup in preparation. Periodicals as far apart as *Nuevo Hombre,* the pro-ERP fortnightly which reappeared with a new series on November 5, 1975, and the Peronist daily *Mayoría* speculated that the developing coup by quotas was likely to end with the so-called "Bordaberryzation" of the government. (In June 1973 the Uruguayan armed forces had shut down congress in a palace coup supported by the legal President, Juan María Bordaberry, whose nominal continuation in office gave a quasi-legal sanction to the operation.) In an editorial in *Mayoría* (14 February 1976) Dr. Julio González, Isabelita's private secretary and virtual head of the government's "inner circle," had reportedly proposed a similar venture to various high-ranking officers. Thus, without altering the legal framework, a new cabinet was to be constituted whose members would be directly chosen by the armed forces.

By the middle of February the army was still divided into two main currents. The hard-liners in favor of generalized, long-term, and violent repression were led by General Ramón Díaz Bessone, commander of the 2nd Army Corps in Rosario, by General Luciano Benjamín Menéndez, commander of the 3rd Army Corps in Córdoba, and by the newly appointed chief of the Federal Police. The moderates in favor of a partial and temporary repression of political and trade union activity were led by General Videla and

Army Chief of Staff Roberto Viola. This second current hoped not only to exhaust all legal possibilities before launching a coup, but also to divide the Peronist movement by neutralizing dissident sectors within its political and trade union branches. It counted on at least passive support from Luder's group in congress and from the backers of Victorio Calabró, the rebellious governor of Buenos Aires.

Faced with Isabelita's refusal to resign and the failure of impeachment procedures against her in congress, the two principal currents within the army finally reached an agreement. Thus the review *Ultima Clave* (25 February 1976) reported that at a reunion of the army's top brass on February 20, at the insistence of General Videla a deadline had been set for overthrowing the government. Among other things, it was agreed that the armed forces should seize power at the earliest opportunity in order to counter the anticipated wave of strikes against Mondelli's new austerity plan and the government's refusal to grant wage increases. Determined to enforce that plan over the heads of organized labor, the military also proposed to intervene the CGT and to dissolve the "62 Organizations." At the same time it hoped to inflict a minimum of damage to the Justicialist movement and to avoid alienating the underlying population. A Pinochet-type solution to Argentina's crisis had been reputedly rejected in favor of "national reconciliation."

Mondelli spelled out the terms of his new austerity plan on March 5. Besides devaluing the peso by 82.5 percent, the plan called for a fifty- or sixty-percent hike in basic foodstuffs, an eighty-percent increase in the price of gasoline, a fifty-percent increase in subway fares and a 100–150-percent hike in taxi and rail fares. As partial compensation for this sacrifice he was asking of organized labor, wages were to be raised by twelve percent. Labor's response came as predicted. By March 10 striking industrial workers had idled seventy percent of productive capacity in the nation's principal cities, which prompted the president to make new concessions by boosting the wage increase to twenty percent and by opening a new series of collective bargaining sessions.

To add to the economic uncertainty, a twenty-four-hour shutdown for the province of Buenos Aires had been scheduled for March 18 by small shopkeepers and retailers protesting the price controls and the government's use of police to enforce them. Since the larger business associations were also considering new shut-downs, there was virtually no sector of Argentine society that had not escalated its organized opposition to the government. Calls for the president's resignation and declarations of her unfitness to rule were heard even louder than before.

The final act in the military's coup by quotas came on March 23 with the detention of the president by a military junta consisting of the three commanders in chief led by the principal inspirer and accepted leader of the coup, General Videla. The army mobilized to occupy not only the federal government, but also the provincial and municipal governments. Congress and the provincial legisla-tures were dissolved; the justices of the Supreme Court and the higher provincial courts were removed from office; the principal leaders of the Peronist Party, the CGT, and "62 Organizations" were rounded up and imprisoned. There was virtually no resistance to these arbitrary measures.

On the first day of the coup a proclamation was issued stating that the purpose of the miltiary take-over was to restore the essential values of the nation, to eradicate left-wing subversion, to promote economic development, and to establish subsequently a "republican, representative, and federal democracy." On the sec-ond day another proclamation by the junta assured the population that its purpose was "to put an end to misgovernment, corruption, and subversion" and that it intended to act exclusively against delinquents or persons who had commited abuses of power. Unlike the Chilean military, the Argentine armed forces had not assumed power for an indefinite period. On the contrary, five days after the coup General Videla was sworn in as the new president for a three-year term. Apparently, there was not going to be a repetition in Argentina of the Chilean bloodbath and flagrant violation of human rights.

The junta claimed to represent the interests of all Argentines, but its actions belied its words. The coup was directed not only against "delinquent" individuals, but also against a "delinquent" class and ideology. While ostensibly aimed only at extremist guerrillas and corrupt officials who had misused their power in office, the coup's principal victims consisted of labor's rank and file and the Peronist and Marxist left. Strikes were declared illegal, revision of past labor codes made it easier to fire people, collective bargaining was proscribed, the government declared that it alone would determine future wage increases, the CGT was intervened and its funds were frozen, and the "62 Organizations" were dissolved. Concurrently, martial law was declared, the heaviest penalties were imposed for inciting violence and engaging in terrorist acts, and military courts were empowered to invoke the death penalty. Five Marxist-Leninist parties were also outlawed: the pro-Peking Communist Party (Marxist-Leninist), the Revolutionary Communist Party (PCR), the Socialist Workers Party (PST), Labor Politics (PO), and the Trotskyist Labor Party.

While the detention of national and provincial leaders of the Peronist movement occupied the headlines, the military also proceeded to arrest labor militants and all persons suspected of having connections with the Montoneros and Peronist Youth. This included cadres of the Authentic Peronist Party who prudently disappeared or went underground. Some 1,800 persons were arrested during the first two days of the coup. A week later this figure had reportedly doubled and by the middle of April was approaching 10,000. While the top political and labor bureaucrats were fleeing by private boats across the River Plate to Uruguay, rank and file militants in the movement were not so fortunate.

The military's overriding preoccupation continued to be its private war against the ERP and Montoneros. If it had taken a tough position toward organized labor, it was in the conviction that the labor conflicts and social tensions growing out of economic disruption and the political "power vacuum" were playing into the hands of leftist extremists. As part of this strategy, the military was determined to throw the Peronists out of office. For even the movement's ultraright wing had established a pattern of concessions to the rank and file that had nullified or seriously undermined the government's austerity programs and efforts to put the economy back on its feet. The military stopped short, however, of outlawing the Peronist movement and the 150,000 member Communist Party of Argentina which had consistently opposed the guerrillas. How long might this tolerance last? In view of the military's strategy of a graduated coup, the army is committed to piecemeal repression aimed at destroying its enemies one by one.

Despite the escalation of repression against the guerrillas in 1975, they were able to increase both their fighting strength and their popularity among the Peronist masses. If anything, they were becoming more rather than less of a headache to the professional army. As Jonathan Kandell reported in *The New York Times* (24 March 1976), the guerrillas, who used to be derided as a university-trained elite, had substantially increased their appeal among factory workers. During the past year twenty-two foreign and Argentine executives had been slain, scores kidnapped, and hundreds more intimidated by bombs or threatening letters and phone calls into granting large wage increases. In December the Montoneros kidnapped Enrique Metz, one of the executives of Mercedes-Benz in Córdoba, and compelled the company to grant an illegal twenty-three-percent wage increase for its 20,000 workers. At the same time they collected a so-called "fine" of four million dollars for labor mispractices by the company, and succeeded in reinstating a hundred workers who had been fired. By March 1976 restive trade-unionists backed by the Montoneros were asking for another forty percent. Is there any wonder that management was worried over the proliferation of so-called factory guerrillas? As Kandell quotes an executive of Fiat in the industrial city of Córdoba: "At this point, the guerrillas can count on the passive or active support of a majority of our workers." This view, he notes, was not isolated but shared by the managers of other large industrial plants including Ika-Renault and the Perkins diesel factory in Córdoba.

From its inception the military coup had the support of employers' associations. For months Argentine businessmen had been calling upon the military to intervene. Finally, their patience exhausted, representatives of the most influential business association, the Permanent Assembly of Employers' Guild Entities (APEGE) unanimously resolved to carry out a nationwide lockout on February 10 if their demands should go unheeded. These demands included the removal of legal fetters discouraging industry and commerce, the reduction of the tax burden, the curbing of inflation, the promotion of exports, and the reestablishment of a favorable business climate. To secure these demands the Permanent Assembly also resolved to suspend the payment of taxes, social insurance, compulsory union contributions, and the like. Paradoxically, these unprecedented resolutions by Argentine business called for the violation of law and order in an effort to enforce them.

What precisely was the APEGE and how did it differ from the Peronist-oriented General Economic Confederation (CGE) which was intervened by the military following the March coup? Originally dominated by employers representing small- and medium-size industries, the CGE came into conflict with the powerful Argentine Industrial Union (UIA) consisting of the biggest employers and business sectors linked to the multinational corporations. In 1955 the CGE suffered repression with other Peronist organizations and did not reemerge as a significant force until after General Onganía's coup in 1966. At that time it began to absorb sectors that had originally belonged to the UIA. Under Gelbard's presidency, it ceased to be an organ mainly of small and medium industry to become the organization of the big bourgeoisie. However, disconcerted by the unbusinesslike results of the Social Pact, the largest industrialists left it after Perón's death to organize the APEGE. Designed to accelerate the process of monopolistic concentration, the APEGE became the principal spokesman for halting the advance of organized labor. And, since its principal concern was to increase the margin of profitability of Argentine business, it also began to call upon the armed forces to intervene in the political process.

In response to business pressures, the military junta announced on April 2 the scrapping of the highly nationalistic and state-oriented economic program of the overthrown Peronist government. In place of state controls it favored a free market economy with special emphasis on the promotion of exports and foreign investment. The junta had previously withdrawn a restrictive Peronist law that had discouraged new foreign investment for the past three years. The new economics minister, José Alfredo Martínez de Hoz, who had served in the same capacity during the military intervention of 1962–63, was preparing a new austerity plan that was expected to overshadow completely those of his Peronist predecessors. Provisions were being made to return nationalized enterprises to the private sector, including the U.S. subsidiary of International Telephone & Telegraph, the First National City Bank of New York, and the Bank of Boston. The door was to be opened to foreign oil exploration and development, the government was expected to resolve compensation disputes with Exxon and Royal Dutch Shell, tax incentives were announced for increasing the amount of land under cultivation, and price controls were eliminated in the effort to boost overall production. To fight inflation the government proposed curbs on the money supply, budget cuts, a reduction in the number of government employees, tax changes aimed at increasing public revenues and reducing the fiscal deficit, and higher prices for public utilities. The austerity plan was expected to hit hardest at organized labor, currently disoriented because of the repressive laws, imprisonment, and disappearance of union officials identified with the Peronist movement. Private estimates indicated that unemployment would at least double under the new plan.

The military coup was evidently partial to the interests of Argentine business. But did it portend a political counterrevolution, like that resulting from the self-styled "Liberator Revolution" of 1955? Or had the traditional political parties of the landowners, bourgeoisie, and petty bourgeoisie exhausted and discredited themselves? In the latter event, the only realistic options remaining were either long-term rule by an independent military bureaucracy or the calling of new elections in which a democratically reorganized and fortified Peronist or Authentic Peronist Party would again carry the day.

Since June 1943 the landed oligarchy had lost most of its political influence in Argentina. Its political organization, the National Democratic Party (PDN), never recovered from the blow inflicted on the so-called Democratic Union in the elections of February 1946. To be sure, the 1955 coup against Perón worked toward a restoration of the traditional balance of political power between the conservative and radical parties. But the conservative party or PDN virtually disappeared as an effective political force, while the radical party or UCR split in 1956 into the anti-Peronist Popular Radical Civic Union (UCRP) and the pro-Peronist Intransigent Radical Civic Union (UCRI). Originally a coalition of the bourgeoisie and petty bourgeoisie, the Radical Civic Union dissolved into one party for the bourgeoisie (UCRP) and into another for the petty bourgeoisie (UCRI).

Instead of the anticipated bourgeois-oligarchical restoration, the country experienced a political counterrevolution of the petty bourgeoisie under Arturo Frondizi (1958–62), followed by a new period of military intervention in 1962–63, and only then by a bourgeois counterrevolution under Arturo Illia (1963–66). Since the bourgeoisie in power were only slightly more successful than the petty bourgeoisie in stemming the Peronist tide, Illia's government was toppled by another military coup in June 1966. By that time the armed forces had exhausted all electoral possibilities of keeping the Peronists from power and had settled for the sole remaining option of ruling on their own.

The transfer of political power to a military bureaucracy independent of other social classes was tantamount to a second edition of the political revolution first launched by the armed forces in 1943. Of course, it was not a national revolution aimed at reaffirming political sovereignty, economic independence, and social justice. The "Argentine Revolution," the banner under which the armed forces baptized their new seizure of power, was written off as exaggerated by representatives of the Peronist and Marxist left. Unlike the armed forces during Perón's first administration, they were determined to halt rather than encourage the advance of organized labor. Onganía's economic program was also downright reactionary. Yet the new regime represented the political hegemony of the same social class that had made the revolution of 1943 and triumphed with Perón in the elections of 1946. Notwithstanding its efforts to strengthen big business, its officers were neither bourgeois nor dependents of the bourgeoisie.

The elections of March and September 1973 did not result in a transfer of political power to a new governing class. Although the military relinquished its monopoly of political power, the new beneficiaries of power belonged to the same class as the old. The armed forces were obliged to share power with the Peronist political and trade union bureaucracies, but this change in the balance of social forces internal to the bureaucracy signified a broader base of support for the bureaucracy as a whole. At the same time, there were important differences between the repressive military regimes that succeeded one another after 1966 and the series of Peronist governments beginning in 1973. The military wing of the bureaucracy was antinationalist as well as anti-Peronist and was allied to the big bourgeoisie and the multinational corporations. In contrast, the Peronist bureaucracy was nationalist in orientation and favored organized labor in opposition to the monopolies and foreign interests.

The still unanswered question is whether the coup that toppled Isabelita will end by favoring a political counterrevolution, like that in 1955, or a new edition of the "Argentine Revolution" of 1966. It is possible that bureaucratic rule is not itself being challenged, but rather the disastrous political and economic course it took under the ultraverticalist and verticalist wings of the

Peronist bureaucracy. On the eve of the March coup the only realistic political options were those limited to the struggle for hegemony between rival sectors of the bureaucratic class. These were basically the following: first, the continued predominance of the FREJULI, whether under the control of the ultraverticalists in Isabelita's political "entourage" or under the verticalist labor bureaucrats in the CGT and "62 Organizations"; second, the decomposition of the FREJULI and the defection of loyalist or "centrist" sectors in favor of the new front of national and social liberation being organized under Authentic Peronist Party leadership, with the support of the Intransigent Party and an assortment of other left-of-center parties; and third, a coup by the anti-Peronist military bureaucracy based on a strategy of alliance with the big bourgeoisie and the multinational corporations.

Two of these options are now thoroughly discredited and are unlikely to withstand the test of time. Despite their initial veneer of moderation, Argentina's new military rulers are relying upon too narrow a social basis to remain in power very long. Eventually, one may expect the divisions within the armed forces to erupt and to pressure the government into calling new elections. The official Peronist movement is also likely to be discredited as a result of past performance and the "Watergate" investigations designed to destroy it politically. It has already lost much of its former mass support. Isabelita will have to stand trial a second time on charges of "embezzlement," while the judge who exonerated her will also have to answer to the military. Hundreds of other government and union officials will have to stand trial on charges of financial corruption and gangster-type methods used to perpetuate themselves in power.

Once the military coup has run its course by antagonizing the underlying population and creating new problems of its own, a reconstructed Peronist movement is quite likely to be its principal beneficiary. Although leaders of the Authentic Peronist Party and the combative trade unions are being detained on charges of subversion, the reemergence of a military dictatorship has again given a semblance of legality and constitutionality to armed resistance. In addition to increased popular support for armed struggle one may anticipate that a reinvigorated and democratized labor movement, in a new version of Ongaro's "CGT of the Argentines," will also emerge to back up the resistance. Together the combative trade unions and the self-denominated authentic wing of the Peronist movement should be able to rebuild their forces and, at the head of a new front of national and social liberation, lead the country in a new direction toward an eventual socialist transformation.

APPENDIX
The Cooke-Guillén Guerrilla Plan of 1955

In September 1951, in response to the aborted military coup against Perón's first administration, Evita Perón called for the organization of popular militias and purchased the first shipment of arms for the CGT with funds from her Foundation. Four years later, in the wake of the aerial bombardment of the Plaza de Mayo and unsuccessful coup of June 1955, the CGT announced to the four winds its determination to organize popular militias in defense of Perón's second administration.

To forestall the arming of the workers, the armed forces pressured the Peronist leadership to call off the plans for popular militias and to surrender the pistols which Evita had purchased. Between June and September most of these weapons were turned over to military arsenals. Thus the Peronist Party negotiated its own downfall by bowing to a military veto and disarming the trade unions.

From his position as secretary of the Peronist Party in the capital city of Buenos Aires, John William Cooke supported the CGT's plans. He foresaw renewed military conspiracies and an easy victory of the armed forces against the Peronist government unless the workers were mobilized for such a contingency. At the same time his developing friendship with Abraham Guillén, the former military commissar of the 14th Division and the 4th Army Corps of the Spanish Republican Army, led him to favor Guillén's alternative of clandestine urban guerrillas.

The beginning of this friendship can be traced from the moment in 1954 when Guillén began collaborating as an economist and political commentator on Cooke's review *De Frente*. On the basis of his experience during the Spanish Civil War of 1936–39, Guillén advised Cooke that any military uprising could be defeated through urban guerrilla warfare with popular support. But he warned

Cooke against organizing militias openly instead of clandestinely. To do so openly would provoke rather than avert military intervention. For Guillén secrecy was imperative to insure that military officers would not react to encroachments on their monopoly of violence. The surprise factor was also crucial: the military should be kept in the dark concerning the training, logistics, and strategy for urban guerrilla resistance. Cooke, who foresaw renewed efforts to launch a coup, was persuaded by these arguments. Thereupon he commissioned Guillén to draw up a secret political-military plan for defending the popular government.

After receiving Cooke's blessing, Guillén's plan was presented to the top Peronist command. Instead of proceeding immediately to implement it, however, the leadership submitted it to the army's general staff consisting of self-styled Peronist officers. Since the proposed clandestine armed vanguard would have been independent of the regular army, the Peronist military vetoed it. Even loyal Peronist officers were displeased by the prospect of a rival military force. But how many were really loyal? In passively accepting the military's veto, the Peronist leadership was henceforth at the mercy of army generals who were shortly to betray both the Party and the government.

Cooke was perfectly aware that his own political force was equal to zero without the support of urban defense groups organized politically and strategically as the people in arms. He knew that the popular government could not be defended against a military insurrection without both regular and irregular armed units working in unison. Accordingly, he instructed Guillén to go ahead with the plan's implementation behind the backs of the Party's leaders.

The plan called for a clandestine armed vanguard based on the youth sector and the principal branches of the Peronist movement: the CGT, the Peronist Party, and the women's branch. In the event of a new military coup this clandestine apparatus was to become the core of a people's army of liberation. By September 1955 only small guerrilla groups, capable of moving through the streets in automobiles, had been structured. These were only a beginning and had yet to become organized in combat units at the level of the company or platoon. Without support from the Party's leadership, they were unprepared for the September coup and were inconsequential in resisting it.

Ideally, the Cooke-Guillén plan should have been implemented by the Party when it was strongest and still in control of the government. The plan would have worked best during the historic period between June and September, when Perón flexed his muscles by mobilizing hundreds of thousands of Argentine workers in repudiation of the June coup. Instead, the plan was adopted by the Party only after the coup which overthrew the government in September. Actually, the Cooke-Guillén plan was accepted by the Peronist leadership only when Cooke took over control of the restructured Party as Perón's personal representative and chief of operations in Argentina. Thus the plan remained mostly on paper until, in January 1956, Perón himself gave the signal for armed resistance.

In an unpublished manuscript written just after the return of the Peronist Party to power in May 1973, Guillén sketched the original guerrilla plan of 1955. That plan was summarized in the following points.

(1) *Armed Popular Vanguard.* An armed vanguard must be organized on the basis of the most politically advanced Peronist cadres. It must be rigorously clandestine, thus avoiding the trap of the much vaunted popular militias which only serve to scare the enemy. The professional army is bound to resist any encroachment on its monopoly of military power. Efforts to organize guerrillas in self-defense and with the consent of a popular government are an invitation to a military coup. The only feasible alternative is to organize guerrilla groups in secret.

(2) *Army and Guerrillas.* Although the regular army is very large and the guerrilla groups are very small, the balance of social forces may nonetheless favor the guerrillas. A great army of repression may be defeated by a popular resistance provided, first, that the armed vanguard sets in motion an insurrectional movement supported by the people and, second, engages in operations within large cities where the guerrillas have the population on their side. Although every guerrilla group stands in need of a sanctuary, jungles of cement afford the same kind of protection as the mountains and forests of rural guerrillas.

(3) *Surface versus Front Line Tactics.* When an enemy is strong

in numbers and fire-power, one can defeat it only by doing the contrary of what it does. If the regular army concentrates most of its forces in one place, one must attack it in other places and in several simultaneously, where it is not prepared to do battle. In order for the guerrillas to be superior in numbers and fire-power, they must rely on surprising the enemy and attacking it in isolated posts, where the guerrillas in fact outnumber it. In other words, the guerrillas must be stronger than the enemy in a given situation. Although the repressive army is stronger in general, it is always weaker in particular engagements in the space and time elected by the guerrillas. The resistance must be stronger than the regular army, but at one point at a time. Little does it matter that the army is stronger everywhere else; there will always be one point where the guerrillas can master it. Thus the guerrillas can defeat the army in one operation after another until they become stronger and the army becomes weaker. That is a fundamental principle of revolutionary warfare.

(4) *Space and Population.* The guerrillas must never cling to, or attempt to defend, a fixed terrain. Confronted with a powerful enemy, they must bite and disappear—the battle tactics of the flea. Since the regular army is superior in the dimension of space, the guerrillas must be superior in the dimension of time. They can become superior by winning over the population. Repressive and counterrevolutionary armies aspire to dominate not only space, but also the people who inhabit it. They will stop at nothing in this effort, including the massacre of defenseless individuals. But this exercise of force, in violation of elementary moral principles and human rights, is a sign of weakness. The guerrillas must take advantage of this weakness by assisting the victims of repression, by encouraging mass resistance, and by political and armed propaganda capable of catalyzing an insurrectional movement. To cede space but to persevere in time—that is the secret. In short, guerrilla warfare must be prolonged until the conscience and will of the people have become transformed, until the armed vanguard has also become a popular one.

(5) *Political Warfare.* Confronted with a military coup against a popular government, it is enough to have urban guerrilla groups go into action in one or several large cities to prevent the army from establishing its own law and order. If urban and rural populations are catalyzed by the guerrillas to support a resistance movement,

then eventually the army will become isolated and forced to retreat. The struggle against a military coup is basically a political one. Immersed in the basic units of the Peronist Party, working-class neighborhoods, and the principal places of work, urban guerrillas can count on a steady stream of recruits for launching recurrent actions against the forces of repression. The political role of the guerrillas is to serve as the engine of the popular train. In this capacity they should be able to persevere in their operations and compel the army to abdicate before a hostile population.

(6) *Politics, Strategy, and Tactics.* If war is the continuation of politics by other means (Clausewitz), then a popular party must resort to it when all legal avenues are closed. When a popular government is threatened or overturned by a military coup, the only effective strategy is that of the people in arms. When peace on one's knees is worse than the risk of death through violence, people should try to overthrow their tyrants. But the violence of the oppressed cannot triumph if they lack a clear vision of their political objectives, if their strategy is improvised, and their tactics are spontaneous. A military uprising against a popular government is an occasion for transforming usurpation into civil war. The Spanish Civil War began in this way and offered multiple possibilities of victory by the popular forces. Since legality was on the side of the Peronist government, it should have been possible to divide the armed forces and police, as in Spain in 1936. One could have defeated the enemy in a few days, before the imperialist powers could intervene in support of the coup. A lightning civil war offers the best strategy: it prevents the enemy from reestablishing law and order; it takes full advantage of the momentary enthusiasm of the masses for combat; it minimizes the extent of damage to the productive forces; it saves the people from prolonged suffering. But for that, popular support is necessary on a national scale.

In the perspective of Peronism restored to power in 1973, Guillén argued that his original plan still carried force. The Montoneros agreed and kept their cadres alerted in the event of an emergency. History might repeat itself, and to some extent it did. Only this time Perón was gone; Isabelita betrayed her husband's mandate; and the Montoneros ended by declaring war against the government for repressing the Peronist left wing. The CGT had no plan for organizing militias in response to the December 1975 coup and there were no leaders of the stature of John William Cooke to lead the resistance against the successful coup in March 1976. Leaders there were, like Raimundo Ongaro, but those who had not been arbitrarily imprisoned had been either murdered or compelled to flee the country. Guillén too had to go into exile to escape assassination by the "Triple A." And under those circumstances the government, whose popularity with the workers had reached an all-time low, was no longer worth defending.

Selected Bibliography

Periodicals

Avanzada Socialista. Buenos Aires, June 1973–July 1974, Nos. 64–111.
Confluencia. Buenos Aires, May 1974, No. 3.
Con Todo. Buenos Aires, May 1974, Nos. 1–2.
De Frente. Buenos Aires, May–July 1974, Nos. 1–10.
El Caudillo. Buenos Aires, March 1974–December 1975, Nos. 16–73.
El Combatiente. Buenos Aires, August 1973–July 1974, Nos. 85–124.
El Descamisado. Buenos Aires, June 1973–April 1974, Nos. 6–46.
El Mundo. Buenos Aires, February–March 1974, Nos. 134–65.
El Obrero. Buenos Aires, April 1974, No. 1.
El Peronista. Buenos Aires, April–May 1974, Nos. 2–4.
El Trabajador. Buenos Aires, April–July 1974, Nos. 4–6.
Estrella Roja. Buenos Aires, August 1973–July 1974, Nos. 23–35.
JOTAPÉ. Buenos Aires, February–April 1974, Nos. 1–3.
Mayoría. Buenos Aires, December 1975–February 1976.
Militancia. Buenos Aires, June 1973–March 1974, Nos. 1–38.
Nuevo Hombre. Buenos Aires, 1st series, September 1973–June 1974, Nos. 47–65; 2d series, November 1975–February 1976, Nos. 1–8.
Noticias. Buenos Aires, May–June 1974, Nos. 184–98.
Patria Socialista. Buenos Aires, July 1973–February 1974, Nos. 1–5.
Posición. Córdoba, November 1973–April 1974, Nos. 10–13.
Prensa Confidencial. Buenos Aires, August 1973–January 1976, Nos. 284–402.
Primicia Argentina. Buenos Aires, July 1974, No. 23.
Semana Política. Buenos Aires, December 1975–February 1976, Nos. 62–67.
Vocero Popular. Buenos Aires, January–April 1974, Nos. 37–38.

Books

Acossano, Benigno. *Eva Perón, su verdadera vida.* Buenos Aires, 1955.
Alexander, Robert. *The Peron Era.* New York, 1951.
Artesano, Eduardo. *Ensayo sobre el justicialismo a la luz del materialismo histórico.* Rosario, 1953.
Baily, Samuel L. *Labor, Nationalism, and Politics in Argentina.* New Brunswick, 1967.
Belloni, Alberto. *Del anarquismo al peronismo.* Buenos Aires, 1960.
———. *Peronismo y socialismo nacional.* Buenos Aires, 1962.

Blanksten, George I. *Peron's Argentina*. Chicago, 1953.

Braun, Oscar, ed. *El capitalismo argentino en crisis*. Buenos Aires, 1973.

Cámpora, Héctor. *El mandato de Perón*. Buenos Aires, 1975.

————. *La revolución Peronista*. Buenos Aires, 1973.

Canton, Darío. *La política de los militares argentinos: 1900–1971*. Buenos Aires, 1971.

Cárdenas, Gonzalo, et al. *El peronismo*, Buenos Aires, 1969.

Cerrutti Costa, Luis B. *El Sindicalismo*. Buenos Aires, 1957.

Ciria, Alberto. *Partidos y Poder en la Argentina Moderna (1930–1946)*. Buenos Aires, 1975.

————. *Perón y el justicialismo*. Buenos Aires, 1971.

Concatti, Rolando. *Nuestra opción por el peronismo*, 2d ed. Mendoza, 1972.

Cooke, John William. *Apuntes para la militancia*. Buenos Aires, 1972.

————. *Correspondencia Perón-Cooke*, 2 vols. Buenos Aires, 1973.

————. *La lucha por la liberación nacional*. Buenos Aires, 1971.

————. *Peronismo e Integración*, 3d ed. Buenos Aires, 1974.

————. *Peronismo y revolución*. Buenos Aires, 1971.

Debray, Régis. *La critique des armes*, 2 vols. Paris, 1974.

————. *Revolution in the Revolution?* trans. by Bobbye Ortiz. New York, 1967.

Fayt, Carlos S. *El político armado: dinámica del proceso político argentino, 1960–1971*. Buenos Aires, 1971.

————, ed. *La naturaleza del peronismo*. Buenos Aires, 1968.

Feinmann, José Pablo. *El peronismo y la primacia de la política*. Buenos Aires, 1974.

Franco, Juan Pablo and Fernando Alvarez. *Peronismo: antecedentes y gobierno*. Buenos Aires, 1972.

Frondizi, Silvio. *La realidad argentina*, 2 vols. Buenos Aires, 1955–56.

Garcia Lupo, Rogelio. *La rebelión de los generales*, 3d ed. Buenos Aires, 1963.

Gerassi, Marysa Navarro. *Los nacionalistas*. Buenos Aires, 1969.

Godio, Julio. *La caída de Perón de junio a setiembre de 1955*, 2d ed. Buenos Aires, 1973.

Goldwert, Marvin. *Democracy, Militarism, and Nationalism in Argentina, 1930–1966*. Austin, 1972.

González, Ernesto. *Qué fue y qué es el peronismo*. Buenos Aires, 1974.

González Jansen, Ignacio. *Argentina: 20 años de luchas Peronistas*. Mexico, D. F. 1975.

Gutiérrez, Guillermo. *Explotación y respuestos populares*. Buenos Aires, 1974.

Hernández Arregui, Juan José. *La formación de la conciencia nacional: 1930–1960*. Buenos Aires, 1960.

————. *Peronismo y socialismo*, 2d ed. Buenos Aires, 1972.

Hodges, Donald C. *La revolución latinoamericana*. Mexico, D. F., 1976.

————, ed. *Philosophy of the Urban Guerrilla*. New York, 1973.

Ibarguren, Federico. *Orígenes del nacionalismo argentino*. Buenos Aires, 1969.

Imaz, José Luis de. *Los que mandan*, 1st ed. Buenos Aires, 1964.

Jauretche, Arturo. *F.O.R.J.A. y la década infame*. Buenos Aires, 1962.

Kilpatrick, Jeane. *Leader and Vanguard in Mass Society: A Study of Peronist Argentina*. Cambridge, Mass., 1971.

López, Alfredo. *La clase obrera y la revolución del 4 de junio.* Buenos Aires, 1945.

Luna, Félix. *Argentina de Perón a Lanusse 1943–1973,* 9th ed. Buenos Aires, 1974.

Lux-Wurm, Pierre. *Le Péronisme.* Paris, 1965.

Murmis, Miguel and Juan Carlos Portantiero. *Estudios sobre los orígenes del peronismo,* 1st ed. Buenos Aires, 1971.

NACLA. *Argentina in the Hour of the Furnaces.* New York, 1975.

Nadra, Fernando. *Un año de gobierno peronista.* Buenos Aires, 1974.

Pan, Luis. *La agonía del regimen de junio a setiembre.* Buenos Aires, 1956.

Pavón, Pereya. *Perón tal como es.* Buenos Aires, 1972.

Peña, Milciades. *El peronismo: selección de documentos para la historia.* Buenos Aires, 1972.

Peralta Ramos, Monica. *Etapas de acumulación y alianza de clases en la argentina.* Buenos Aires, 1972.

Perelman, Angel. *Como hicimos el 17 de octubre.* Buenos Aires, 1961.

Perón, Eva. *La razón de mi vida.* Buenos Aires, n.d.

Perón, Juan Domingo. *Actualización política y doctrina para la toma del poder.* Buenos Aires, 1973.

———. *Conducción Política.* Buenos Aires, 1973.

———. *Doctrina Peronista.* Buenos Aires, 1973.

———. *Doctrina Revolucionaria.* Buenos Aires, 1974.

———. *El Pueblo Quiere Saber de que se Trata (Discursos).* Buenos Aires, 1973.

———. *El Pueblo ya Sabe de que se Trata (Discursos).* Buenos Aires, 1973.

———. *Juan D. Perón 1973–1974 (Discursos).* Buenos Aires, 1974.

———. *Juan Perón en la Argentina 1973–1974 (Discursos),* 2 vols. Buenos Aires, 1974.

———. *La Comunidad Organizada.* Buenos Aires, 1974.

———. *La Fuerza es el Derecho de las Bestias.* Buenos Aires, 1958.

———. *La Hora de los Pueblos.* Buenos Aires, 1974.

———. *La Tercera Posición Argentina.* Buenos Aires, 1974.

———. *Latinoamérica: ahora o nunca.* Montevideo, 1967.

———. *Tres Revoluciones Militares.* Buenos Aires, 1972.

Prieto, Ramón. *Correspondencia Perón-Frigerio 1958–1973.* Buenos Aires, 1975.

———. *De Perón a Perón (1946–1973).* Buenos Aires, 1974.

PRT. *El Peronismo ayer y hoy.* Mexico, D. F., 1974.

Puiggrós, Rodolfo. *El peronismo: sus causas.* Buenos Aires, 1969.

Ramos, Jorge Abelardo. *De octubre a setiembre.* Buenos Aires, 1959.

———. *Revolución y contrarrevolución en la Argentina.* Buenos Aires, 1961.

Reyes, Cipriano. *Qué es el laborismo.* Buenos Aires, 1946.

Senén González, Santiago. *Breve historia del sindicalismo argentino 1857–1974.* Buenos Aires, 1974.

———. *El sindicalismo despues de Perón.* Buenos Aires, 1971.

Snow, Peter G. *Political Forces in Argentina.* Boston, 1971.

Spilimbergo, Jorge E. *Juan B. Justo o el socialismo cipayo.* Buenos Aires, n.d.

———. *Nacionalismo oligárquico y nacionalismo revolucionario.* Buenos Aires, 1958.

Strasser, C., ed. *Las izquierdas en el proceso político argentino.* Buenos Aires, 1959.

Terragno, Rodolfo. *Los 400 días de Perón.* Buenos Aires, 1974.
Weil, Felix. *Argentine Riddle.* New York, 1945.
Whitaker, Arthur P. *Argentine Upheaval.* New York, 1956.
Zuleta Alvarez, Enrique. *El nacionalismo argentino,* 2 vols. Buenos Aires, 1975.

Index

201